LIBRARIES AND ACCREDITATION IN INSTITUTIONS OF HIGHER EDUCATION

LIBRARIES AND ACCREDITATION IN INSTITUTIONS OF HIGHER EDUCATION

Proceedings of a Conference held in New York City
June 26-27, 1980

Edited by
Julie Carroll Virgo
and
David Alan Yuro
1981

ASSOCIATION OF COLLEGE AND RESEARCH LIBRARIES

International Standard Book Number: 0-8389-6480-X
Association of College and Research Libraries
A division of the American Library Association
Chicago, Illinois 60611

CONTENTS

Introduction
Julie Carroll Virgo

Accreditation teams in higher education evaluate the library component of colleges and universities as part of the overall evaluation and accreditation process. Regional accrediting organizations do not officially adopt the standards of particular professional associations. Rather, they develop their own guidelines for evaluating each component, such as the library, and these guidelines are necessarily somewhat brief. Such guidelines can serve not only as tools for evaluating library services but, just as importantly, can be used to assist the libraries in evaluating themselves.

The Association of College and Research Libraries (ACRL), a division of the American Library Association, has developed standards for two and four year college libraries and, most recently, for university libraries (see Appendix B). These standards focus on the specific requirements of libraries serving the three distinctly different types of institutions in higher education. The standards provide an extensive vehicle which can be used by the institutions and library staffs to assess their libraries internally and which can provide guidance to external agencies as they evaluate the library component of a college or university.

Since libraries in higher education are evaluated as a part of the overall institutional accreditation process, the Standards and Accreditation Committee of ACRL proposed an invitational meeting which would bring together libraries and accreditation groups. The Commission on Postsecondary Accreditation (COPA), which evaluates the postsecondary educational accrediting activities of institutional and accrediting associations, shared the ACRL opinion that more informed accrediting teams can be of valuable assistance in improving library service in academic libraries. For this reason COPA and ACRL agreed to co-sponsor a workshop which would bring together staff from the six accrediting agencies and librarians who serve in the pool of candidates used by the regional accrediting agencies in forming accreditation teams.

A two-day workshop was planned to improve the self-study and evaluation of libraries. The ACRL Board of Directors approved the funding. Invitations were sent to the six regional accrediting associations and to librarians who had been nominated by the accreditation agencies as having been effective accrediting team members.

Forty-seven people participated in the meeting. They represented staff and commission members from five of the six regions (the sixth was having its Board meeting on the workshop dates) and from librarians throughout the United States. The librarians were evenly distributed from among the different types of institutions that academic librarians serve.

The content of the workshop included: an overview of the accrediting process; the reasons for the development of standards to supplement the accrediting associations' guidelines; a discussion of different types of standards — qualitative, quantitative, and checklists; the rationale underlying the three different sets of ACRL standards; the processes by which they were develop-

Julie Carroll Virgo is the executive director of the Association of College and Research Libraries.

ed; how they are currently used; how they relate to the self-study process; their relationship to other library standards; how an accreditation team evaluates a library when there is not a librarian on the team; and, how the accreditation process can be improved from the viewpoints of a team member, the accreditation agency, and a librarian who has successfully completed the accreditation process.

The workshop included general sessions for all participants and small group discussions for a more comprehensive examination of particular issues, such as specific standards for the three types of libraries.

This publication includes the formal presentations, summaries of the small group discussions, and conclusions as viewed by one of the participants.

James Dodson, Chair of the Standards and Accreditation Committee was most helpful in initiating the conference and providing suggestions along the way. Appreciation is also owed to Kenneth Young, who was the current Executive Director of the Council on Postsecondary Accreditation, and to Brooke Sheldon who served as facilitator to the group. Lastly, and very importantly, the speakers and participants contributed significantly to the success of the conference.

Overview of the Accrediting Process
Kenneth E. Young

In reviewing the literature on accreditation, it has been discovered that virtually no one understands accreditation, not even many of those involved in the process. This is the case, perhaps, because the word "accreditation" is used in other settings. (Diplomats, White House correspondents, hospitals, and prisons are accredited). Also, like any dynamic process, educational accreditation has been evolving, in subtle but important ways, over the approximately eighty years that it has been around; and, in fact, it continues to change. Finally, the corps of individuals, professionals, and volunteers who have been actively involved in accreditation have been so busy making the process work that they have had little or no time to spend in educating others as to its values, its limitations, and its changing emphases.

There are two particular problems in achieving a general understanding of educational accreditation — faulty definitions and faulty assumptions.

Faulty definitions:

There are four important terms in accreditation which suffer from problems of definition:

Institutions of postsecondary education:

There was a time when there was agreement on what was a college or university. These institutions essentially offered the same kinds of programs and degrees and served the same kinds of students. However, "higher education" now has become "postsecondary education." In fact, one of the more fundamental, but as yet not fully appreciated, evolutions occurring in society during recent years has been the changing definition of "higher education" (degree-granting colleges and universities offering traditional academic programs and primarily serving full-time students recently out of high schools) into "postsecondary education" (an expanding variety of institutions, programs, and delivery systems in many different settings and under various forms of sponsorship serving a growing diversity of learners of all ages with a multiplicity of educational objectives). Although the expansion of higher education into postsecondary education has taken place over time, and in fact still is occurring, the Education Amendments of 1972 for all practical purposes made the change official.

It is still possible to identify institutions of higher education, but this distinction can become artificial if one fails to recognize that many traditional degree-granting colleges and universities are engaging in a growing number of educational activities not directly related to production of degreed students; and at the same time, a variety of nontraditional institutions are beginning to award academic credits and degrees. Almost all of these types of postsecondary education are seeking accreditation. The institutions involved are graduate, baccalaureate, associate, and nondegree (certificate-granting) in level; public, private nonprofit, and proprietary in governance; liberal arts, vocational, and professional in orientation; complex or single-purpose, freestanding or part of a system in organization. In addition, other social institu-

Kenneth E. Young was the president of the Council on Postsecondary Accreditation.

tions that are not primarily educational in purpose (government, business and industry, labor unions, churches, voluntary associations) also sponsor education and training in support of their primary purposes.

It is not commonly understood that the regional commissions now are accrediting proprietary schools, technical/vocational institutes, and free-standing professional institutions as well as traditional colleges and universities. The regional accrediting commissions, for example, have accredited or are considering for accreditation such institutions as the Rand Graduate Institute for Policy Studies (sponsored by the Rand Corporation), the Arthur D. Little Management Education Institute, Inc., the Community College of the Air Force (which bills itself as "the largest accredited, degree-granting institution in the world"), ICS-International Correspondence Schools, and Western State University College of Law at San Diego.

Furthermore, in addition to the nine postsecondary educational accrediting commissions of the six regional associations, there are several national bodies that accredit various kinds of specialized institutions. Such organizations as the American Association of Bible Colleges, the Association of Independent Colleges and Schools, the National Association of Trade and Technical Schools, and the National Home Study Council accredit several thousand worthy institutions of their kind, including (just to suggest the variety) the Moody Bible Institute, the New York School of Dog Grooming, the National College of Business, and the Gemological Institute of America. A number of the national professional organizations that accredit educational units located within colleges and universities also accredit free-standing professional schools in such fields as art, chiropractic, law, medicine, music, optometry, osteopathy, podiatry, psychology, and theology.

Accreditation now is expected to evaluate and assure the educational quality of everything from a one-man school of welding to a statewide system of postsecondary education, from a hospital offering its own training programs to a state agency awarding degrees by examination, from institutions that operate campuses across the world to institutions that have no campuses at all. Surely no social enterprise in history has faced such a dramatic expansion of and change in its universe in such a relatively short period of time as has educational accreditation in just the last ten years or so.

For purposes of accreditation, an institution of postsecondary education must have at least three basic characteristics:

(1) A lay governing board, or an acceptable equivalent, to represent the public interest;

(2) A faculty that functions collectively to assure educational standards and plays a meaningful role in determining admissions requirements, graduation standards, curricular offerings, etc.;

(3) A clear statement of educational objectives that are postsecondary in nature and that lend themselves to evaluation.

Educational quality:

Quality, like truth and beauty, essentially is undefinable. Robert Pirsig, in his book, *Zen and the Art of Motorcycle Maintenance,* describes a man's search for the meaning of quality; he eventually comes to the realization that quality is like the Holy Grail — something that everyone, consciously or subconsciously, is searching for in every aspect of life. We cannot define it, but we almost always recognize and appreciate quality when we come across it. So, too, accreditation in a very real sense is an organized search for educational quality. People make a serious error if they believe that the accreditation process begins with a definition of educational quality, expressed in terms of standards, and then proceed to apply that definition to institutions and programs. Educational quality, rather than the beginning, is the result of the accreditation process — at least when it is practiced correctly.

Accreditation:

One basic flaw in much thinking about accreditation has already been suggested. In addition, many people see accreditation as an external monitoring or regulating mechanism; and, as often is the case with federal and state government officials, they attempt to use accreditation in ways that would divert and distort it from its primary purpose. Accreditation inherently is an evaluative process, and, by its very nature, it is nongovernmental. Accreditation is the process by which an institution of postsecondary education formally evaluates its educational activities, in whole or in part, and seeks an independent judgment that it substantially achieves its own objectives and is comparable to similar institutions or specialized units. Essential elements of the process are:

(1) A clear statement of educational objectives;

(2) A directed self-study focused on these objectives;

(3) An on-site evaluation of a selected group of peers;

(4) A decision by an independent commission that the institution or unit meets established minimum qualifications.

Library:

In addition, the term "library" is increasingly subject to problems of definition. Libraries long ago became something more than collections of books; but they now are challenged by the rapid development of new knowledge, new technologies, and interdisciplinary approaches that ultimately will produce new disciplines and new taxonomies. People are forced to think of libraries as systems for conserving and communicating information, and these changes in perspective produce a challenge not only for librarians and the institutions they serve but also for the accreditation process.

Faulty assumptions:

One can identify three faulty assumptions that have particular relevance for accreditation:

Assumption 1: That there will be, or should be, a return to "the good old days," that the future will be the same as the present — "more of the same" — or that change will occur but in only one particular area of life.

Everyone on occasion slips into a kind of thinking representing the third of these elements. This is called single-track, rather than multi-track, thinking; and it is particularly dangerous in this period of history because of the move into a post-industrial society which will be radically different in *all* respects due to significant developments in such areas as space, computers, and television.

Postsecondary education, for example, will be greatly changed in terms of sponsors, clienteles, and delivery systems. "Lifelong learning" will be more the rule than the exception. Persons in the professions and specialized occupations (which means most people) will have to continue their education in order to keep pace with new developments. Last year, degree-granting institutions had more part-time adult students than full-time undergraduate and graduate students; this shift to part-time students will continue.

How are changing libraries, dealing with changing technology and content, going to serve changing institutions in a changing society — when change is so rapid and so multi-dimensional? And how are those people in accreditation going to determine what is a "good" library or a "bad" library? Certainly not by counting books or square feet.

Assumption 2: That the "quality" of one segment or aspect of an institution can be evaluated and improved without considering the relationship of that part to the whole.

Arthur Godfrey, one of the most popular radio personalities, attributed his success to an early realization that although he was heard by many people, from the perspective of the individual listener it was a one-to-one conversation.

There is an important lesson here for accreditation. Even though accrediting agencies deal with hundreds of institutions, any one of those colleges and universities is concerned only with what happens to it.

The Council on Postsecondary Accreditation regularly receives telephone calls, letters, and personal visits from institutional presidents. They have many concerns, an underlying theme of which is that accreditation — as it affects their institutions — appears to be an uncoordinated process.

All accrediting agencies accept as basic principles that (1) the primary purpose of accreditation is to evaluate and improve the educational quality of the institution, and (2) the institution is evaluated in terms of its own scope, level, and objectives. The institution has good reason to ask, then, why it should not follow that any accrediting activity — no matter what its special focus or sponsorship — should function in a complementary manner with all other accrediting activities at that institution.

The ideal situation for accreditation, as it relates to the institution, can best be described by the word "coherent," which means "composed of interdependent or related parts, or consistent." The problem, of course, is that bringing coherence to a process involving more than fifty accrediting bodies and an additional number of sponsoring and collaborating organizations is not an easy matter. COPA took steps to address this problem several years ago, first by the appointment of a Task Force on Interagency Cooperation, then by a major conference on the same subject. Out of those efforts came agreement that cooperation and collaboration are highly desirable, if not essential, in accreditation and that COPA should see this as a major priority. The accrediting community also agreed on *Interim Guidelines for Interagency Cooperation:*

It is COPA's intention to encourage and assist these and other cooperative efforts and to develop models for consideration by others in the accrediting community. A new Task Force on Interagency Cooperation is working toward this goal. In addition, COPA is revising its *Provisions and Procedures for Becoming Recognized as an Accrediting Agency for Postsecondary Educational Institutions or Programs* and will strengthen its requirement that member agencies demonstrate how they meet this objective.

Assumption 3: That "quality" or "good practice" can be successfully imposed upon or required of an institution by some form of external regulation.

Accreditation can be properly understood only as it is seen as a preeminent form of self-regulation, and the importance of self-regulation can be appreciated only when one realizes that this is what civilization is all about. Civilization began when a group of cave people were crouched around a fire gnawing on cooked animal legs. One person probably burped, and the others frowned; thus, for the first time, an individual was forced to contemplate the need to shape his or her behavior in a way that would take into consideration how it might affect other people. That is a basic definition of civilized man, and that principle is at the heart of self-regulation.

Any system of *coercive* external regulation (whether federal, state, or both) is bound to fail. Our experience with Prohibition should have taught that. External regulation can be successful only when it builds upon a basis of self-regulation. An example of this comes from the campuses of the 1960s. College administrators who were constructing new buildings soon found that it was best to wait and determine where students and faculty walked before putting in the sidewalks.

Furthermore, a large number of colleges and universities want to do "the right thing" if they only are made to know what that is. And a substantial majority (all, in fact, but a fringe few) will voluntarily follow certain agreed-upon forms of behavior if they fear that failure to do so will expose them to the criticism of their colleagues.

These beliefs have led this author to promulgate six premises for a system of self-regulation in postsecondary education:

1. To the maximum extent possible, colleges and universities should regulate themselves.

2. Colleges and universities should feel an obligation to report institutions that fail to regulate themselves.

3. As one of their major, continuing responsibilities, national and regional nongovernmental higher education associations should assist colleges and universities in becoming self-regulating.

4. Students should be informed about their opportunities, their rights, and their obligations and should have mechanisms for filing grievances.

5. Through their chartering and licensing authority, states should prevent the operation of fraudulent and ineffective institutions, take action against law violators, and provide for basic student consumer protection.

6. The federal role in higher education should be limited to providing funds in behalf of achieving specific national objectives and assuring that these public funds are properly expended and accounted for.

The American Council on Education has established an Office on Self-Regulation Initiatives, headed by Elaine El-Khawas. The Office is collecting codes of good practice, identifying areas where such codifications of generally accepted behavior should be developed or updated, working with other appropriate groups to prepare new or revised codes, and planning dissemination and education activities. For example, the National Association of College and University Business Officers has developed proposed guidelines for tuition refund policies.

Accreditation is a centerpiece to, but not the whole of, an effective system of self-regulation. Given established codes of good practice in such areas as in-stitution—student relations, institution—donor relations, and academic standards, and the regional accrediting bodies can, as a regular practice, ask their member institutions if they subscribe to these codes. If an institution does not, it can be asked to state in writing to what policies and procedures it does subscribe. The accrediting agencies then can expect the instituion to "be what it says it is and do what it says it does" and can deal with those instances where the institutions fail to live up to their own declared standards.

The accrediting associations, of course, have very small staffs and function through the extensive use of volunteers, so they cannot monitor or regulate ongoing institutional behavior. They can only deal with problems as they are identified at the time of regular review or as they are called to the attention of the appropriate accrediting body by way of a complaint. This is where other institutions must feel increasingly a responsibility to call problems to the attention of the accrediting agencies.

The future foresees increasing problems with institutional behavior. The combination of declining enrollments of eighteen-to-twenty-two years old students, inflation, and restricted government funding is going to cause many more instances of (1) institutional bankruptcy or closing, (2) cutbacks in the funding of maintenance, libraries, support services, etc., that eventually will affect the quality of education, and (3) questionable practices in the recruit-ing and admission of students, the offering of credit for experiential learning or previous education in noncollegiate settings, and grading practices. The academic community must gear up to police itself, and the accrediting agen-cies will have to be prepared to make some tough decisions in the immediate years ahead.

The Evolution of College and University Library Standards
Jasper G. Schad

The years immediately preceding and following the turn of the century were marked by enormous growth and change in higher education. Accompanying this change came diversity so extreme that many colleges were little more than secondary schools; undergraduate programs themselves were not standard, sometimes requiring three years' work, sometimes four. These conditions made it necessary to choose between continued chaos or standardization in the most literal sense of the word. Choosing the latter, a host of foundations, associations, and even governmental agencies undertook to develop standards for colleges and universities.[1] These first standards had little or nothing to say about libraries, but it was not long before things changed. The North Central Association decided in 1908 to undertake inspection and accreditation of institutions of higher learning and, a year later, approved the first set of standards for any of the regional accrediting associations. These criteria stated simply that the library should be adequate to support the institution's instructional program.[2]

Although other regional accrediting associations moved in the same direction, it was not until after World War I that the accrediting movement gained full momentum. Standardizing agencies proliferated and standards became increasingly specific, listing essential minimum resources and conditions for effective instruction. For libraries, these typically called for holdings of at least 7,000 to 10,000 volumes, adequate facilities, competent staff, funds for new acquisitions, and sometimes a minimum appropriation per student.[3] Joining the bandwagon, the American Library Association first took an active interest in standards with the appointment in 1919 of a Committee of Five to survey actual conditions in American libraries with the expectation that this work would eventually lead to standards.[4] It did not, but there were many other studies undertaken during this period,[5] one of which did. That one surveyed the budgets of 100 college and university libraries and was published in 1929 under the title *Budgets, Classification and Compensation Plans for University and College Libraries*. Although not called standards, in fact, that is what this document was. It set two conditions for all college and university libraries: an expenditure of not less than 4 percent of the institution's educational and general spending and a minimum of either twenty or twenty-five dollars annually per student, depending on the number of students enrolled. In addition, there were detailed staff and budgetary requirements for different sized institutions.[6] Two years later, the concerns of junior college librarians about the adequacy of their libraries and the low figures contained in accrediting association standards led the Junior College Round Table to develop standards for collection and staff size, as well as for current acquisitions.[7]

Up to that point, standards had been essentially quantitative. Whether prepared by the regional accrediting associations or ALA, all were about the same, differing only in that ALA's figures were a little more generous and a little more detailed. The early 1930s brought a fundamental change. Recog-

---

Jasper Schad is director of the Wichita State University Library/Media Resources Center.

nizing that innovations in curriculum and instructional methods since 1900 had had an important impact on libraries, the Carnegie Corporation first supported a number of library studies in the 1920s,[8] then established an Advisory Group on College Libraries in 1928 to administer grants for the purchase of books. The Advisory Group soon became concerned about "some really pitiful conditions" in college libraries and saw the need for an entirely different kind of standards, ones that set forth what a college library should be and do and how it should be supported. These 1932 Carnegie standards abandoned numerical minima altogether, choosing to stress that the college library must be supported adequately because it is an essential part of the school's educational program, and even calling for formal instruction in library use.[9] For many years, these pioneering qualitative standards served as the principal model for the college library.

At the same time, the North Central Association began to move in a similar direction. Responding to growing criticism that its standards were rigid and inflexible, the Association undertook an extensive statistical study of fifty-seven institutions.[10] Concluding that revision would serve only to perpetuate existing problems, the old standards were replaced in 1934 by new criteria, different from the earlier ones in many respects. They were general rather than specific, stressed quality rather than quantity, were more elastic, and were based on objective observation that revealed characteristics associated with institutional excellence. Another major difference was that the revision abandoned the goal of standardization, the very basis of accreditation since its inception.[11] In fact, the term "standard" was discarded as being conceptually alien to the spirit of the new approach to institutional evaluation.[12] Finally, the new criteria were based on the assumption that institutions would be judged as a whole, rather than by specific standards for particular functions. This point was especially important, because it meant that part of a college or university, say the library, could be inadequate, but the institution could still be accredited.

The 1934 criteria specified only that the library must support adequately the institution's educational program.[13] This requirement, however, was supplemented by an elaborate procedure for evaluation, using check lists to determine the quality of the collection and various statistics to measure the adequacy of support and use. Statistical norms were established for four categories of institutions: junior colleges, four-year colleges, those with master's programs, and universities.[14] Although the objective of the new criteria was to make it possible to distinguish between libraries that functioned as a vital part of the educational program and those that did not,[15] the result was only partially successful, simply because there really was no measure of excellence for libraries. This difficulty led to considerable criticism of the 1934 criteria.[16] At the same time, the efforts of regional accrediting associations that continued to employ quantitative minima proved no more satisfactory, and those, too, were attacked for being so low as to serve little, if any, purpose.[17]

Librarians were not alone in attacking accreditation.[18] Criticism was inherent in the process because there was no guarantee of quality. It worked well for schools committed to quality, but provided no real way to deal with those that would not or could not provide adequate library service. Too frequently, the result was little more than explaining away less than adequate library service. Thus, while librarians and others were often frustrated, no less so were the regional accrediting associations, which found libraries to be one of the most difficult institutional components to evaluate adequately.[19]

In light of these circumstances, there was growing concern over the plight of the many inadequately supported college libraries.[20] This situation led librarians to take a more active role in standards development, bringing to conclusion a project launched in 1939, but interrupted by World War II, to develop quantitative standards for junior colleges, four-year institutions, and universities. These *Score Cards,*[21] as they were called, were identical in format and intended for self-evaluation, making it possible to rate or score individual libraries on staff, collections, book budget, and hours of service.[22] While the *Score Cards* represented a definite step forward, their value was limited because they were purely numerical. By the mid-1950s, it was obvious that something more had to be done. Budgetary stringency was becoming a matter of growing concern, library buildings were all too often antiquated and overcrowded, and librarians worried that rapidly rising enrollments in the decade ahead would further exaggerate the problems of already inadequate libraries.[23] Increasingly, they saw the need for sound criteria to enable administrators to determine how well libraries support the instructional program at their colleges.[24] Responding to this need, the Association of College and Research Libraries first made a series of changes by which the Committee on Budgets, Compensation, and Schemes of Service evolved into the Committee on Standards,[25] which in 1957 began work on college library standards.[26] Equally pressing were the needs of two-year colleges. In 1953, the Junior College Library Section established a committee that prepared standards,[27] which were referred by the ACRL Board of Directors in 1959 to the Committee on Standards.[28]

What emerged in 1959 and 1960, respectively, were two sets of standards, one for four-year and the other for two-year schools. Similar in form and content, both emphasized quality rather than quantity. Each contained a carefully delineated set of principles describing adequate library service, augmented by a few minimum quantitative standards for budget, collections, staff, and facilities.[29] Unlike the *Score Cards,* these standards were not intended primarily for internal use, but were directed principally to college administrators, board members, and others in higher education.

While both sets of standards had an important impact during the 1960s,[30] that decade also witnessed profound change in higher education: larger enrollments, curricular expansion, the emergence of new disciplines, a stronger emphasis on research, and greater diversity among the nation's colleges and universities. These were accompanied by a staggering growth in the amount of published information and the beginnings of a serious inflationary spiral. Libraries were similarly affected; new responsibilities and services emerged and growth in collections and staff produced vastly more complex organizations. Nowhere were these changes more profound than in two-year colleges, where emerged the concept of the learning resources center, a merger of library and audiovisual services that better served the needs of campuses committed to instructional improvement.

The impact of the 1960s was nothing short of revolutionary. Thus, although it was originally felt that the passage of time would have little effect on the 1959 and 1960 standards,[31] the events of the 1960s abruptly destroyed the idea that standards could be permanent.[32] Committes were established to revise both sets of standards in 1966[33] and 1968,[34] respectively. First to be completed was *Guidelines for Two-Year College Learning Resources Programs*,[35] approved in 1972. These differed from the 1960 standards in several important respects, the most obvious being their emphasis on combining print and nonprint services. Another difference, related in part to this emphasis, was the decision to seek the involvement and endorsement of both the American Association of Community and Junior Colleges and the Association for Educational Communications and Technology. A third difference was the absence of numerical standards. The committee recognized their importance, but there had been criticism of the way quantitative measures in the 1960 standards had been used and there was not enough research to support better figures. Consequently, the committee decided to limit the guidelines to a description of an adequate learning resources program and that quantitative measures should be developed sometime in the future. Further, it was assumed that two-year college learning resources centers would continue to change, making it necessary to review the guidelines annually.[36]

Taking a similar approach, the committee working on the college library standards was less successful. Quantitative standards were the principal stumbling block. Some felt they were no longer necessary, but the euphoria of the 1960s was rapidly fading. Draft standards, completed late in 1970,[37] met strong opposition from librarians, because they were very general in nature and entirely without quantitative measures.[38] A second effort proved successful. These 1975 standards resembled the earlier ones in many ways, but there were important differences. Numerical measures, again, were a source of concern. The committee recognized that standards ideally should contain measures reflecting effectiveness rather than financial support, but there was neither enough research nor data on which to construct such standards. This left no alternative other than the traditional input measures. At the same time, no longer would a single minimum suffice. The years since 1959 witnessed growing institutional diversity (particularly, the emergence of many large, state supported institutions, some with over 30,000 students and a broad range of professional programs at the bachelor's and master's levels, as well as limited doctoral offerings), which precluded the possibility of a single numerical standard in many cases. Thus, the formulas for resources, staff, and facilities were based on enrollment and programmatic elements. Further, recognizing the need for something more than minima, they introduced graded levels of quality.[39]

Although by 1975 ACRL had been actively developing standards for nearly twenty years, there were still no university library standards. The enormous diversity among those institutions made it especially difficult to agree on standards. In fact, work had begun in 1967,[40] but it took twelve years and two separate efforts[41] before a joint committee of ACRL and the Association of Research Libraries successfully completed its work. Again, a major obstacle was quantitative standards. At length, it was decided that none could be applied to the entire range of institutions covered, although an extensive appendix dealing with quantitative analytical techniques was added.[42]

In the early 1980s, as throughout the last fifty years, two major themes continue to concern academic libraries. The first is statistical measures of library adequacy. Like a pendulum, standards have swung back and forth, sometimes emphasizing quantity, sometimes quality. Available figures suggest a relationship between financial support and quantitative standards — greater emphasis, when fiscal support is low or declining, less in better times — but the figures are not sufficiently complete to confirm this relationship. Nevertheless, it is clear that there is now a strongly felt need for better statistical measures of library effectiveness. Even though ACRL standards contain figures that are based on the judgment of persons with unquestioned competence to discriminate between good and bad libraries, these figures are hard to defend and are often challenged. Consequently, ACRL soon established committees to expand or revise both the community college and college standards.[43]

A supplementary document for two-year institutions was completed in 1979. It contains formulas based either on existing statistics or professional judgment for staffing, collection size, space requirements, and equipment.[44] Efforts to revise the college library standards have also focused principally on statistical analysis of available data. Up to this point, however, there has been no basic change in numerical standards, but only the prospect that something better will ultimately emerge from the new literature, oriented toward library effectiveness, often involving performance measures, and based on operations research or systems engineering. The lack of adequate measures of effectiveness is a problem not unique to libraries. In fact, there is no better evidence to prove the value of college and university libraries than there is to measure the impact of higher education itself. The second major issue of the 80s is institutional diversity. At present, the three existing sets of standards have difficulty embracing the wide range of institutions they are intended to cover, and the matter is getting worse. Neither problem is overwhelming. A growing body of research on library use eventually will make possible better statistical measures of library effectiveness just as future standards will certainly reflect the growing divergence in postsecondary education. In turn, these will make possible better evaluation of one of higher education's fundamental components.

References

1. Conditions at this time are reviewed in many histories of higher education. See, for example, John S. Brubacher and Willis Rudy, *Higher Education in Transition: A History of American Colleges and Universities, 1636-1976*, 3rd ed. (New York: Harper & Row, 1973), Chapters 7, 8, 12, and 17; George F. Zook and M. E. Haggerty, *The Evaluation of Higher Institutions: 1. Principles of Accrediting Higher Institutions* (Chicago: University of Chicago Press, 1936), pp. 19-26.

2. "Report of the Committee on College Standards," *Proceedings of the Fourteenth Annual Meeting of the North Central Association of Colleges and Secondary Schools* (Chicago: North Central Association, 1909), pp. 52-54.

3. W. Stanley Hoole, "Library Standards," *Southern Association Quarterly,* 12 (February 1948), pp. 118-119; "Standards of Accredited Institutions of Higher Education," *North Central Association Quarterly,* 1 (June 1926), p. 20.

4. William W. Bishop, "(Letter to persons invited to serve on a Committee of Five)," *Bulletin of the American Library Association,* 13 (March 1919), pp. 32-33. The results were published in *Survey of Libraries in the United States,* 4 vols. (Chicago: American Library Association, 1926-1927).

5. Carl H. Milam, "Suggestions for Minimum College Library Standards," in *College and Reference Library Yearbook: Number Two* (Chicago: American Library Association, 1930), pp. 90-94, summarizes 28 such studies published between 1920-1929.

6. American Library Association, Committee on Classification of Library Personnel, *Budgets, Classification and Compensation Plans for University and College Libraries* (Chicago: American Library Association, 1929).

7. Eleanor M. Homer, "A Junior College 'Measuring Stick'," *Bulletin of the American Library Association,* 24 (August 1930), pp. 296-297.

8. George Alan Works, *College and University Library Problems* (Chicago: American Library Association, 1927); William M. Randall, *The College Library* (Chicago: American Library Association and The University of Chicago Press, 1932).

9. Carnegie Corporation, Advisory Group on College Libraries, *College Library Standards* (New York: n.p., 1932). These were based principally on the work of Randall. See *College Library,* pp. 140-142.

10. Douglas Waples, *The Evaluation of Higher Institutions: IV. The Library* (Chicago: University of Chicago Press, 1936).

11. "Statement of Policy Relative to the Accrediting of Institutions of Higher Education," *North Central Association Quarterly,* 9 (July 1934), pp. 40-46.

12. Zook and Haggerty, *Evaluation,* pp. 94-97.

13. "Statement of Policy Relative to the Accrediting of Institutions of Higher Education," *North Central Association Quarterly,* 9 (July 1934), p. 43.

14. For a description of the evaluation process, as it evolved over a 20-year period, see Manning M. Pattillo, "The Appraisal of Junior College and College Libraries," *College and Research Libraries,* 17 (September 1956), pp. 398-400.

15. *Ibid.,* p. 400.

16. G. Flint Purdy, "The New Library Accrediting Policies of the North

Central Association," in *College and University Library Service: Trends, Standards, Appraisal, Problems,* ed. by A. F. Kuhlman (Chicago: American Library Association, 1938), p. 58; L. H. Kirkpatrick, "Wanted — A Revision of Library Standards," *School and Society,* 52 (November 9, 1940), pp. 464-466.

17. David C. Weber, "Criteria for Evaluating a College Library," *Association of American Colleges Bulletin,* 43 (March 1957), p. 629.

18. By World War II, many favored abandoning accreditation altogether. Major criticism is summarized in Allan O. Pfnister, "Regional Accrediting Agencies at the Crossroads," *Journal of Higher Education,* 42 (October 1971). pp. 558-559.

19. Pattillo, "Appraisal," p. 397.

20. American Library Association and Association of College and Reference Libraries, College and University Postwar Planning Committee, *College and University Libraries and Librarianship* (Chicago: American Library Association, 1946), Chapter II "Library Expenditures and Standards of Support," pp. 7-21.

21. The *Score Cards* were developed to supplement American Library Association, Board on Personnel Administration, *Classification and Pay Plans for Libraries in Institutions of Higher Education,* 2nd ed., 3 vols. (Chicago: American Library Association, c. 1948).

22. American Library Association, Board on Personnel Administration, *Library Score Card: Supplement to Classification and Pay Plans for Libraries in Institutions of Higher Education,* 3 vols. (Chicago: American Library Association, 1950).

23. Robert Vosper, "Foundation Support of College Libraries," *College and Research Libraries,* 17 (March 1956), p. 141; Felix E. Hirsch, "Facing the Future: On the Way to New College Library Standards," *College and Research Libraries,* 19 (May 1958), p. 197.

24. Weber, "Criteria," p. 630.

25. Arthur T. Hamlin, "Notes from the A. C. R. L. Office," *College and Research Libraries,* 13 (January 1952), p. 65; and "The Year Ahead for ACRL," *College and Research Libraries,* 15 (October 1954), unpaged insert following p. 428.

26. Hirsch, "Facing the Future," p. 197.

27. "National Standards of the Junior College Section of the Association of College and Reference Libraries — American Library Association, June, 1956," *School Library Association of California Bulletin,* 28 (May 1957), pp. 10-14.

28. James O. Wallace, "Two-Year College Library Standards," *Library Trends*, 21 (October 1972), pp. 222-223.

29. "Standards for College Libraries," *College and Research Libraries*, 20 (July 1959), pp. 274-280; "Standards for Junior College Libraries," *College and Research Libraries*, 21 (May 1960), pp. 200-206.

30. James S. Coles, "A College President and the Standards for College Libraries," *College and Research Libraries*, 22 (July 1961), p. 267; Wallace, "Two-Year Standards," pp. 223, 225.

31. Helen M. Brown, "The Standards and the College Library in 1965," *Drexel Library Quarterly*, 3 (July 1966), p. 204.

32. Margaret E. Monroe, "Standards — Criteria for Service or Goals for the Future?" *ALA Bulletin*, 56 (October 1962), pp. 818-820.

33. "ACRL Board of Directors . . . Brief of Minutes, July 14, 1966," *College & Research Libraries News*, 27 (September 1966), pp. 107-108.

34. "ACRL Board of Directors . . . Brief of Minutes, January 9, 1968," *College & Research Libraries News*, 29 (March 1968), p. 64.

35. "Guidelines for Two-Year College Learning Resources Programs," *College & Research Libraries News*, 33 (December 1972), pp. 305-315.

36. Wallace, "Two-Year Standards," p. 228; "Guidelines for Two-Year Learning Resources Programs," pp. 305-306; "ACRL Board of Directors . . . Brief of Minutes, January 27, 1972," *College & Research Libraries News*, 33 (April 1972), p. 81.

37. *Guidelines for College Libraries* (Working draft of the Association of College and Research Libraries, Standards and Accreditation Committee, approved for distribution — January 21, 1971), lithographed (November, 1970).

38. Helen M. Brown, "College Library Standards," *Library Trends*, 21 (October 1972), p. 215.

39. "College Library Standards: Questions and Answers," *College & Research Libraries News*, 35 (November 1974), pp. 249-250); "Standards for College Libraries," *College & Research Libraries News*, 36 (1975), pp. 277-279, 290-295, 298-301.

40. David R. Watkins, "Standards for University Libraries," *Library Trends*, 21 (October 1972), p. 194.

41. "Report of ARL-ACRL Joint Committee on University Library Standards," xerographed (May 28, 1974).

42. "Draft: Standards for University Libraries," *College & Research Libraries News* 39 (April 1978), p. 89: The final version, approved by the ACRL Board, January, 1979, was published in *College & Research Libraries News,* 40 (April 1979), pp. 101-110.

43. "Committee Appointed to Write Quantitative Standards for 'Guidelines for Two-Year College Learning Resources Programs'," *College & Research Libraries News,* 36 (October 1975), p. 283; "Highlights of the Annual Conference Meetings of the ACRL Board of Directors," *College & Research Libraries News,* 38 (September 1977), p. 226.

44. "Draft: Statement on Quantitative Standards for Two-Year Learning Resources Programs," *College & Research Libraries News,* 40 (March 1979), pp. 69-73.

An Overview of The Guidelines for Two-Year
College Learning Resources Programs
James O. Wallace

The assessment of quality is never easy. An excellent hotel, a fine automobile, or an educational institution must all meet difficult standards covering all discrete elements which should be considered. The process involved in the evaluation of an educational institution poses special problems. Whether the assessment is for internal direction and planning or for external appraisal, acceptable criteria must be utilized for all aspects of the institution. Two-year colleges are fortunate to have such criteria for one distinctive element in the *Guidelines for Two-Year College Learning Resources Programs*[1] and the related *Statement of Quantitative Standards for Two-Year Learning Resources Programs*.

Any criteria used for evaluation of quality must meet the tests of the authority of the authors, the appropriateness of the criteria, and their flexibility as applied to diverse institutional settings. As to the first of these tests, the *Guidelines* have the distinction of being jointly developed and endorsed by the three national organizations most concerned with learning resources services in two-year institutions. While the initiative was taken by the Association of College and Research Libraries, there was from the beginning the full participation of the American Association of Community and Junior Colleges. The Association for Educational Communications and Technology was unable to participate until later phases of the development of the document, but they more than made up for the initial delay by providing funds for a task force to work with the other two associations. The resultant document is a statement of the highest authority about services in two-year institutions.

Guidelines is concerned with the quality of learning resources services provided by the institution, not merely with library services. The criteria contained in *Guidelines* reflect this campus-wide approach to services but pose a problem for two-year institutions where the regional accrediting association has standards relating primarily to traditional libraries. The criteria do reflect, however, the long trend in the two-year colleges away from any focal emphasis solely on print-related or traditional library services for its learning resources program. This trend was addressed in the introduction to *Guidelines* where it stated that

> contemporary Learning Resources programs in two-year colleges are supportive of institution-wide efforts. Such programs should provide innovative leadership coupled with a multiplicity of varied resources which are managed by qualified staff who serve to facilitate the attainment of institutional objectives. Paramount to the success of such programs is the involvement of Learning Resources staff with teaching, administrative, and other staff members in the design, implementation, and evaluation of instructional and educational systems of the institution.[2]

The qualitative criteria statements throughout *Guidelines* represent the combined opinions of experts concerned with all aspects of the learning resources

---

James O. Wallace is the director of the San Antonio College.

programs with wide participation from educators, librarians, media specialists, and other interested parties. Under these circumstances the appropriateness of the criteria statements for the evaluation of quality at an individual institution must be considered to be convergent. Departures from recognized norms by any institution can be clearly identified in relation to the statements contained. For example, the first section of the "Objectives and Purposes" of *Guidelines* states: "The College makes provision for a Learning Resources Program." With *Guidelines'* explanatory notes and glossary to provide the necessary clarity, it is possible for any institution to determine whether it provides or ignores campus needs.

Since *Guidelines* recognizes the diversities that exist among the two-year colleges, they are sufficiently flexible so that they may apply equally to private junior colleges, public community colleges, technical institutes, lower-division branches of four-year colleges and universities, and even private business and trade schools. Variations in organizational structure from consolidated administration of the learning resources program under a single administrative head to independent units for traditional library and audiovisual services do not affect the application of the criteria. *Guidelines* is not related to institutional structure but rather to the quality of the services provided campus-wide by a program which provides for learning resources of all types to meet instructional, individual, and institutional needs.

Guidelines was adopted in 1972 following a process which included wide dissemination of draft copies, hearings at the national meetings of all three associations, review of suggestions for improvement or amplification from many correspondents, and finally passage through the labrynthine sequences involved in securing adoption by all of the organizations. Recently a task force from the Association for Educational Communications and Technology made a complete reevaluation of the wording of the document. They found no need for any major changes and only suggested elimination of some phrases which could be interpreted as sexist (though not so intended) along with minor shifting and polishing.

Four basic assumptions are made in *Guidelines*. First, it assumes that the institution at which they are being used will have as one of its objectives the provision for quality education. *Guidelines* proceeds to outline what information specialists, communications specialists, and two-year college administrators perceive to be necessary aspects of learning resources to support quality education.

The second assumption is that the provision for learning resources throughout the campus is more important than administrative structure. There are strong statements on services to be provided and no definition of organizational structure to be used to provide the services. An institution defines for itself the units included in the learning resource program and the administrative channels by which such units are linked.

The third assumption is that learning is an essential ingredient in all services provided. Involvement in the instructional role, including any appropriate classroom teaching, is understood. As a corollary of this, the staff have appropriate professional or technical training to make learning possible, and all professional staff members have equivalent faculty status, benefits, and obligations.

Finally, it is assumed that, should some provision become impossible because of institutional objectives, administrators and staff will be able to identify such criteria and, after documenting their inappropriateness, will disregard them. One example of this assumption is the statement relating to multi-campus districts which is clearly without any possibility of application to a single-campus institution. This assumption, however, does not imply that neglecting to provide some service or to follow recommended procedures is acceptable.

What we have, then, in *Guidelines* is a significant document of the highest professional status which every institution should utilize at the campus level to make comparisons there between existing provisions for services and a model for quality learning resources programs. It was never expected that this statement should be an isolated, external measurement for accreditation. On the other hand accreditation agencies should be concerned that *Guidelines* and the supplementary *Quantitative Standards* are not ignored in the self-study process that precedes accreditation.

Other speakers will address the use of these documents in accreditation. It suffices for the use of this paper to point out that a self-study which ignores the recommendations of the three national associations most directly concerned with learning resources in two-year institutions can scarcely be expected to meet any objective for quality educational experiences.

It may be desirable to point out some things missing from *Guidelines*. There is no organizational structure. On one campus it will be desirable for the chief administrator of the program to be a Dean with corresponding authority and responsibility; on the another campus with few students, the responsibilities can effectively be performed by an individual with some other title. These are decisions which can be determined best by the institution and not by national statements.

There is also no provision that the program be funded in a single budget account. Statistical groups, such as the Department of Education in the HEGIS report series, often miss the significance of this statement. It is rarely the case that all provision for library or learning resources services on a campus comes from a centralized budget. Not only are learning resources provided through grants and gifts, but the various departments also purchase through their budgets items that constitute part of the learning resources program. The *Guidelines* point out, for example, the potential for rental of materials to meet needs; on many campuses, film rentals are charged to department budgets and not to a central account. A method must be developed by each institution to recognize and include such expenditures as part of the learning resources program expenditures as the support given is considered as a percentage of the institutional budget.

Guidelines does not prescribe the administrative units that constitute the program; the collge must determine what units should be identified as part of the program. At San Antonio College, a language laboratory and a learning laboratory are part of the central services, but the campus program includes multimedia laboratories in chemistry, reading, business technology, and nursing for which personnel are supplied by the departments, although the central services purchase and catalog the materials and purchase and service the equipment as part of the learning resources program. A computer laboratory is separately operated; even here there has been some discussion that this might possibly become part of the overall learning resources program.

Finally, *Guidelines* does not provide quantitative standards. At the time in 1972 when they were issued, the most prevalent criticism was that no quantitative items were included in the document. There were good reasons for this. The document was designed to measure quality, not quantity. More significant was the lack of statistical basis for any quantitative evaluation. It was not until 1975 that the HEGIS report asked for specific details about materials other than books and serials. Without some statistics representing actual two-year college holdings of various types of audiovisual materials, it was impractical to attempt to develop collection standards. The committee which developed *Guidelines* did not believe that inclusion of partial quantitative standards, given the information available, would add anything to the document.

A further reason that quantitative standards were not included in *Guidelines* was the awareness that such standards often become dated. When the first junior college standards were published in 1960, one of the quantitative statements was that every junior college library should have 20,000 volumes. There was tremendous furor about this simple statement. Three-fourths of the administrators who spoke up at a meeting of the American Association of Junior Colleges in Denver in 1961 attacked the quantity as unrealistic. It must be admitted that at that time fewer than 10 percent of all two-year colleges had that many volumes; today fewer than 5 percent have fewer than 20,000 volumes. San Antonio College, this author's institution, probably the largest today, has 235,000 volumes of printed materials and, including audiovisual materials, more than 300,000 cataloged items.

Although no quantitative standards were included in *Guidelines*, the desirability for such standards to supplement them was recognized from the beginning. By the late seventies a joint committee of the Association for Educational Communications and Technology and ACRL began developing quantitative statements as the expected supplement. The final draft of the *Statement on Quantitative Standards for Two-Year College Learning Resources Programs*[4] was approved in June 1979. *Guidelines* was changed in no way by this quantitative statement.

The standards deal with staff, collection size, equipment for distribution, and production levels. There are brief statements about budgets and space requirements. The latter accepts by citation the comprehensive study of space needs prepared in California by the Learning Resources Association of the California Community Colleges.[3] The budget statement recognizes that until concise determination of budget account elements to be included has been made, comparable budget figures must be very generalized.

The 1975 HEGIS statistics, including as these did all types of learning resources, were used extensively in developing standards for collection and staff. The two levels identified, "good" and "minimal," identify the points where fell the upper and lower quartiles in studies of data from all major public two-year college states. The quartiles as developed relate to full-time equivalent enrollments. The resulting standards apply to a single campus where services are provided for twelve months. Collection size is expressed in bibliographical units, not volumes. This approach is appropriate for two-year institutions but has not been used for the standards for other types of academic institutions. Provision in the collection is made for all types of materials: motion pictures, videotapes, kits, slides, models, art prints, bound volumes, microfilms, and other catalog items. Rented motion pictures are accepted as an alternate to purchased motion pictures in determining collection size.

Since the key element in the quantitative standards is the full-time equivalent enrollment, as a matter of illustration take the standards for a campus with 2,000 full-time enrollment with no outside cataloging, no unusual additional learning resources units, and no commercial-level production facilities. For such a two-year college, staff would range from a minimum of three professionals to a good level of five professionals on the staff. Fewer than three would indicate that services are likely to be poor while more than five would indicate that the institution was in the upper 25 percent of all similiar institutions. Total staff would number at the minimal level ten persons and at the good level nineteen.

Similiarly, collection size in bibliographical unit equivalents would be expected to range from a minimal level of 45,000 items to a good level of 66, 000 items. Of these 70 percent would be printed materials, including periodical subscriptions and microfilms. The remaining 30 percent would be recorded materials, motion pictures, videotapes, and other audiovisual media.

In terms of space the facilities would be slightly over 16,500 square feet, with from 50 to 70 percent for print areas, 5 percent for related instructional services, and the remainder for use in audiovisual production and services. Production capabilities, moving into the intermediate level, would include two-camera video production, black and white photographic processing, and the making and editing of sound recordings.

What do such details mean in determining quality of learning resources programs? First of all, if the institution moves above the "good" level, probability of quality services increases, possibility for quality instruction in the classroom which utilizes advanced instructional techniques is enhanced, and the dedication of the institution to the improvement of institutional capabilities is demonstrated. This does not mean that other elements in the institution do not need to be examined, but they are examined with the consideration of demonstrated planning for quality.

Both *Guidelines* and *Statement* are significant documents which should be used by every two-year institution for planning and for evaluating qualitatively and quantitatively an institution's learning resources program, and as significant documents to be used in a self-study process.

References

1. American Association of Community and Junior Colleges — Association for Educational Communications and Technology — American Library Association, "Guidelines for Two-Year College Learning Resources Programs," *Audiovisual Instruction,* 18 (January 1973), pp. 50-61; *College & Research Libraries News,* 33 (December 1972), pp. 305-315.

2. *Ibid.* Introduction, ¶2.

3. Learning Resources Association of the California Community Colleges, *Facilities Guidelines for Learning Resources Centers: Print, Non-print, Related Instructional Services,* 1978.

4. Association of College and Research Libraries, "Statement on Quantitative Standards for Two-Year College Learning Resources Programs," 1979.

Standards for College Libraries: Trends and Issues
Patricia Ann Sacks

The tutored and pious speak of standards as vision and mental flying. They are schooled in the word-by-word testing and tasting that standards demand, diligently identifying the parts, then elevating their selection to stand for the whole. Caught in the need to pin and measure, and baste the stitch, they define standards as the word (trimmed of its selvedge), the line (gathered by the paragraph), and the text (bound with professional papers). On occasions it has been difficult to compose a document addressing each notion. But they have designed, cut, tailored and worn . . . and somehow have moved from the pioneering formulas of Clapp/Jordan (which challenged the data in the 1959 *Standards for College Libraries* with a formula constructed on listings of basic and subject collections)[1], and avoided the extremes of *Farewell to Alexandria*.[2] The standards which have evolved — and are evolving — are neither hollow nor hallowed. Rather they are deeply embedded in the academic library's tradition and purpose, and the academic librarian's professional wisdom. Librarians need to record and shelve the printed line, variable within its rigor, and proclaim the library's once and future dimensions.

This presentation addresses college library standards and covers:

1. A brief survey of the development of college library standards in the United States;
2. Current conditions and trends affecting the development and use of standards;
3. Issues which require study and resolution;
4. A few specifics of the college library environment which challenge and bind librarians.

There is a curiosity about the past that no future can satisfy. Some pasts, like classification systems, are invented; others like accession books and neat handwriting, are remembered. The invocation of the past, with its chronicles, summons the present, with its problematic corollary, prophecy. The starting point in contemporary history is 1959 when the ACRL Committee on Standards, under the chairmanship of Felix Hirsch, published *Standards for College Libraries*.

> These standards [were] designed to provide a guide for the evaluation of libraries in American Colleges which emphasize[d] four-year undergraduate instruction, and may or may not have graduate program leading to a Master's degree. They [were] not applicable to junior college libraries, or to libraries of academic institutions stressing advanced research.[3]

The document, addressed to librarians, college administrators, and budget-approving authorities, was the first comprehensive guide for the evaluation of college libraries. It was considered a major influence on the Higher Education Act of 1965, Title IIA, which provided — and still provides, in decreasing amounts — financial support upgrading the collections of academic libraries.

Patricia Ann Sacks is the director of the Cedar Crest and Muhlenberg Colleges Libraries.

The revision process, influenced by the managerial, organizational, and technological advances of a decade, resulted in an interim document, *Guidelines for College Libraries,* which was rejected by the membership of ACRL in 1971.

The approved edition, *Standards for College Libraries,* produced by a committee chaired by Johnnie Givens, and endorsed by ACRL in 1975, includes qualitative and quantitative criteria. Organized on the basis of the major functions and supporting requirements of the college library, the eleven page statement covers: Objectives; Collections; Organization of Materials; Staff; Delivery of Service; Facilities; Administration; and Budget.[4] Each standard is followed by a commentary explicating the standard. Three of the standards — collections, staff, and facilities — are accompanied by specific formulas. Since a copy of this document is included in this publication, it is not necessary to paraphrase its contents. Neither should one remain content with its suitability because the present is an irritable reaching after certainty and perfection — a cord that tethers the unruly elephant in our field.

Directing the college library in the face of the unknown brings with it certain mixed blessings as secondary compensation. The talismen include the computer, ANSI Z 39 standards, self-studies and guides, and better managerial techniques which place evaluation on a par with planning and implementation processes. Counterbalancing the charms are several sleep-stealing monstrosities ... cobwebs spun by conflicting objectives, shortages of space, the upward spiral of inflation on acquisition and service costs, reduced financial support, the crumbling of pulp paper bookstock, and the necessity for institutions to relinquish some autonomy to achieve common objectives. The latter in the form of cooperation is a positive charge which forces the seeking of guidelines and standards which encourage collective commitments, and the effective use of new technology and managerial techniques.

The talismen and the bogey-beasts (their form and character reflect Western value systems) collide to set the trends which influence the future course of the *College Library Standards.*

Trend 1: a movement to standards based on individuality, addressing an academic community's needs rather than absolute ideals. This development suggests needs assessment, analysis of resources, and coordination with the goals and objectives of the academic community. It reflects commitments toward user services, including instruction in the use of library resources and services.

The ARL's Office of Management Studies has pioneered the development of programs which assist academic libraries to conduct self-analysis studies and plan programs based on institutional needs. The programs which are designed for libraries covered by the *College Library Standards* are:

a. The Academic Library Development Program (ALDP), a comprehensive review process focusing on services, operations, and management of mid-sized academic libraries; and

b. The Planning Program for Small Academic Libraries which assists the library with a professional staff of fewer than ten to examine and strengthen its role in the instructional processes of its parent institution.

Trend 2: a user-oriented evaluation process emphasizing outputs, the services the user receives. Increased resources do not necessarily improve services.

An evaluation of effectiveness is an evaluation of user satisfaction and efficiency of resource allocation. This presupposes the existence of stated objectives against which a service or program can be measured. It requires objectives that are tangible and susceptible to precise definition. Major contributors to this development include F.W. Lancaster, Donald King and King Research, Michael Hamburg, Michael Buckland, and pioneers J.A. Raffel, P. Shisko, J.C. Licklider, F. Leimkuhler, and P.M. Morse. Library literature now reports experiences which convert theories into practices.

Trend 3: the development of normative standards. The emphasis here is on ranges of adequacy in terms of quantitative measures rather than absolute levels for quantitative standards. This approach allows an individual library to compare itself to other libraries similar in purpose, size, staff, collections, and facilities. It is a process by which a library can develop standards appropriate to its unique situation rather than submit to a national statement of arbitrary numbers. The trend was advanced by Deprospo's study, *Performance Measures for Public Libraries*[5], and is reflected in the Appendix (Quantitative Analytical Techniques) to *Standards for University Libraries*[6].

The Task Force on Library Costs and Service Analysis affiliated with the Council for the Advancement of Small Colleges is providing a support system for the college library in this area with activities that:

a. provide each participating college with operating and analytical data for short and long-range planning purposes;

b. support an ongoing data collection and dissemination service that permits colleges to analyze local and national trends;

c. develop a national data base on libraries and independent liberal arts colleges that can be used to influence public policy formulation and funding.

The users manual, *Managing Costs and Service in College Libraries,* provides an overview of the module, and describes methods for analysis, interpretation, and use.[7]

Trend 4: an awareness of the need to address standards on a continuous revision process. An ACRL Ad Hoc Committee was established as a recognition of this need and is currently between the folds of computer printouts reporting an analysis of the 1977 National Center for Educational Services (NCES) data prepared by Ray Carpenter of the University of North Carolina.[8] The study, directed at determining to what degree more than 1,100 academic libraries meet the quantitative criteria of the 1975 *Standards*, is not ready for publication, but the preliminary findings indicate some major disparities between *Standards* and existing conditions in the categories of volumes held, staffing, and budget support. For example, 52 percent of the libraries have fewer than 100,000 volumes. And 84 percent of the libraries are allocated less than 6 percent of their institutions' educational and general budgets. The distress is compounded by this statement from the introduction to the *Standards*:

The *Standards* . . . do not prescribe [an] unattainable ideal. They rather describe a realistic set of conditions which, if fulfilled, will provide an adequate library program in a college.

In identifying key issues which are subjected to these trends, one still needs standards (or their methodological substitutes) for college libraries; standards should identify the means for evaluating performance and effectiveness. The library's goals, according to F.W. Lancaster, should be:

> To maximize the accessibility of resources to the user;
> To maximize the exposure of the user to the resources;
> To use efficiently available funds to accomplish accessibility and exposure.[9]

The issues requiring study and resolution are:

Issue 1: contradictory applications and expectations of standards. A standard requires purposeful definition and application. It cannot be all things to all people. The dimensions of the standard-setting process are presented in Figure 1 adapted from Charles McClure's article in *Library Research*.[10] Confusing one purpose with another is a primary issue to be addressed in standards' development.

Issue 2: the availability of an agreed-upon terminology and data bases which support comparative studies regarding resources and services, and identify inputs *and* outputs. The draft on *Library Statistics* from the American National Standards Institute Z 39.7 has been prepared

> to assist librarians and researchers to collect user statistical data on libraries by indicating and defining appropriate measures for obtaining quantifiable information to improve accountability.[11]

The document is deficient in several areas, particularly in its identification of output measures. Its use of the intellectual unit of measure is certain to be debated by the profession, but its recognition of needs and pioneering efforts are steps in the right direction. Other advances in this area include the compilation of the *Handbook of Standard Terminology for Reporting and Recording Information About Libraries* scheduled for publication as a field edition by the American Library Association in fall 1980. This publication acknowledges the working document of the National Center for Higher Education Management Systems, *Library Statistical Data Base Formats and Definitions* (1977) and its *Glossary* (1978). Although these documents help stabilize definitions and formats and comprehensively identify library inputs, none of them helps measure the impact of library services on our communities. The question to be addressed is, "How does the library perform related to the needs of its users?"

Issue 3: the role of the library profession (ACRL) and the postsecondary accrediting associations regarding the development, adoption, and use of college library standards. This relationship is complicated by the movement to standards emphasizing empirical research, local needs, and individualized goals. Complications, however, should be viewed as opportunities, not threats. There is need to build on variation as a strength and to share experiences.

Issue 4: the acceptability of the self-study documents and locally-determined levels of adequacy as substitutes for or replacements of standards. Are locally-determined levels of adequacy an acceptable means of determining adequacy? Are they an alternative or a substitute for standards?

The foregoing identification of the trends and the key issues without an acknowledgment of some of the specifics of the college library environment would

A. *Origin of Standards*
1. Library Profession
2. State agency
3. Academic library
4. Academic community
5. Accrediting Assn.

B. *Basis*
1. Expert opinion
2. State, federal regulations
3. Local, information needs
4. Empirical data

C. *Level of Standard*
1. Minimum
2. Adequate
3. Average
4. Range of levels
5. Maximum

D. *Type of Measure*
1. Qualitative
2. Quantitative
3. Professional judgement

E. *For Library Type*
1. College
2. University
3. Community/Jr. College
4. Branch
5. Subject
6. Special Collection

F. *Criteria of the Standard*
1. Provision of services
2. Storage of documents
3. Provision of information
4. Basic resources, staff,
   collection, facility, etc.

G. *Intent*
1. Encourage
2. Comply
3. Self-assess
4. Improve
5. Control

H. *Anticipated Result*
1. Increase resources
   (input)
2. Increase services
   (output)
3. Maintain status quo
4. Facilitate cooperation
5. Establish goals

I. *Primary Purpose*
1. Planning
2. Measuring
3. Comparing
4. Allocating resources

J. *Target Audience*
1. Librarians
2. College administrators
3. Governing bodies
4. Academic community

Figure 1: DIMENSIONS AND EXPECTATIONS OF LIBRARY STANDARDS

McClure, Charles R. "From Public Library Standards to Development of Statewide Levels of Adequacy," *Library Research* 2 (1980–81), p. 51. Several of the terms cited by Dr. McClure are changed to reflect the academic library environment.

be somewhat like defining a table as composed of largely empty space populated by sub-atomic particles rushing about in waves. One's shins experience the corners of a solid object with definite boundaries. The dimensions are immediate and particular. The specifics which have a critical bearing on what kind of academic library, and ultimately what kind of college exists, include:

1. Funding acquisitions within an environment where the number of print and non-print titles increases and inflation erodes purchasing power. This is more crucial where it is known that the great majority of library materials in active use are fewer than ten years old, yet most college libraries are buying fewer new publications;

2. The deterioration to which all printed materials are subjected, especially wood fiber papers. We need a comprehensive program of conservation, saving what is used and what is unique, withdrawing what is necessary, and insuring adequate preservation procedures;

3. Applying the new technology. The traditional means of providing access to library holdings is being overtaken by the computer. The costs and the benefits are not as clear as it would be hoped they would be, and sometimes seem beyond the grasp of the college library. Yet the commitment made in this decade to automation will determine how prepared and able the library functions in the 1990s;

4. The change in the production, storage and retrieval of information. The text of 3,200 books could be contained on a single two-sided video disc. This raises questions not only about the library's future, but about the publication, storage, dissemination, and assimilation of such quantities of information;

5. Fundamental changes in student populations. The number of students enrolled in continuing education programs (credit and non-credit) exceeds the number of full-time, matriculated students,[12] yet libraries — and standards — are often unaware of this new majority, their needs, and their impact on the future.

Imaginatively and wisely supporting the curriculum of the college, seeing that students develop self-reliant skills in locating and using information, making the library exceptional for its service and responsiveness to student and faculty needs are essentially the challenges before standards and the purposes to which evaluative activities are directed. Finding the means for improving documents and processes requires broad recognition of needs and constraints, and systematic approaches for sharing knowledge, exposing views, and developing working relationships which support better libraries.

Where does that leave the unruly elephant? With a memory minding the proceedings and measuring the distances between one word and another. The shift from the elephant to the subject of standards is not the crux of the matter, but the conjunction of both gives a sense of the Jumbos and jungles of meaning. The lines nearing judgment deliberately jingle.

References

1. Verner W. Clapp and Robert T. Jordan, "Quantitative Criteria for Adequacy of Academic Library Collections, *College and Research Libraries,* 26 (September 1965), pp. 371-80.

2. ACM Conference on Space, Growth and Performance Problems of Academic Libraries, Chicago, 1975, *Farewell to Alexandria: solutions to space, growth, and performance problems of libraries* (Westport, Conn.: Greenwood Press, 1976).

3. Association of College and Research Libraries, Committee on Standards, "Standards for College Libraries," *College and Research Libraries,* 20 (July 1959), pp. 274-80.

4. "Standards for College Libraries," *College and Research Libraries News,* 36 (October 1975), pp. 277-79, 290-95, 298-301.

5. E. Altman, E.R. DeProspo and E.C. Clark, *A Data Gathering and Instructional Manual for Performance Measures in Public Libraries* (Chicago: Celadon Press, 1976).

6. Association of Research Libraries and the Association of College and Research Libraries, Joint Committee on University Library Standards, "Standards for University Libraries," *College and Research Libraries News,* 39 (April 1979), pp. 107-110.

7. Council for the Advancement of Small Colleges, *Managing Costs and Services in College Libraries: A Users Manual* (Washington, D.C.: The Council, 1979).

8. Ray Carpenter, "Measures of College Libraries and the ACRL College Library Standards," Unpublished draft (University of North Carolina, 1980).

9. F.W. Lancaster, *The Measurement and Evaluation of Library Services* (Washington, D.C.: Information Resources Press, 1977), p. 6.

10. Charles R. McClure, "From Public Library Standards to Development of Statewide Levels of Adequacy," *Library Research* 2 (1980-81), pp. 51-52.

11. *Draft of Library Statistics.* Prepared by American National Standard Z 39.7 for discussion (June 1980), p. 2.

12. American Council of Education, Committee on the Financing of Higher Education for Adult Students, *Financing Part-time Students: The New Majority in Post-Secondary Education* (Washington, D.C.: American Council on Education, 1974).

A Review of the Development of
the Current University Library Standards
Richard J. Talbot

Most of the current developments in library standards, especially academic library standards, seem to arise from the seminal article by Verner Clapp and Robert Jordan entitled "Quantitative Criteria for Adequacy of Academic Library Collections" which was published in *College & Research Libraries* in September 1965. This article was eagerly seized upon by library administrators and university officials who were seeking a quantitative method for evaluating library collections. In the context of the sixties this was easy to understand. The relative affluence of higher education led many institutions to attempt to strengthen their libraries, and in the midst of competing priorities it is always necessary to define how much is enough for any one segment of the institution. Nevertheless, the eagerness with which the Clapp-Jordan formula was taken up suprised even Verner Clapp. According to a recently retired ARL Director who knew him well, Mr. Clapp viewed this formula as a trial balloon, something which other researchers or practitioners might perfect.

Indeed, this did happen to some extent. The formula was adapted and refined by many institutions, most notably Washington State. Even today, if you compare the Washington State formula with the ALA *Standard for College Libraries* you will see that they are essentially the same. Clapp-Jordan's original notion of assigning minimual values per student, per faculty member, per program, etc., was adopted and accepted by much of the library world without a great deal of discussion and debate.

With the universities, however, it was a different story. A joint ARL/ACRL committee on university library standards was appointed as early as 1968 under the chairmanship of Robert Downs, but it was not until 1978 that a report of a succedent committee under the chairmanship of Eldred Smith produced a report which was finally accepted both by ARL and ALA.

Why did it take so long? The principal reasons were stated by Dr. Downs as early as 1969 in a report on *University Library Statistics* which he prepared for ARL. He said, in part:

> At the present stage, in fact, considerable skepticism exists as to the feasibility, or even the desirability, of setting up standards for university libraries. Among the reasons are: the "institutional environment" and "mission" of individual universities vary greatly; standards applicable to comprehensive universities may be invalid for specialized institutions; and stated minima may come to be regarded as maxima, thereby impeding the growth of a given library.

To put the matter more bluntly, the larger libraries feared that any standard would tend to be a kind of average which would set threshold limits considerably below the level of support which they already enjoyed. Libraries of truly inter-

Richard Talbot is the director of the libraries at University of Massachusetts at Amherst.

national scope feared, with some justice, that their budgeting officials would seize upon such standards as a justification for lowering or at least not raising their budgets. Wiser officials of what might be called "emerging" university libraries realized that if the standards were set too high, they would be seen by their budgetary officials as impossible of attainment and consequently disregarded. Those in the middle were more impressed by a paragraph from the Clapp-Jordan article which is worth quoting:

> When . . . standardizing authorities omit or refuse to set standards in quantitative terms, the budgeting and appropriating authorities, who cannot avoid quantitative bases for their decisions, are compelled to adopt measures which, though perhaps having the virtue of simplicity, may be essentially irrelevant.

In other words, every institution of any size will adopt some kind of quantitative measure to apply to its libraries. So it seemed better to most of the libraries of middle size to attempt to devise some kind of useful standard rather than to have something thrust upon them.

Dr. Downs and his committee agreed, and they offered to ARL in 1976 the Washington State standard, but this again met with the same objections as before and the issue remained unresolved. Nevertheless, given the growing budgetary pressures of the seventies, ALA and ARL decided to try once again to achieve a set of university library standards, so a new joint committee was formed under the leadership of Eldred Smith.

The members of the new committee, not surprisingly, held views representative of the various factions in the debate. A majority seemed to be in favor of quantitative standards, but the representatives of the larger library point of view were adamantly opposed. So it was decided to experiment, to test what would happen if quantitative standards were applied to university libraries.

But what are university libraries? Pragmatically, they are the academic libraries which do not fall under the ALA *Standards for College Libraries,* the libraries of institutions which offer Ph.D. degrees in ten or more disciplines, the ones which are listed as such in the Carnegie Commission's *A Classification of Institutions of Higher Education* (Berkeley, 1973). There are 172 of these institutions in that list, and this was thus the population to examine.

The next issue was: What formula should be applied? One obvious candidate was the Washington State formula in the version proposed to ARL by Dr. Downs in his 20 December 1974 report of the ARL/ACRL Task Force on University Library Standards. Another candidate was suggested by Mr. Melvin Voigt, who was a member of the committee and who had published his own formula for adequacy of collections in the July 1975 issue of *College & Research Libraries.* Finally, there was the work on regression analysis of library data which was published by Professors Baumol and Marcus in their book *Economics of Academic Libraries* (Washington: American Council on Education, 1973). A review of the literature produced no other promising formula candidates, and there was neither the time nor the resources to develop now ones, it was decided to use these three. Survey questionnaires were sent to the 172 institutions in the Carnegie Commission list and to the seven Canadian institutions in ARL. One hundred fifteen responses were received, or a response rate of 64 percent.

Recalling the pattern of the Washington State formula or the ALA *Standards for College Libraries* and being familiar with regression analysis, one sees at a glance that the Washington State formula could lend itself to empirical validation by regression analysis. In fact, this is a point which R. Marvin McInnis makes about the Clapp-Jordan formula in a very interesting article which was published in the May 1972 issue of *College & Research Libraries*.

Ultimately, all formulas of the type being discussed must be considered as either predictive or normative. By predictive it is meant treating them either as true regression formulas or quasi-regression formulas in which one or more known variables are used to predict an unknown quantity. By normative it is meant the implication that some kind of absolute standard can be adopted and applied to the data. In the case of libraries, normative standards are inevitably subjective or Delphic. Delphic methods are not to be despised. In the hands of skilled practitioners, they have proven to be useful in several disciplines. But it seems that once normative standards derived by a Delphic process are transplanted out of the environment in which they originated, they cease to satisfy. Perhaps this is because one person's or one group's subjective judgments are limited by his or its own experience. These normative formulas may be valuable in their own areas, but they should not be extended beyond them without being modified for local conditions. Thus, the Washinton State formula, taken as a normative standard, may be valid in Washington State, but it should not be applied normatively outside of Washington State without taking into account local conditions.

So in looking at the results of the survey for the Washington State and Voigt formulas, this author treated them as predictive and not normative. This means that if the formulas are useful predictors, then the variables generated by the formulas should be close to the actual numbers. In fact, this turned out not to be true: the results obtained showed so much variability between what was predicted and what was actually the case that the committee rejected both the Washington State formula and the Voigt formula. They we judged not to be useful.

The committee turned its attention to the application of the regression formulas derived by Baumol and Marcus. However, since the response from the non-ARL libraries was much less satisfactory than that from ARL libraries, the committee limited the application of these formulas to ARL libraries. And it produced results for the population with which it was concerned which had higher R^2 values than Baumol and Marcus found in their sample. (The R^2 measures the reduction in variation accounted for by the variable used.) Regression techniques are useful for making succinct comparative judgments and as a managerial tool for indicating what differences among similar institutions are worth analyzing, but they are obviously not standards themselves. They are not intended to be.

So the end result of this examination left the committee with the problem which it had now come to accept as usual. The majority of the committee would like to have discovered quantitative standards which would be intellectually defensible, but its researchers had yielded nothing which it could propose. On the other hand, the effort to find a quantitative standard had deepened the appreciation of the committee for the use of quantitative measures. This led to the development of the strategy which was finally employed in drafting the standards.

First of all, the committee really abandoned the notion of trying to define a standard in the traditional sense of a criterion which could be applied uniquely to libraries as one applies a yard stick to something which can be easily measured. Realistically, library standards cannot be compared to physical standards. This is a proposition which anyone will admit as soon as it is enunciated, but when attention shifts to evaluation one swiftly falls into the trap of acting as if what is called library standards are physical measures. They are not; they can never be. They can only be guides. The most that could be claimed for library standards is that they are immanent in the practices of "good" libraries and represent a kind of consensus on what constitutes adequate service or adequate collections. This ought to be measurable, as Verner Clapp hoped it eventually would be, but it is not yet. Librarians simply do not have the data or the means to compile the data to measure these practices adequately. More importantly, many of these practices are constantly changing, so their measurement ought to be flexible.

If one accepts the notion that library standards are not physical but merely comparative (and even comparative measures, to be useful, must be easily modifiable as conditions of change), then one will concentrate on attempting to provide guidance on how to determine what good practice is. And that is essentially what the *Standards for University Libraries* are, a general statement applicable in various ways to various institutions. They are an effort to assist those who must make evaluative decisions. They offer only guidance and suggestion, even in the statistical appendix which accompanies them. To the extent that they are valid, they are valid only for a time, until practices change or until librarians are better able to qualify and measure the phenomena with which they deal.

To illustrate: Section B.1 of *Standards* is concerned with collections which are most susceptible to the application of quantitative measures. Yet, the standard simply says:

> A university library's collections shall be of sufficient size and scope to support the university's total instructional needs and to facilitate the university's research programs.

This is a rather obvious statement, and in the commentary which follows only very general advice is given. The user is urged to make qualitative judgments on the basis of very general principles and is cautioned about the use of quantitative measures, as follows:

> Attempts have been made to identify precise quantitative measures of adequate collection size and growth rates for a university library. No such formula has yet been developed which can be generally applied. At present, such formulas as exist can only yield approximations which indicate a general level of need. If they are applied arbitrarily and mechanically, they can distort the realities of a given situation. Nevertheless, qualitative measures are increasingly important in guiding the qualitative judgment that must ultimately be applied to university libraries and their collec-

tions. One technique is the use of regression analysis to facilitate the comparison of similar libraries to one another; another of some general applicability is the "index of quality" developed by the American Council on Education for relating library collection size to graduate program quality.

Even the appendix to the standards offers only a general indication of the kinds of measures which could be used.

So the intent here in B.1, as throughout, was to indicate that a library should be compared, not to some absolute or normative standard, but to a comparative standard derived from an examination of an appropriate peer group. The selection of the appropriate peer group is left to the user. Such an examination requires a qualitative and subjective judgment, but this kind of judgment can be aided by the quantitative measures whose use is advocated.

The committee would have liked to have gone beyond this advise to suggest the application of performance measures in addition to merely comparative ones, but as the appendix says:

> Performance measures are . . . still in the early stages of their development. They may eventually prove to be most useful in making intra-institutional rather than interinstitutional decisions.
> In sum, there are no simple solutions, no ready panaceas, no easily available substitutes for intelligent analysis of available data.

Current Uses of Standards
Johnnie E. Givens

Introduction

To ask people to focus their thinking at this time in the *Proceedings* on the uses of standards in the accreditation process is a challenge. They have made numerous uses of standards in a variety of ways. They are participating in the *Proceedings* because of the contribution which can be made to this problem of standards from positive experiences and successful interaction with others engaged in the accrediting process.

By accepting the invitation to contribute time and ability, people have joined the effort toward reaching a goal articulated by ACRL in the early seventies – to work toward improving the functioning of libraries in the accreditation problem of higher education. The assignment here is to function in a so-called "think tank" mode. At the conclusion of the *Proceedings,* people will return to their usual schedule of assignments and activities within which, because of their professional responsibilities, they will become emissaries. The information they will share from their experience here should help to expand the understanding of libraries and accreditation in higher education institutions, an understanding which is unevenly held in the academic world.

The following silhouette of the uses of standards, not as new information, but as a review, is offered.

Various Constituents of Higher Education

Communities of higher education consist of several constituents. They include:

    (1) Librarians, both library directors and staff members;
    (2) Academic administrators at various institutional levels;
    (3) Teaching faculty, representing the perspective of the individual disciplines and sometimes the double viewpoint as members of a library advisory policy committee;
    (4) Students: undergraduate, graduate, and post graduate researchers;
    (5) Fiscal officers;
    (6) Governing Boards; ·
    (7) Coordinating Commissions with staff;
    (8) Accrediting agencies and their subsequent visitation committees;
    (9) Legislators, generally as members of study committees.

Each of these at times and in ways becomes a shareholder with a stake in the academic institution. This interest and involvement necessitate that they respond to and interact with the accreditation process. The link between libraries and accreditation is fundamental, and people have been particularly informed by the previous papers on the relationship standards hold with the two.

Current Uses of Standards

When reviewing the heritage of philosophical concepts and the pragmatic pressures surrounding each group of constituents, one should not be surprised by the acknowledgement that the use of standards in the academic community can have both a positive and negative charge. Given a specific situation, each

Johnnie E. Givens is a consultant with the Metrics Research Corporation.

group can employ the standards either way. Neither use nor response is always likely either to support or question the value of a specific use of standards.

Enumerated here are some uses while left to the readers is the mind-awakening task of identifying the constituent group. Readers will surely be able to contribute other uses accidentally omitted. Standards are used:

(1) as an evaluative instrument to measure a library program;

(2) as a basis for budget planning and leverage for requesting increased fiscal support

(3) as the structure within which to compare the standing of one institution with peer institutions or with competing institutions either to pass a judgment as in the review for accreditation or as a stimulus to an ego-conscious administration;

(4) as justification for limiting the expansion of a library program considered by some to be out of proportion to other demands on inflation riddled funds;

(5) as justification for raiding the library budget or resisting the raid when there are fiscal cutbacks;

(6) as the basis for state- or system-wide long range planning;

(7) as documentation for fund raising in support of improving collections, buildings, or other resources and services;

(8) as substantiation for status in the academic environment.

Commonly Held Objectives

Neither individuals nor groups tend to be neutral about standards or their use. Response is substantial. But even when there appear to be adversary positions, regardless of the constituent group their objectives seem to be commonly held. Everyone wishes to provide for quality library service. No one argues against improving library services, even when the expectation is to be reached without cost. Individuals and groups together understand the benefits of effective planning even when the projected outcomes may not please everyone uniformly. Standards have been, are, and will continue to be used for meeting these general objectives.

Standards as a Language for Communication

These *Proceedings* had their evolution as an idea in 1975. The participants represent various constituent groups in higher education; all of whom are interested in what the accreditation process can mean to academic institutions in the 1980s. Sharing another's perspective improves understanding. As people work together, one use for standards is proposed which can form a comprehensive framework for all other uses. Think of standards as a language to provide a means of communication for developing a widely held understanding. People have an opportunity to develop and expand this communication use now.

The Assisted Self-Study Approach
To Improving Academic Libraries
Duane E. Webster

Introduction and Background

Academic libraries are entering the 1980s with the prospect of continued financial constraints, rapid technological change, increased competition for public and institutional support, demands from users for different and enhanced services, and pressure from college and university administrators for greater cost accountability. Libraries concerned with developing their capabilities and improving their performance in the face of these pressures can use a number of alternative change agents and processes.

1. The accreditation process, for example, exerts pressure on an institution to meet commonly-accepted, minimal levels of performance and resource commitment.
2. The external consultant may be used for objective assessment of the current situation, technical advice on library operations or introduction of new technology, organizational problem-solving, training and development of staff, or as a counselor on introducing the managing a change process such as management-by-objectives.[1]
3. The faculty committee provides an excellent opportunity for a key client group to help solve problems, advise on strategic development of the library, or encourage better institutional support of the library program.
4. Key staff can introduce fresh perspectives, different experience, and possibly a commitment to change.
5. Internal library committees and other group problem-solving efforts can involve the staff in responsible efforts to improve the situation.
6. Individual administrative leadership traditionally is seen as central to the shaping and directing of the process of library improvement.
7. Collective bargaining uses confrontation and pressure to secure improvement in library operations.
8. A process known as assisted self-study combines several of these change agents and strategies – key staff; committees composed of faculty, administration, staff, and students; external consultants; and library leadership – in a process that identifies and deals with problems. The assisted self-study approach recognizes that the library staff and administration are in the best position to gather and analyze information and make recommendations for change, assisted by a limited amount of direct consultation.

Library Improvement and Assisted Self-Study

The Academic Library Program designed and operated by the ARL/OMS enables academic libraries of all sizes to use assisted self-study to deal with pressures for change. Libraries participating in the program employ tested self-study methodologies to examine managerial and operational practices, focusing on workable recommendations for improvement. Libraries choose study

Duane Webster is the director of the Office of Management Studies at the Association of Research Libraries.

modules that best deal with their current and evolving needs. Each participating library receives on-site consultation, staff training, manuals, and other support materials from OMS as it conducts a study, which normally takes somewhere between three months and one year.

The self-improvement strategy of assisted self-study takes into account the unique strengths and weaknesses of a typical academic library. For example, libraries tend not to have the money to retain consultants, although frequently there are small funds available within the institution for faculty development or special projects. Library staff do not tend to have extensive training or experience in institutional research. Frequently they lack skills related to analytical problem-solving and interpersonal conflict negoitation and resolution. Yet these staff are industrious and hard working. They display considerable dedication and are committed to helping the library achieve its goals.

The demands of day-to-day library operation are overwhelming, and working at or above capacity does not allow staff to remain abreast of current and potential demands for user service. Yet the need for planning and for an enlarged role for the library within the college or university seems obvious and is generally accepted as an important goal for improvement by library staff.

On another front some of the problems present in these libraries can be traced to historical or personal factors and are so woven into the fabric of the institution that it is difficult for those directly involved to be objective or to come up with fresh ideas. The stimulation and objectivity achieved through a defined study process and the help of external experts is essential to overcoming the limits of this perspective.

The assisted self-study procedure addresses these several concerns by building on the strengths of the local situation. Central to the philosophy of assisted self-study are two notions. The first is that involvement in problem-solving and decision-making leads to commitment to action. The best ideas can prove useless if not implemented. Thus the assisted self-study approach deliberately secures the direct the involvement of key groups and individuals in the process of data-gathering, analysis, and preparation of an action plan. This is done with a scheme that allows efficient blending of individual and group efforts, all of which are focused on organizational development and useful change that deserve implementation.

The second notion central to the philosophy of self-study is that groups tend to make better decisions than individuals, particularly when a problem is so complex and involved that no one person has all the information necessary to resolve it and when no clear cut answers are readily available. With a study procedure aimed at the systematic examination of issues, the prospects of effective group decision-making is very good. In fact, our experience suggests that the group process produces more than a simple combination of individual efforts.

The study process provides for staff training in group problem-solving, program-planning, report writing and various interpersonal and analytical skills. This training is accomplished through a series of three on-site visits strategically timed to be of most assistance to the participating libraries. The study process is staged to avoid drastic demands on staff time that interfere with ongoing operations. While the time requirements for self-study are high, the rewards of direct involvement as well as the benefits for library development are generally regarded as being worth it. The methodology of systematic data-gathering, analysis, and idea development allows for creative problem-solving even in the most traditional self-study. The presence of an external advisor also helps in focusing on issues and productive outcomes. A recently-published book by Ed Johnson and Stuart Mann evalutes one of these study procedures.[2] The costs of doing a study are quite modest, typically $3,000-4,000 for Program resources and assistance. The library must also be prepared to contribute staff and faculty time.

Academic Library Program Options and Study Modules

Libraries participating in the Academic Library Program choose from modules within a number of self-study programs, based upon their particular interests and needs.[3] The Office of Management Studies assists libraries in making this initial decision. Current programs include:

a. *Organizational Screening Program*. This program assists libraries in conducting a rapid assessment of their current situation to determine whether a more comprehensive analysis is needed.

b. *The Management Review and Analysis Program (MRAP)*. This is a systematic examination of the management functions that are a part of most mid-sized and large academic libraries. The program modules from which libraries select include: planning; budgeting; policy-making; management information; supervision and leadership; organization; personnel practices; staff development; and executive leadership.

This program is for those libraries with fifty or more staff which are interested in either a full-scale study of their management and operational practices or an intense study of particular aspects of those practices.

c. *The Collection Analysis Project (CAP)*. This project is designed to help academic libraries assess their collection development practices and policies and includes modules on: collection history and description; collection objectives and policies; material fund allocation; organizational and staffing of collection development functions; collection assessment; preservation; and resource sharing.

This program was designed as a comprehensive study for research libraries, but now is available to libraries with smaller collections and those interested in completing specific modules such as collection assessment or collection policies and objectives.

d. *The Academic Library Development Program (ALDP)*. This study is geared to the smaller and mid-sized academic library and provides a comprehensive review of all aspects of library programs. It includes procedures for assessing operations, services, management practices, facilities, and changing technological needs.

The program is appropriate for libraries with staffs of more than fifteen, but fewer than fifty. Individual study modules may also be used.

e. *Small Library Planning Program*. Under development, this study will help libraries examine such services as reference, circulation, interlibrary loan, reserve book, and bibliographic instruction. It draws upon the College Library Program sponsored by the Council on Library Resources, the National Endowment for the Humanities, and the Council's Library Service Enhancement Program.

In each of the studies listed above, the participating library follows certain basic steps including:

(1) planning and designing the analysis;
(2) collecting data on the current situation;
(3) analyzing the situation for strengths and weaknesses;
(4) developing action-oriented solutions to build on strengths and overcome weaknesses;
(5) preparing a report that describes the situation and outlines a recommended course of action;
(6) deciding on an implementation strategy.

Academic Library Program Study Strategy

The library appoints a series of working groups with designated responsibilities for specific portions of the self-study. These groups are composed of library staff and teaching faculty who carry out the study with consultative support and materials supplied by the Office of Management Studies. With this approach the work is shared, and the variety of individuals involved in data-gathering and analysis provides a broad perspective. The actual size and number of study groups, as well as the time required to perform the study, vary depending upon the library's size and the design of the particular program.

The library receives procedural manuals and support publications throughout the study, including state-of-the-art reports, conceptual papers, and data-gathering instruments. Consultants provide on-site training for staff and both on-site and telephone consultation on developing a workable procedure and on reviewing results and recommendations. The Office's consultants concentrate on providing guidance in following study techniques and utilizing data collection instruments, and they also may assist in designing special instruments or procedures, critiquing reports, or simply acting as sounding boards. Consultants do not prescribe soultions to given problems. Rather, they facilitate the library's development of solutions.

The most important criteria for participating in the Program are a commitment to work toward improvement of the library and a desire or need to initiate significant change. A library and its parent institution must be ready to contribute energy, time, and support in order to ensure an effective study.

Combining Developmental Strategies

Bringing together the periodic accreditation process with the self-improvement studies of the Academic Library Program offers a number of intriguing possibilities. Such a combination could well build on the recognized strengths of each approach.

The accreditation process contributes:
(1) pressure for change and improvement;
(2) standards for analytical comparison;
(3) external objectivity and ideas;
(4) attention from key groups in institutions;
(5) incentive for taking action.

The ALP self-improvement studies:
(1) provide tested methodologies designed for use in the unique setting of the academic library;
(2) give structure and direction to the study process;
(3) ensure production of analytical and data-based reports and recommendations;

(4) introduce current technology for conducting specified analysis such as personal availability or user satisfaction;

(5) make available supporting information on library practices elsewhere;

(6) give timely and direct assistance to libraries as they are conducting the study to allow efficient and effective execution of the procedure;

(7) develop staff capabilities in improved management which is an investment in the future.

Fundamentally, both approaches are seeking the same goal – improved library capabilities and performance. And there is some concrete evidence that the two processes can be successfully combined. Over the past two years, the Office has made some effort toward bringing together these two processes.

A representative of the Southern Association of Collages and schools (Grover Andrews) was a member of the Advisory Committee that assisted the Office in the design of the Academic Library Development Program. This study is for mid-sized academic libraries, and as result of the initial design work, the Southern Association is willing to accept applications for using the ALDP design for the library component of the institutional self-study.

A representative of the Middle States (Robert Kirkwood) was a member of the Advisory Committees for two self-studies (Carnegie Mellon University and Drew University) and had the chance to see first hand the assisted self-study process.

A representative of the North Central Association of Colleges and Secondary Schools (Patsy Thrash) was a member of the Advisory Committee for the University of Wisconsin-Parkside study. As a result of this involvement, North Central is also willing to accept application for using the ALDP design for the library component of the institution's self-study.

At Seattle University, the self-study report was presented to the accreditation visiting team as part of the institution's self-study. The visiting team's report commented:

> During the visit of the Evaluation Committee, a document entitled *Academic Library Development Program, Report of the Self-Study,* was issued by the library. Representing a year's work and the involvement of virtually the entire library staff, the ALDP Report is a wholly admirable detailed analysis, objective, balanced, and clear-sighted, of the strengths and weaknesses of the University library. More than that, the *Report* also presents a thoughfully considered blueprint for the improvement and future development of the library. As such, it deserves attentive reading by all those in the campus community who rely upon the library for services, and thus who have a vested interest in making the library as strong as possible. Furthermore, the *Report* certainly deserves no less than the careful continuing consideration by those in the University administration who have the responsibility of making decisions affecting the future of the library. It is strongly recommended that the report be so used.
>
> The *ALDP Report,* together with the library section of the institutional self-study, makes the need for comments in the Evaluation Committee's report almost supererogatory. However, for the sake of

emphasis, the following observations and recommendations are presented.[4]

What else can be done? That is probably best answered by the participants in these *Proceedings*. The accrediting agencies may want to examine more closely the use of assisted self-study as an approach to strengthen the libraries' portion of the accreditation process. Librarians may want to propose their institutions use the assisted self-study process to allow maximum impact for the accreditation event and for staff development and organizational development purposes.

References

1. Duane E. Webster and John Lorenz, "Effective Use of Library Consultants," *Library Trends* (Winter 1980), pp. 345-362.
2. Edward Johnson and Stuart Mann, *Organization Development for Academic Libraries* (Westport, Conn.: Greenwood Press, 1980).
3. The material describing resources available in the Academic Library Program is taken from OMS brochures which are available for distribution to interested groups.
4. Northwestern Association of Schools and Colleges, *Evaluation Committee Report Seattle University* (Seattle, Wash., April 17-19, 1979).

Evaluation of Libraries in the Accrediting Process from the
Standpoint of the Accrediting Association
Patricia Thrash

The task is to provide information on the evaluation of libraries in the accrediting process from the standpoint of the accrediting association. Preparation consisted of consultation with peers — the executive staff officers of the nine postsecondary accredition commissions of the six regional accrediting associations — inviting them to submit the sections of their accreditation policies and manuals that related to the evaluation of libraries along with their comments about what seemed most important and perplexing to them in the evaluation of libraries as a part of the institutional accrediting process. A review of all these materials and comments was made in an attempt to develop a series of common expectations and concerns regarding the evaluation of libraries.

Also reviewed were ACRL's standards: *Guidelines for Two-Year College Learning Resources Programs* and *Statement of Quantitative Standards for Two-Year Learning Resources Programs; Standards for College Libraries* and *An Evaluative Checklist for Reviewing a College Library Program;* and *Standards for University Libraries* with its appendix, *Quantitative Analytical Techniques for University Libraries.* Part of the inquiry led to the discovery that there were also *Guidelines for Library Services to Extension Students* and that these 1967 guidelines are currently being examined for possible revision.

All these materials provided an informational underpinning. The first step was to attempt a summary analysis of the various guidelines of the regional accrediting commissions and the ACRL standards. (See Appendix A.)

Then came the difficult task of assimilating the information and the points of view contributed by colleagues into a coherent document which would serve a variety of purposes: first, to provide those unfamiliar with regional accrediting commission criteria and procedures an overview of those policies and processes; second, to supply members of regional accrediting commission staffs detailed information on both the library criteria of the nine commissions and a summary of library association standards so that they might consider developing common statements and expectations concerning the evaluation of libraries; third, to suggest through comments on the evaluation of the library in the institutional accrediting process some of the concerns that professional library associations might wish to consider as they review their own standards; and, finally, to offer professional librarians some ways in which they might be more fully and productively involved in the regional commissions' evaluative processes.

The attempt to accomplish those purposes is organized in the following fashion:

(1) Regional accrediting commissions for postsecondary education — an overview;
(2) Regional accrediting commissions — common criteria for evaluation of libraries;
(3) ACRL Standards — some observations;
(4) Evaluating the library in the institutional accrediting process;

Patricia A. Thrash is the associate director of the North Central Association's Commission on Institutions of Higher Education.

(5) Suggestions for librarians who serve as evaluators;

(6) Conclusion.

Regional accrediting commissions for postsecondary education — an overview:

The nine regional commissions for postsecondary education are components of six regional accrediting associations that also include accrediting commissions for schools. The postsecondary commissions are characterized by a high level of communication and coordination among the executive staffs. In the late sixties and early seventies staff members met regularly as members of FRACHE (Federation of Regional Accrediting Commissions in Higher Education) and developed a series of policy statements on the purposes and practices of institutional accreditation. With the creation of COPA in 1975, the regional staff officers continued to meet on an informal basis. They have also coordinated the participation of their respective commissions in several national projects related to assessment in terms of outcomes through institutional self-study, evaluation criteria and processes for nontraditional education, and examination of military base programs. These common endeavors have encouraged and reinforced common, or at least consistent, approaches to accreditation. Consequently, while there are variations in procedures, the general criteria or guidelines do not differ widely across the regions.

A review of the publications of the nine postsecondary accrediting commissions reveals common purposes, criteria, or standards for accreditation that are congruent, and procedures for evaluation and accreditation which are similar.

Purposes: The postsecondary accrediting commissions are organizations of member institutions joined together for two fundamental purposes:

1. To establish and apply criteria or standards for the accreditation of postsecondary education institutions so that public assurance can be provided concerning the educational quality and integrity of member institutions;

2. To assist affiliated institutions in the improvement of their educational programs and related activities.

The commission also recognize as Candidates for Accreditation and assist in their development non-member institutions judged to be capable of achieving accreditation in a reasonable time.

The accreditation process: The primary means utilized to achieve the purposes of the regional accrediting commission is the accreditation process, a program of periodic (at least once every ten years) evaluation which included these steps: (1) Institutional self-study and submission of a self-study report to the commission; (2) an on-site evaluation visit by a team of professional peers who prepare a report and recommendation for the commission; (3) submission of an institutional response to the team report; (4) review of the report and response by another group of experienced educators appointed by the commission; and (5) accrediting action taken by the commission or its designated board. There are also procedures for appeal of the decision by the institution. This many-layered process is designed to ensure a fair evaluation for the institution and to provide assurance of the validity of the accrediting action taken. At the successful conclusion of this process, the institution is listed as a member of the association in the public documents of the commission.

Criteria (standards) for accreditation: Although there are variations in the degree of specificity and the amount of detail in the criteria for accreditation of the accrediting commissions, the criteria of all are designed to provide public assurance that an institution recognized as a member meets certain conditions:

(1) has the organizational and educational characteristics commonly associated with a postsecondary education institution as exemplified in the various standards or criteria of the commission;

(2) has a mission which is clearly and publicly stated and is appropriate to a postsecondary education institution;

(3) has an educational program and offers certificates or degrees appropriate to its mission;

(4) has a program for recruitment and admission of students which is congruent with the institution's mission and consistent with its educational program;

(5) has the resources (human, educational, physical, fiscal) and processes (organization for decision-making, evaluation, and planning) appropriate to its mission and adequate to support its educational programs (inputs);

(6) is achieving its purposes at a satisfactory level (educational outcomes);

(7) demonstrates through the level of its resources and the adequacy of its processes the stability and continuity and planning that provide assurance that the institution can be expected to continue to achieve its purposes effectively in the future.

Regional accrediting commissions: common criteria for evaluation of libraries:

An examination of the policy statements and the self-study handbooks of the regional accrediting commissions for postsecondary education reveals that (1) all have statements regarding the centrality of the library to the eductional institution, (2) all have specific criteria or standards for libraries, with varying degrees of detail required for demonstrating the adequacy of the library as a primary learning resource of the institution, and (3) there are common threads concerning the evaluation of libraries among the criteria.

Examples of the perception of the library as central to the institution are statements from four of the commissions:

a. The effectiveness of the library as a learning center is of paramount importance ... The library/learning resources center is the chief resource of the faculty and student body ... in the best sense [it] is also a classroom, and the best librarians are those who consider themselves teachers ... (Middle States)

b. The library is a vital instrument of instruction. It serves as an indispensable agent not only in general but also in the cultural development of students, faculty, and the community it serves ... (Northwest)

c. The quality of the library facilities and collections and the degree to which the library is used by the students and faculty are particularly important ... (New England CVTC)

d. The library is central to the total educational program ...

(Western ACCJC).

Each of the regional accrediting commissions has clear expectations of libraries. These are communicated in the form of general statements or more explicit standards. Here is a brief review:

a. Middle States has an extensive section on Library/Learning Center in its Policies and Procedures and in its Self-Study Handbook.

b. Both the New England Commission on Institutions of Higher Education and the Commission on Vocational, Technical, and Career Institutions have a standard on libraries and in their self-study guides request specific quantitative information on the library's organization and resources.

c. North Central's Commission on Institutions of Higher Education has a general statement in its handbook, now being revised, but an extensive section in its Basic Institutional Data forms requesting specific quantitative information on libraries.

d. Northwest has a library standard. Alone among the regionals, it notes: "The Northwest Association considers the standards of the American Library Association for two-year, college, or university libraries useful guidelines."

e. The Southern Association's Commission on Colleges has Standard Six, "Library," which provides illustrations and interpretations of the standard in the areas of staff, budget, resources, services, and institutional relationships. SACS' Commission on Occupational Educational Institutions also has a Standard Six; and its self-study guidelines request specific quantitative information on library resources, as well as an analysis of those resources.

f. The Western Association's Commission on Senior Colleges and Universities has an extended Standard Five, "Library and Other Learning Resources," with four subsections and components listed under each as examples. The Accrediting Commission for Community and Junior Colleges has an extensive section on Learning Resources. The guidelines require a description and appraisal according to a suggested list of questions and request plans for the future. Specific quantitative information is also requested.

In addition to the specific statements on the evaluation of libraries, all of the regional materials include statements on the importance of adequate library and other support services for off-campus programs; and many have specific requirements for such programs.

An analysis of the accrediting criteria or standards of the regional commissions indicates a marked similarity, with the differences lying largely in the amount of detail and explicitness required to demonstrate library effectiveness. Here is a summary of those "common threads."

Common Criteria among the Regional Accrediting Commissions for the Evaluation of Libraries:

1. The library/learning center should be of central and crucial

importance to the institution as a primary learning resource.

2. The library should be directly related to the institution's mission and its programs of instruction. It should realistically relate to the institution's constituency, enrollment, program diversity and complexity.

3. The expanded role of the library to include non-print materials of all varieties and to serve as a learning development center for students and faculty is acknowledged and encouraged.

4. The institution should have its own library or collection of learning resources. While cooperative relationships and arrangements with other institutions or agencies are encouraged, the institution's facility should have the basic resources to support its purposes and programs and to enhance the intellectual and cultural development of its faculty and students.

5. Library collections should be housed in an accessible, well-lighted, well-ventilated, adequately equipped and well-maintained building, with sufficient seating capacity and study carrels to support the needs of students and faculty. The library should be open at hours convenient and adequate to the needs of the users. Materials should be organized for easy access and use, and appropriate supporting equipment for utilizing print and non-print materials should be provided. The assistance of competent staff should be provided. The assistance of competent staff should be available to enhance the use of the library's resources.

6. The library should be administered by a professionally qualified staff with adequate support staff. Professional staff should be appropriately recognized as full members of the academic community.

7. The director of the library and the professional staff are responsible for administering the total program of library services within an institution. They should have the counsel of the representative advisory committee of faculty and students to assist them in the planning, utilization, and evaluation of library resources to achieve the library's objectives.

8. The budget should include all expenditures related to the operation and maintenance of the library. Sufficient funds should be provided to support a sound program of operation and development, with planning for subsequent years and a systematic program for culling obsolete materials.

9. If an institution has off-campus programs, it should provide adequate library resources and support services to serve students in those programs.

10. Services of the library should be evaluated regularly to determine the library's effectiveness through the nature and extent of its use. Circulation and acquisition statistics should be maintained for all library resource materials. User surveys should be conducted periodically, for use is primary evidence of

a library's effectiveness. In the self-study process which is part of the periodic institutional evaluation and accreditation process, the library should examine its own statement of purposes and provide an assessment of its strengths, concerns, plans to remedy concerns identified, evidence of effectiveness, and plans for the future.

ACRL Standards — some observations:

While this review of the criteria of the regional accrediting commissions for the evaluation of libraries was undergirded and reinforced by the author's experience as a professional staff member of a regional accrediting commission, the examination of the various standards of ACRL was largely a "paper process," in which the written materials were surveyed without benefit of experience in their application. Therefore, it is not the intention here to provide an exhaustive appraisal of those standards. Instead, the brief comments will pertain to the standards seen in relation to the regional accrediting commissions' criteria.

The various standards of ACRL at the two-year, college, and university level have to do with objectives and purposes, administration, collection, organization of materials, staff, budget, delivery of services, and evaluation. In broad outline, the library standards and the institutional accrediting commissions' criteria are consonant. The distinct difference lies in the library associations' use of formulas and specific quantitative measures as a means of providing evidence of library effectiveness. The difference is understandable, for the focus of the regional accrediting commissions is on the general place of the library in the total institutional scheme of things, while library professionals are quite naturally concerned with developing and maintaining superior libraries.

The librarian is a member of a professional guild. Judging by a review of the various library standards, it is important for this guild to see that its members are properly trained (i.e. have a degree from an ALA-accredited program), appropriately recognized (through the *Standards for Faculty Status for College and University Librarians),* and that libraries are adequately staffed (one librarian for each 500 FTE). There must be enough books in the library (basic collection, 85,000 volumes), and the library must be organized to serve the institution (with grades of A to D, according to how quickly the library can provide what percent of its volumes as requested). The faculty must be adequate (see Formula C, which calculates library size on the basis of a formula which considers the size of the student body, requisite administrative space, and number of physical volumes in the collections). Further, the library must be administered in accord with the spirit of the ALA *Library Bill of Rights.*

These documents are impressive on several counts. First, they are clearly the documents of professionals who are dedicated to the ideal of superior libraries related to the educational institution's mission, adequately staffed and supported, and continuously evaluated. Second, each of the documents is developed through a meticulous process that includes development of an initial draft by committee, circulation of the draft for review, revision, development of a final document that is approved by the Board of Directors of ACRL, and publication and wide circulation of the standards. Third, all the documents are extremely well-written so that they can be understood, even by non-librarians.

The documents include introductions, definitions, explicit standards with supporting commentaries to assist in their interpretation, and supplementary checklists or quantitative analytical techniques to assist in the application of the standards.

There are some elements in these materials which cause concern or at least raise questions. First, there is what could be characterized as an exquisite level of detail. Almost every eventuality seems to be covered, with little left to chance. As one of the documents cautions, the standards set forth ideals impossible to achieve in their ultimate form. At the same time, the enumeration of fastidious and explicit standards can create the expectation that such achievements are not only possible but are also mandatory. A second concern shared by many in the regional accrediting commissions is the "numbers game" apparent in the formula constructions. While the yearning for specificity and certainty is understandable, as is the idea that the number of volumes and periodicals has a bearing on the library's adequacy, the quality of those publications and the extent of their utilization seem to be more direct measures of a library's effectiveness. The data gathered on the checklists, unless widely understood and carefully interpreted, can lead to simplistic and sometimes erroneous conclusions. Third, there is a high level of protectionism for librarians as professionals. This is understandable, though, for a guild whose members have often been misunderstood and poorly recognized by their academic colleagues. Librarians should be a part of the faculty, of the decision-making apparatus of a university; they should be recognized and treated as full members of the academic community.

A fourth and final concern is one which can also be expressed about the regional accrediting commissions: most of the standards have to do with "inputs" or process criteria, with relatively little indicated about "outcomes" or evidence of effectiveness. Librarians appear to make the same mistake that institutional accreditors make: of assuming that, if certain conditions are present and processes in place, good librarians (or good institutions) will occur. To the credit of both, however, library associations and regional accrediting commissions have recognized the need for more tangible outcome information, and have begun to develop better ways for obtaining this concrete evidence of effectiveness.

Library associations should be complimented for recognizing their standards as guides to assist librarians in the development and maintenance of superior learning resources without resorting to an accompanying structure of self-study reports, on-site visits, and accrediting bureaucracy and have spared institutions one more costly duplication of effort.

Evaluating the library in the institutional accrediting process:
As a first principle, it should be remembered that the regional accrediting commissions are concerned with the evaluation of a total institution — its purposes, programs, resources, and processes — to determine its effectiveness and to provide assurance that it meets the accrediting criteria of those commissions. The library, although a primary educational resource of an institution, is but one of the components to be examined as the team makes its determinations. As one of the components, the library will be reviewed in terms of the relationship of its purposes to those of the institution; its organization,

evaluation, and planning processes will be scrutinized as they relate to the total institution and support it; and its resources will be examined for their adequacy in supporting the educational programs of the institution.

It should also be noted that not all evaluation teams have librarians as members. While some of the regional commissions routinely have librarians or learning resource professionals on their teams, others have librarians as team members infrequently. In constructing teams, however, all the commissions include a mix of professional educators deemed competent as a group to evaluate the total institution. One or more persons who are considered able in the evaluation of libraries are on every team making a comprehensive institutional evaluation. All team members are expected to visit an institution's library and to comment on its adequacy in team discussions; all evaluation team reports contain sections on the evaluation of libraries.

As indicated earlier, every regional accrediting commission has general criteria or specific standards for libraries. The institution's self-study process is expected to include an examination of the library, and the self-study report always contains a section on the library. The initial task in the evaluation of the library, then, is to validate the institution's assessment of the library, applying the commission's criteria for evaluating libraries. While team members are advised not to apply ACRL standards as such in their evaluation nor to refer specifically to these standards in the team report, it is clear that many of the library self-studies are written to demonstrate that these standards are met. As Thurston Manning has commented,

> ... most of the standards of the various library associations are process-resource criteria rather than outcome criteria. By their nature, such standards are not purposive; that is, they do not relate to the institution's purposes in an obvious way ... My experience is that library information in a self-study report often offers too much in the way of certain kinds of statistics and too little in the way of other sorts of analysis that would be very useful in making a determination of the library's effectiveness. This in because libraries are easy sources of some kinds of statistics: the number of volumes, expenditures, and books that go in and out. Staffs are trained to gather these data. Because these statistics are easily available, they are also the ones used in library self-studies to determine whether the library's resources meet the standards of the regional accrediting commissions.
>
> ... On the other hand, libraries in general have not always collected some statistics that would be quite useful: circulation patterns over time; the number of book circulations to freshmen as opposed to upper classmen or faculty. The nature and use of books within the library when books are not checked out is another area of interest. In-library usage of open-shelf areas may be very important information, but it is difficult to come by. Finally, the actual usage of the library for a number of purposes beyond direct use of the library's material is important and revealing — the library's use as a study hall, or for recreational reading, or for social purposes. It is important to know how much of the usage of the library's resources goes in these varied directions and to what effect.

Robert Kirkwood underscores this point: "We need new criteria for measuring the quality and effectiveness of libraries. We've got to get away from counting the books." Willaim MacLeod emphasizes that " . . . the availability of resources is not the only or major problem, but the use of resources is . . . ."

Regional accrediting teams are of course expected to examine the collections and to make a judgment as to their adequacy; but they are not expected to make that judgment on the basis of numbers alone. The important issues are the relatedness and currency of the materials and the quality and quantity of the use of the library's resources.

The evaluators of the library will want to know whether professors encourage library use through their course syllabi and assignments. They will try to determine, too, the adequacy of library materials for the professional development of faculty. Another area of concern is the extent of involvement of faculty and students in the selection and evaluation of materials for the library.

One way that teams test collections, of course, is to have individual team members examine the print and non-print materials in their academic areas. In this process, they also sometimes make the discovery that an institution is spending a great deal of money for publications that are not used, perhaps in response to some external expectation that certain kinds of back issues should be a part of every library.

If the visit is to an institution with off-campus programs, these sites are often visited; and a part of that visit is always devoted to determining whether library resources and assistance are adequate and used.

An integral part of the library evaluation is the observation of the library activity so that a determination can be made about the quality of service to students and faculty. How is the library used? Do a variety of things happen there? How satisfied are students with it? Are faculty often present? These are some of the questions that evaluators will explore.

In summary, evaluators will look carefully at the library, but in the context of its relatedness to and impact upon the total institution. They will apply the same questions about purposes, processes, resources, and outcomes that they apply to other areas. Because of the nature of the library, they will probably spend more time reviewing data and statistics than in any other area of evaluation, with the possible exception of their review of the institution's fiscal resources. In the final analysis, though, the evaluators will be most concerned with finding or confirming evidence of the library's effectiveness through the quantity and quality of its use as a primary learning resource of the institution.

Suggestions for librarians who serve as members of evaluation teams:

First, remember that you were chosen because of your abilities as generalists who can make determinations about the overall quality of an institution in addition to your professional abilities as librarians.

Second, while your expertise as librarians and your knowledge of ACRL standards are valuable resources for the team, don't let yourselves be pigeon-holed as some people with a single area of competence. Use this opportunity to test your skills in other areas and to broaden your experience and ability as evaluators.

Third, if you know other librarians who would be excellent evaluators, recommend them freely and generously to the executive officers of the regional accrediting commissions. In your nominations, stress the board range of your colleagues' abilities. Because institutional evaluators must be generalists, those with many areas of competence are especially desirable.

Finally, librarians are in an enviable position to educate their colleagues on the team to the ever-expanding universe of information and technologies designed to respond to rapid change and to serve the needs of adult and non-traditional learners who rely on those resources. It is hoped that during the "free" time of the team's visit, you may stimulate some of your colleagues from sleepier places or more eternal disciplines to consider how they may assimilate this flood of new information, master the emerging technologies, and alter their teaching strategies to meet the needs of lifelong learners. This will surely be a major challenge to librarians in the enormous upheaval that is happening even now in postsecondary education.

Conclusion:

This paper has been an attempt to provide and synthesize information on the evaluative criteria for libraries as they affect accrediting associations, professional library associations, and librarians themselves. Suggestions for improvements in the process and greater involvement of librarians in accreditation activities have been offered; addressing the context in which accreditation agencies operate and those larger issues which will surely change or at least modify all that they do has been avoided. A brief comment in closing seems appropriate.

Some of these issues are political — the amount of federal involvement in postsecondary education and the agencies that serve institutions, state funding and control — but many issues are directly related to postsecondary education institutions themselves. Effective institutions in the years ahead will be those able to comprehend and respond to change — rapidly expanding knowledge, almost unimaginable technologies, new kinds of learners, and the emergence of lifelong learning as a concept demanding new strategies. One important role of the institutional accrediting agencies and the evaluators who serve them is to encourage and to monitor institutions' understanding of and responsiveness to these developing realities. Everyone will be the better for it!

Evaluation of Libraries in the Accrediting Process
—From the Standpoint of the Library
George M. Bailey

The comments of forty librarians in academic institutions on the subject of evaluation of libraries were solicited, and all of the regional accrediting associations which are represented in these proceedings were contacted in order to secure the statements concerning libraries and learning centers in their regional manuals and instructions.

The accrediting association statements and the answers received from librarians will be frequently noted, but the selection of sources does not imply that other associations agree or disagree with the statements made, or that the words of a librarian reflect the thoughts of a majority of librarians. The statements merely reflect or enforce some of the thinking which has been noted during years of contact with the subject of regional accreditation and libraries.

The following topics will be covered briefly:
   (1)   the role of the library in the academic institution;
   (2)   the role of the accrediting process for the library;
   (3)   the ACRL standards and guidelines;
   (4)   the regional accrediting association statements and their relationship to the ACRL standards and guidelines;
   (5)   the role and value of the ACRL standards in preparation for the accreditation visit;
   (6)   the role of the librarian in the accrediting process;
   (7)   Possible action.

Role of the Library:
Eli Oboler, University Librarian at Idaho State University, emphasized that the academic library is a service agency within the campus. If the library suits the needs of its patrons, it is a good library. If not, it is not a good library. In his 1977 publication, *Ideas and the University Library: essays of an unorthodox academic librarian,* he notes that the collection should reflect the campus and curricular needs, service should be provided enthusiastically, and there should be a good rapport with students, faculty, and administration.[1] The library needs to have a good public relations program and must show efficient use of resources in today's budget crunch.

As *Standards for College Libraries* states, "Their role has ever been to provide access to the human records needed by members of the higher educatrion community for the successful pursuit of academic programs."[2]

The *Accreditation Handbook* of the Northwest Association of Schools and Colleges' on Colleges states that "The library is a vital instrument of instruction. It serves as an indispensable agent not only in general education but also in the cultural development of students, faculty, and the community it serves."[3] This statement is expressed again in a bit more detail in the draft of the *Standard and Self-Study Guide on Library and Learning Resources,* now under preparation by a Committee for the Commission: "The purpose of a library and

George Bailey is the associate director of the Claremont Colleges Libraries in California.

learning resources program is to facilitate and improve instruction and learning in a manner consistent with the philosophy and evolving curricular programs of the institution. Its goals and objectives shall be compatible with and supportive of the institutional goals and objectives. It shall be a central support of the entire educational program ... facilitate innovation, learning, and community services, resources, and facilities which encourage and stimulate individualization of instruction, independent study, and effective use of resources . . . ."[4]

Role of the Accrediting Process:

With these few statements as background, what does the role of the accrediting process have to offer for the library and learning resources center? The *Manual for the Institutional Self-Study Program* of the Southern Association of Colleges and Schools' Commission on Colleges states that "The essential purpose of the Institutional Self-Study Program is the improving of educational effectiveness in institutions of higher learning. The procedures of that program are designed to help institutions reassess their objectives, measure success in attaining objectives, explore ways and means by which educationl efficiency may be improved, and prepare for the ever-increasing demands by society,"[5]

The *Handbook of Accreditation* of the Accrediting Commission for Senior Colleges and Universities of the Western Association states that "The heart of accreditation lies in periodical self-appraisal by each member institution."

The *Handbook of Accreditation* of the North Central Association's Commission on Institutions of Higher Education notes that the purpose of accreditation is to foster excellence in postsecondary education, encourage institutional improvement, assure that the institution has clearly defined and appropriate educational objectives, provide counsel and assistance, and to protect institutions against encroachments which might jeopardize effectiveness or academic freedom.[6]

The "Commission Procedures" of North Central state that "the accreditation process subjects an institution to an external evaluation by persons from peer institutions whose task is to validate the institutions own assessment of its effectiveness and to certify that the institution meets the criteria for accreditation set forth by the Commission."[7]

"The certification statements are *not standards,* because they are not definite measures that can be applied without extensive exercise of judgment. The statements are more appropriately called criteria, a term similar to standards, but applying to less definite, more general tests (or rules) that form a basis for judgment."[8]

The programs try very hard to "protect both universal standards of excellence and individualized educational philosophy and practice."[9] The accrediting process is meant only to benefit the library and the institution, to encourage the library, through the self-study process, to make an in-depth look at itself and write a detailed report stating how the library is fulfilling its role and what it might do to perform that role better. The report provides a basis for other experts in the field to take a look at the library and make some suggestion to help the library strengthen its role in the parent institution.

ACRL Standards:

Librarians of various institutions were asked to comment on the usefulness of their appropriate standards in their self-study and the accreditation visit. Comments were mixed as they always are. Only one librarian was found who had used the recently published *Standards for University Libraries* .[10] He indicated that they were very useful, especially the statistical appendix, although he did not provide any detail for his comments. College librarians' comments varied from one librarian who stated that the ACRL standards change too often and are too specifically quantitative to be useful to others who state that they are very helpful, especially the logically developed checklist of factors for self-evaluation. The quantitative standards are very useful in presenting the data requested by the accreditation teams. There is much sensitivity to references to the standards of any organization other than those of the regional accrediting association. However, one can make references to points in the ACRL standards which are often acceptable to other members of the team. On one visit, members of the team insisted that the percentage of general and educational expenditures for support of the library needed to be increased even though the amount of support had increased drastically in the past several years, since the percentage had remained the same.

One librarian stated that the numbers game often penalizes a good collection in the small college library where there is an annual inventory and an active on-going weeding process. In one library there had not been an inventory taken for many years, and a rough count by sections seemed to indicate that approximately 25-30 percent of the volume count was missing. It is quite possible that some inadequate libraries meet every quantitative standard, but some excellent libraries do not.

Another librarian stated that the ACRL standards are strictly formula and several noted that they have insufficient qualitative evaluation. What most of these librarians are saying is that the ACRL standards provide an excellent yardstick for measuring the effectiveness of the library in the institution. They are valuable for self-study, but are still considered unrealistic by the regional accrediting associations. Possibly more contact might have been made with educational administrators in the preparation of the standards, although this may be difficult to do. According to one librarian, the ACRL Committee which developed *Standards for College Libraries* largely ignored some of the very good advice given by educational administrators outside of libraries. As a result, *Standards* has not been widely accepted. The standards and guidelines must be used critically and must be applied in context and perspective.

Accreditation Statements:

The statements in the regional accrediting association manuals and handbooks vary a great deal, although there is much in them that relates to the ACRL standards. However, the librarians who commented still have some strong feelings about accrediting association statements.

One librarian stated that the accrediting association statements were even more vague than the ACRL standards. Another noted that the regional association statements are expressed in general terms, with no formulas or numerical guidelines. In some standards, more provision needs to be made for audio-visual facilities, computer service, and other learning resources. In some instances, little is said about space needs in libraries.

Another librarian, who felt the pattern of the ACRL standards was very useful for the college or small university library, indicated that the regional standards were arbitrary in design and do not conform to the traditional categories librarians use in describing and evaluating the library. This regional statement, the librarian noted, does not provide a clear cut place for discussion of objectives, administration, or budget.

In another regional accrediting area, a librarian also noted that the statement regarding libraries is so vague and general as to be next to useless. These statements essentially note that a library should set its own goals and objectives and that it should be judged on that basis. This is too general even for a librarian to use as a basis for evaluation in a short time.

One librarian only wanted to emphasize that the regional accrediting programs do not give attention to the role of the library as a teaching program other than to collect materials and make them available.

Despite the above comments, the regional statements do cover the subjects of concern in the ACRL standards and guidelines in a variety of ways. The subjects covered in the several ACRL statements are as follows and, in reviewing the accreditation association statements, one will note how many of them cover the same subjects:

(1) Objectives — covered by two of the regions;
(2) Collections — covered by five of the regions;
(3) Organization of materials — covered by two regions specifically;
(4) Personnel — covered by four of the regions;
(5) Services — covered by three of the regions;
(6) Facilities — covered by all six of the regions;
(7) Administration and governance — covered by two regions;
(8) Budget — covered by four regions;
(9) Cooperation — covered by two regions.

This selection of what is coverage of the subject and what is not can be considered rather arbitrary and subject to different reactions. There are some instances where one might argue that there is sufficient indirect reference to a subject to suggest that the visiting team should cover it. However, some of the regional statements might be more specific.

Have the regional associations attempted to make some comparison of their statements with those of other regions? Has there ever been any attempt of the regional associations to develop a statement on libraries that might be used for all the regions? It appears that the Northwest Association's Committee on Standard and Self-Study Guide for Library and Learning Resources is attempting to do this in developing the current *Draft Copy of Revised Standard and Self-Study Guide*. The Western Association's *Standard* for libraries, published in January 1979, is a much more specific statement than previously used, although it still omits some points which should be considered by the visiting team. However, librarians have achieved a much closer relationship with the Regional Accrediting Associations than existed ten to fifteen years ago when the ACRL Committee was holding luncheon meetings with representatives of the local regional association when the ALA meetings were held in an area.

Role of the ACRL Standards and Guidelines in the Accreditation Process:

As far as the regional associations are concerned, the ACRL statements are not used in the accrediting process. At least one region states specifically that the visiting team should "never cite the formulas or requirements of other agencies. Their ideas often are useful to the institution, but the Commission is not their enforcement agent, nor are their rules considered to be uniformly applicable."[11]

Most librarians indicated that they made use of the ACRL standards or guidelines in preparation for the visit and in the self-study if they were involved in the preparation for the visit. They made such comments as:

"Standards are a much more important tool for internal evaluation."

They are "a useful framework within which to examine our activities, whether for purposes of long range planning or evaluation of programs."

"The *Standards for University Libraries* are not adequate and mostly not measurable for such a process."

"Absolutely no use was made of them (the college standards) in the accreditation here. . . . I don't think the ACRL Standards were directly involved in any preparation I've been involved in . . . If the ACRL standards were applied first in any survey there would then be at least an acceptable minimum. I have been on some visits where the library was extremely poor yet in context of the institution, teaching methods, etc. seemed to be doing all that was expected."

In summary, the ACRL standards and guidelines appear to be most beneficial to librarians in preparing the library part of a self-study report for the association team visit and to the librarian who is part of the team, but are still often ignored by a number of visiting teams. More time to secure more information from different regions might reveal that the summary of experiences vary more from one region to another.

Role of the Librarian in the Accrediting Process:

There is an amazing variation of experiences of librarians in the accrediting process. One librarian, who has served as a member of visiting teams, stated: "I have not been involved to any extent with any accreditation here (at the home institution). The first time I spent ten minutes . . . in the Board Room. The last time, a member of the team spent five minutes in my office. I had barely started to explain how our libraries are organized, when she said: 'I have to get to the 2:30 meeting.' I did not sit in on any of the meetings and was not asked to supply any details (other than basic statistics) for a self-study report or for accreditation team room background information . . . Perhaps someone assumes that the library is o.k., but I would welcome an impartial scrutiny by a qualified librarian, so that the library's problems (inadequate staff, space, funds, etc.) would be brought officially to the attention of the Board of Trustees."

Oddly enough, another librarian in the same region is currently deeply involved in the preparation of the self-study. Although he declined to chair the committee on the library part of the study, he "did most of the work on that part of the report; prepared an outline and all statistical appendices, wrote a draft of the report, and after review by the committee, incorporated their revisions and recommendations. The committee functioned mainly as a sounding board."

In at least two other regions, librarians differed in their statements about the role of the librarian. In each case, some would state that the director had almost no role in the accrediting process, or that the library member of the team spent relatively little time in the library, while others would state that the librarian was much involved in the preparation of the self-study report. In one instance, the part of the report devoted to the library covered thirty-six pages, written by the librarian.

It would be very interesting to do a detailed survey of the involvement of library directors in the several kinds of academic libraries in the accreditation process, both from the preparation of the self-study and during the team visit. It appears that the role of the librarian in the preparation of the report may depend on the status of the librarian on the campus and on his or her aggressiveness in getting involved in the process and secondly on the attitude of the institution about the importance of the library in the accreditation process as well as on the attitude of the team about the importance of the library in the fulfillment of the educational objectives.

Recommendations:

1. Regional associations should be encouraged to include a librarian on every visiting team. The Middle States make it a practice of including a librarian, and the Western Association attempts to do this in most cases, although some regions insist that every member of the team must be thought of as a generalist, and if a librarian is on the team, that person must assume responsibility for other parts of the visit. This author always has been assigned other responsibilities in addition to the library, including such things as a subject department, administration of the campus, personnel, finances, student services, etc., in some instances working closely with another member of the team on some aspect of the visit. These visits have been of tremendous personal and professional benefit.

2. One librarian commented that ACRL might take some collective action to have its various groups, colleges, community colleges, and universities approach the accrediting organizations in an effort to try to get agreement on the establishment and use of quantitative measures. This is the old question of qualitative versus quantitative. It would be great if this group could come to some consensus.

3. As suggested before, contacts which have been made among the accrediting associations in an attempt to bring some uniformity to their statements regarding libraries, as the Northwest Association is now trying to do, would be useful. It would be valuable for ACRL to do a more careful study of the statements of regional associations, unless this has already been done, and publish a report of the findings so that librarians would be talking about actual facts rather than making what appear to be generalizations.

4. A survey of librarians to learn more about their experiences in the preparation of the self-study for the accreditation visit, as well as with the visiting team in looking at the library during the visit, should be considered.

The librarians whose comments constitute this paper must be thanked for their contribution to the growing relationship between themselves and the regional accrediting associations.

References

1. Eli M. Oboler, *Ideas and the University Library: Essays of an Unorthodox Academic Librarian* (Westport, Conn., Greenwood Press, c1977).

2. "Standards for College Libraries," *College & Research Libraries News,* 36 (October 1975), p. 277.

3. Northwest Association of Schools and Colleges, Commission on Colleges, *Accreditation Handbook,* (Seattle, Washington, 1978), p. 29.

4. Committee on Standard and Self-Study Guide for Library and Learning Resources, Northwest Association of Schools and Colleges, Commission on Colleges, *Draft Copy of Revised Standard and Self-Study Guide,* (Seattle, Washington, May 23, 1980), p. 1.

5. Southern Association of Colleges and Schools, *Manual for the Institutional Self-Study Program of the Commision on Colleges,* (Atlanta, Georgia, 1974), p. 1.

6. North Central Association of Colleges and Schools, Commission on Institutions of Higher Education, ed. by Joseph J. Semrow, rpt. with corrections, *Handbook on Accreditation,* (Boulder, Colorado, September 1977), p.7.

7. Patricia A. Thrash, North Central Association Commission on Institutions of Higher Education, *Commission Procedures for Evaluation and Accreditation, 1980-81,* (April 14, 1980), p. 1.

8. *Ibid.,* p. 3.

9. Accrediting Commission for Senior Colleges and Universities, Western Association for Schools and Colleges, *Handbook of Accreditation,* (Oakland, California, January 1979), p. 1.

10. "Standards for University Libraries," *College & Research Libraries News,* 40 (April 1979), pp. 101-110.

11. *Ibid.,* p. 80.

How Can the Evaluation of Libraries Be Made Effective?
Harold E. Wade

It is an honor participating in these proceedings and a welcome opportunity to share some thoughts on how at least one regional accrediting association might improve its performance as it relates to effecting meaningful evaluations of libraries in higher education institutions. The thoughts which follow are not intended to represent either the Southern Association of Colleges and Schools (SACS) or even for the Commission on Colleges of the SACS; they are entirely this author's, although they have been influenced to a degree by the expressed opinions of several professional librarians informally polled during accreditation-related visits in the spring of 1980.

In order to address satisfactorily the question of how to serve best the library evaluation function from the standpoint of at least SACS, a brief review of the essential components of the Institutional Self-Study Program of the Southern Association's Commission on Colleges is the best place to begin. These components are (1) the Standards of the College Delegate Assembly, (2) peer evaluation, and (3) institutional self-study.

A brief description of the processes and procedures currently employed by the Commission on Colleges as they relate to the evaluation of degree-granting colleges and universities precedes an attempt to analyze the above-mentioned components.

Like all regional accrediting associations, the Southern Association accredits institutions as a whole as opposed to programs or schools within educational institutions. The College Delegate Assembly of the Commission has approved eleven standards which are applied to postsecondary degree-granting colleges or universities in the SACS region which are seeking Candidate status, initial membership, or reaffirmation of accreditation. In addition to the standard called Library, the College Delegate Assembly has, over the years, authorized review committees to develop, adopt, and revise periodically standards which focus upon purpose, organization and administration, educational program, financial resources, faculty, student development services, physical resources, special activities, graduate program, and research.

The current Library standard has, in addition to a principles section, five illustrations or criteria which relate to staff, budget, resources, and institutional relationships.

On most Commission-authorized teams of evaluators, librarians are accompanied by various other professionals who spend two to four days on campuses interviewing constituents of the institution being visited and reviewing records and documents. One of the responsibilities of a staff member of the Commission on Colleges is to select varying types of professional educators to serve on Commission-authorized Committees. Among those selected are first a chairman, a business manager, and a librarian, and then other personnel as needed. In some cases, the Chairman is a professional librarian. Regardless of size, however, nearly all committees representing the College Commission will include at least one librarian.

Harold E. Wade is the associate executive director of the Commission on Colleges of the Southern Association of Colleges and Schools.

Campus visits by teams of evaluators are, in most cases, preceded by a comprehensive, institution-wide self-study. The report of the study is shared with the visitors prior to their arrival on campus in an effort to acquaint evaluators with the strengths and weaknesses of every aspect of an institution's operations. During the visit, committee members seek primarily to (1) validate the information and data contained in the self-study report, (2) determine the extent to which the institution is in compliance with each applicable standard, and (3) suggest and recommend, both verbally and in writing, ways of effecting compliance with standards.

Briefly that is the process of accreditation as it is carried out by the Commission on Colleges of the SACS. Next is an evaluative discussion of each of the earlier mentioned components of that process in the context of library evaluations.

First, the standards. Many librarians have, in a very courteous, diplomatic, and professional manner, expressed some dismay with SACS current library standard. The chief criticism has been that the standard, in its present form, is completely void of quantitative elements.

Many people are no doubt aware that the College Commission of the Southern Association has made a conscious attempt during the past several revisions to eliminate from the standards almost all quantitative criteria. With the exception of criteria pertaining to degrees held by teaching faculty, all of the standards are qualitative in nature and the concept of "adequacy" has replaced previously required minimums.

Those who have complained about the current standard have typically confined their expressions of dissatisfaction to one general area: collections. That is, the inclusion of minimums for basic collections in the current standard would probably have the effect of silencing most critics. For example, very few librarians have expressed concern over the fact that the library standard requires no minimum number of professional librarians nor have librarians mentioned the removal of the seating space requirement from the standard. In fact, in the libraries or the colleges and universities this author has visited recently, you could act like the gorilla — sit anywhere you want.

One is always treading on dangerous grounds when one suggests that causal relationships may exist between and among events. It seems to be more than a coincidence, however, that at about the time accrediting agencies recognized the reality of the enrollment crunch, they witnessed the onset of grade inflation along with a significant increase in the number of vacant seats in most college and university libraries.

Should a regional accrediting body like the SACS then reconsider its commitment to promote standards which are essentially qualitative in nature? It should not. In other words, if one had to choose between standards or criteria which are expressed in qualitative terms as opposed to quantitative terms one would definitely choose the former. Fortunately, however, it is a choice that does not have to be made.

The best statement on this subject appears in ACRL's *Standards for College Libraries.*[1] It purports that

> quality and quantity are separable only in theory: it is possible to have quantity without quality; it is not possible to have quality with-

out quantity defined in relation to the purposes of the institution.

That says it well and says it all. It is, to say the least, a very powerful commentary. It is one which serves to facilitate an understanding of how the standards of both ACRL and SACS are meant to be applied in the context of accreditation.

Both sets of standards are adequate for the purposes they are intended to serve. The most recently adopted standards of ACRL are certainly not incongruous with the Standards of the College Delegate Assembly of SACS. Such key terms as "adequate" and "sufficient" are commonplace in both sets of standards. Congruity is the most that can be hoped for as it relates to SACS and ACRL standards. There is merit in seeking to arrive at greater consistency in the requirements of the Library standard among regionals because their purposes are similar. The goals, needs, and constituences of the regionals and ACRL, however, differ sufficiently to make differences in their standards both necessary and desirable.

One valid criticism, however, of the College Delegate Assembly's standard is that the current standard lacks the capacity to honor the concept of the "Learning Resource Center. An attempt was made six years ago to have the name of the Library standard changed to reflect the trend toward LRC's which most people associate with the two-year college movement. The proposal to change the name of the standard was responsible for a lengthy and at times heated debate during a meeting of the Executive Council of the Commission on Colleges as long ago as 1974.

The present name for the standard, combined with the fact that such components as the media center, telecommunications, and instructional development are not accommodated in the standard, should suggest the outcome of that debate.

The point to be made here is that accrediting agencies must begin to come to grips first philosophically and then operationally with the reality of the "learning resource" movement if they are to serve clientele effectively.

One final note on the subject of standards which may be of interest: at its 1979 annual meeting, the College Delegate Assembly authorized the Commission to plan and implement a project aimed at effecting a single set of standards which embraces the educational outcomes concept and which will be applied to all types of institutions. All of the standards as well as the policies and procedures of the current process of accreditation will be thoroughly studied and there is likely to be significant revisions in the standards. It is expected that what is now referred to as "THE Project" will be completed in two to three years.

On to the second component of the Institutional Self-Study Program of the Commission — peer evaluation. Many regard this aspect of the accrediting process as the most important; this feeling is perfectly understandable.

After seven years and over two hundred accreditation-related visits to institutions in the Southern Association region, this author continues to be amazed by the dedication and conscientiousness of those who render their service as peer evaluators in the self-study program of the Commission.

With a very few exceptions, most librarians observed in this context could serve as models for other team members. Librarians typically come to the institution being visited thoroughly prepared and well-organized to carry out their function and tend to waste little time and energy. Simply stated, professional librarians are generally quite competent.

Now that most librarians have — for the most part — ceased the practice of attempting to apply American Library Association standards on SACS visits, only a few suggestions come to mind in the spirit of promoting the improvement of library evaluations.

Librarians serving on evaluation teams visiting higher education institutions should seek to change an image — deservingly or not — librarians have as evaluators. The image referred to here relates to what many regard as an unusually zealous commitment to protect and advance the cause of librarianship.

A logical response might be, "Why is that a problem? Is that not what might be expected of any professionals with similar concerns and goals?" One reaction would be that it *is* a problem because when that perception is held by other team members, credibility tends to be reduced. There are those who contend that they know so well what the librarian on the committee is going to recommend that they could themselves write that section of the committee report. Critics say that librarians can be counted on to recommend faculty rank for librarians, a greater percentage of the institution's budget for the library, and an increase in professional and support staff.

Experience says that this is not altogether true, but experience also says that this is not altogether untrue. It shall suffice to say that a significant number of people who serve on evaluation teams hold that perception, and for them that perception represents reality. Efforts to improve library programs and services will not succeed unless the conclusions and recommendations are so carefully documented that there is no room for suspicion.

The second suggestion deals not with the kind of circulation which perhaps comes first to mind, but rather with librarians themselves circulating more during the committee visit. That is, many librarians spend far more time with library personnel and in the library facility than is perhaps either desirable or necessary. Granted, it takes a fair amount of time to observe records, minutes, and the like. More time should be spent interviewing other constituents in other locations on campus, rather than interviewing students or faculty in the library.

Why? Because in the interview process you can educate. The librarian on the campus being visited, for example, may never have the opportunity to interact face-to-face with the chief executive officer of that institution. As a member of a visiting committee, however, a librarian should have little trouble seeing the president or any other top-level administrator. Such individuals need to be seen, made sensitive to the peculiar needs of the library, and informed about the appropriate role of the library — especially as it relates to meaningful involvement in the budgeting and planning process. Librarians should take advantage of every opportunity to perform that function.

Many higher education institutions, especially those with severe financial problems, have begun to plan and implement what personnel within them view as attractive educational programs. Such programs quite often reach the operational stage without any input from a librarian. Many of these new programs require resources which are quite essential and quite expensive. Yet, most recent program prospectuses include grossly inadequate projections for library expenses — if they include them at all.

The final suggestion would be to spend more time with other members of the

visiting team in order to effect a more thorough analysis of each program area —
especially where majors are offered. This kind of collaboration is now more an
ideal than a reality. Just as librarians should spend a greater portion of their
time outside the library, other team members can contribute in positive ways to
an evaluation of the library. There are of course exceptions but most non-
librarians tend to trust the librarian on the committee to assess the adequacy of
library holdings and resources in his or her area of responsibility and simply
share that information in executive sessions of the Committee. That is
unfortunate.

Therefore, it might be a good idea, when next serving on such a visiting team,
to solicit the help of colleagues in the library evaluation. That approach may
serve, in fact to cause the recommendations of librarians to be supported by
other team members because those members will have gained first-hand
knowledge of problem ares in the library.

So far discussed have been the tools of the trade (standards) and the crafts-
manship (peer evaluators). The final component to be discussed then is that of
self-study. If properly conducted, the self-study aspect of the accreditation
process has the potential to maximize the benefits to be derived from evaluation
activities. Rarely are effective external evaluations performed without the
benefits normally associated with a well-done internal or self-evaluation.

One glaring weakness of this aspect of the accreditation process is that many
self-study efforts fall short in terms of achieving objectives related to effecting
the broadest possible involvement in the process. Bob Kirkwood had this to say
about self-study involvement:

> The size of a college or university affects the numbers and percent-
> age of the whole participating in self-study. Good judgment and
> praticality determine the point of diminishing returns with respect
> to numbers engaged, but involvement must be representative of the
> institution's constituencies. Faculty and administrators are
> essential participants in self-study activities, and so are trustees
> and students. Alumni may have a role as well as representatives of
> the local community. Whatever the actual numbers and representa-
> tion of the participants, the total effort will tell much about the insti-
> tution's commitment to self-study and the accrediting process.[2]

Many people regard self-study as little more than a necessary but burdensome
and boring task which must be completed before a report can be written so that
visiting team members will know something about the institution or program
prior to arriving on campus. The real meaning and value of self-study is missed
entirely by those who harbor such feelings.

The need to educate constituents was mentioned earlier. Top-level administrators who are not librarians by profession need to be made to appreciate the
contributions of a quality library. The self-study is a vehicle which can be effectively used to achieve that kind of objective.

To those who will have the opportunity to serve as a resource person on the
library committee when it is time again for self-study: do whatever you can to
influence decisions about the number and types of persons who will serve with
you on that committee. A study usually reflects the attitudes and abilities of

those charged with the responsibility of carrying out the task. Committee appointments of this kind are usually made by the institution's chief executive or someone designated by him. The sad reality is that if commitment to self-study is lacking at that level, that attitude tends to permeate the entire structure for the duration of the study.

In summary, the Institutional Self-Study Program of the Commission on Colleges of SACS and possible improvements of evaluations of libraries have been discussed.

In reverse order, the suggestions have been

(1) to seek to achieve greater involvement of constituent groups in library self-evaluations;

(2) that librarians serving the peer evaluation function should seek to effect greater collaboration with other visiting team members;

(3) that librarians, while visiting institutions, should spend a greater percentage of their time interviewing non-library personnel;

(4) that librarians seek to rid the profession of the "we take care of our own" image.

Also implicit was a suggestion that the Learning Resource concept and its implications for standards or evaluative criteria be dealt with firmly.

In all of the foregoing were generated only four explicit suggestions and one implicit suggestion. That speaks well for the state of the art as it relates to library evaluations. Besides, those who are familiar with the way SACS' Commission on Colleges distinguishes between recommendations and suggestions know that they do not have to respond to suggestions.

References

1. "Standards for College Libraries" adopted by the Association of College Research Libraries (July 3, 1975), p. 5.

2. Robert Kirkwood, "Institutional Responsibilities in Accreditation," *Educational Record,* Vol. 59, No. 4 (1978), pp. 298-299.

How the Evaluation of Libraries Can Be Made More
Effective in the Accreditation Process from the
Standpoint of the Accrediting Association Team Member
Phoebe Oplinger

The evaluation of a library program is at best a rather subjective process. Every visiting team member responsible for the library standard has probably at some time or other wished for some quantitative statements to use as a guide in evaluating a library.

A review of the library standards of the six regional accrediting associations makes it evident that most of the evaluation process is left up to the visiting team member. In general, this probably works pretty well.

There are considerations that should be helpful to the visiting team member and that should make the evaluation of libraries more effective in the accreditation process.

The remarks here are divided into three sections: the responsibilities of the institution and the library in preparing for a committee visit; the responsibility of the visiting team member in preparing for and executing a committee visit; and advice and assistance from the regional accrediting association.

Responsibilities of the institution and the library:
The attitude of the library staff as well as the attitude of the administrative staff of the institution toward the accreditation process set the tone and atmosphere of the accreditation visit. The staff must believe in what it is doing, and the administration must be committed to supporting this attitude. The accrediting association team should be viewed as helpful, professional consultants who are dedicated to their task of surveying all aspects of the library's services, observing and praising strengths and noting weaknesses that need to be corrected. The team's role is supportive rather than critical and destructive, and this approach need to be understood and appreciated.

Occasionally, there is an initial wariness and reluctance on the part of the library director and members of the staff to discuss library concerns. If emphasis could be placed on the helpful role of the visiting team prior to the visit, some of this anxiety might be alleviated.

Library staffs that show a negative attitude or fail to cooperate wholeheartedly with the visiting teams defeat the process and frustrate the work that must be accomplished.

The visiting team forms its first impression of the institution and the library by reviewing the self-study report. This document should be very carefully organized to provide clear, complete responses to the questions asked by the self-study manual and the standards of the accrediting association.

The visiting team members should not have to waste their valuable time searching for answers that belong in the report. All relevant information about the library should be contained in the chapter dealing with the library. The data should be current and factual. For instance, the team member should not have to determine whether the library's organizational chart reflects actual working relation-

---

Phoebe Oplinger is the director of the Central Piedmont Community College Library.

ships, or whether it is an idealized version of the way things should be.

The organization of the report, the clarity of the writing, the documentation of opinions with supporting data—all these characteristics provide the visiting committee with evidence of the ability, or lack of ability, of the institution to look at itself, to analyze its programs, and to make judgments about the success or failure of these programs.

It is essential that the institution mail the self-study to the visiting committee several weeks before the scheduled visit. Committee members cannot be adequately prepared to survey, analyze, and make judgments unless they have had sufficient time to read and think about the self-study before the visit.

Visiting team members are required to meet and confer with a large number of people and to inspect a wide variety of facilities in a limited number of hours. The effectiveness of a visit is improved greatly when library staff members are available for interviews, when an office is provided for meetings, and when all major documents are collected in one area for review. All library records, annual reports, surveys, etc., should be available and well organized for easy access.

Library directors who anticipate the needs of a visiting team member and arrange in advance for these needs to be met will create an effective and efficient atmosphere in which the team member may execute assigned tasks. This preparation enables the visiting team member to concentrate on the work at hand, rather than spend frustrating hours collecting the tools needed to perform an effective evaluation.

One part of the responsibility of the visiting team is to determine the quality of services provided by the library to the faculty, staff, students, and other constituencies. Some evaluation of library services can be acquired superficially by the visiting team through on-the-spot interviews with faculty and students. However, the ability of a visiting team to evaluate adequately the extent to which a library is providing instructional support for its clientele is enhanced greatly by the availability of a well-developed survey. Such a survey should be comprehensive; the data should be analyzed clearly, and conclusions derived from the analysis clearly stated. This activity, if properly executed, is very helpful to the visiting team, and most informative for the library staff. On-the-spot interviews by the team members may serve consequently to reinforce or contradict the results of the survey.

Responsibility of the visiting team member:
When preparing for the visit, the team member should read the complete self-study to understand the college's purposes and its programs and should concentrate on the chapter concerned with the library. In order to assess the effectiveness of the library, the team member must view the library operation in the context of the total institutional program and the purposes of the college. Thus, the visiting team member will be able to determine how well the library is supporting the programs of the college.

While reading the self-study, the visiting team member should attempt to determine whether it reflects the actual library operation and programs. Sometimes a college administration will handpick a small self-study committee and give it instructions not to show how bad things really are. In such a case the library can be particularly vulnerable. The team member should be aware also that some college presidents tend to think of the library as a finished product instead of a living, growing department. This attitude might be reflected in the library's operational budget.

The visiting team member should clearly understand the total learning resources program, audio-visual services, the learning laboratory, and production services and facilities, whether these areas are a part of learning resources or not. Some of this information may be found in a chapter of the self-study other than the one on the library standard.

The most effective visiting team members will decide before the visit whom they want to interview and what questions they want to ask. These decisions can be made after a careful reading of the self-study, noting whether there are divergencies from the standards.

The visiting team member should know the structure of the committee responsible for the library chapter of the self-study report, noting departments or divisions represented. It is helpful to interview as many of these committee members as possible.

It is important to plan to spend time talking with the library director and as many of the library staff members as possible. Care should be taken to interview younger staff members as well as older.

The visiting team member should be able to identify evidence of dissatisfaction within the library operation. If the team member detects areas of concern or criticism, this will provide an opportunity to pursue such concerns further.

Frequently, visiting team members discover serious conflicts within an institution or a department that reduce the effectiveness of the overall educational program. When this type of problem is evident, it is imperative that the institution admit frankly and openly that the problem exists and that specific corrective measures are being contemplated.

Team members need to be aware of any problems of this type that are related to the library staff, library services, or library administration. Staff members should share these problems with members of the visiting team with complete candor. Failure to do so might mean that the problem could be discussed with the committee by someone outside the library, thereby presenting a possibly biased point of view.

At this point it should be stated that visiting team members should always be non-committal in interviews with the faculty and staff.

The opportunity to observe library operations at different times during the day and evening is important. Many community colleges have a lesser commitment to the night program, but often a larger percentage of students attend class at night. The team member should interview some of the students who attend night classes exclusively and faculty who teach at night only, to gain a proper perspective of the extent to which the library is meeting needs of students and instructors.

When evaluating the success of the library operation the team member should assess the following: types of media available, the extent to which the collection supports the curricula, the usefulness of the arrangement, the authenticity of statistics, and the hours of the library operation, with special attention to nights and weekends.

A key to the success of the library program is the extent of the support given the library by faculty members. Library use as a logical component of classroom assignments is an essential factor in helping determine whether the library is fulfilling its role as a support service. As one of the accrediting agencies says so succinctly, ". . . use is the key to fulfillment of (the library's) goals and objectives. Nothing matters if the facilities are not used."

The written report of the visiting team member should be qualitative rather than quantitative; the library should be discussed in terms of the function and purposes of the institution. An overview of the library operation should be included, with a brief description of staff, physical plant and auxiliary services.

The situation should be described accurately with reference to the standards. Any weaknesses, negative matters or non-compliance with the standards should be enumerated and discussed. To paraphrase instructions from one of the regional accrediting associations, the report should analyze, interpret, give perspective, and provide a detached point of view. It should recognize strengths as well as problems, while concentrating on matters of significance.

Advice and assistance from the accrediting association:

It is important for the accrediting associations to conduct periodic training sessions for new or potential team members. Some committee chairmen give little or no guidance to new team members. Relatively few chairmen understand the role and function of the library. Unless the library is really outstanding or obviously in trouble, the chairman usually pays little attention to it. In these cases, the team member responsible for the library standard has to rely almost totally on his own initiative, judgment, and assessment of the situation. The help and advice received in well-conducted workshops would be invaluable to new team members who otherwise would possibly find it difficult to make a worthwhile and effective evaluation.

An examination of the library standard from each of the six regional accrediting associations indicates that each association provides very general guidelines for the library standard; however, there are, significantly, more similarities than differences.

It seems appropriate to end with a paragraph from *Instructions to Members of Evaluation Committees* from one of the regional accrediting associations:

Approach the evaluation as a colleague, not as an inspector. The commission has no formulas to apply or patterns to impose. As a colleague, the evaluator helps to identify the institution's significant strengths and discover how to solve its most critical problems. Approach the task humbly. No one knows all the answers. The evaluator's detached position is a distinct advantage.

Improving the Accreditation Process — A Librarian's Perspective
Jay K. Lucker

The intention of this paper is to offer some suggestions as to means by which the accreditation process might be made more effective from the perspective of the library in the institution that is being evaluated. Implicit in this assignment is the belief that improvement is possible and that the process by which libraries study themselves and are, in turn, studied by others is not perfect. Lest there be any uncertainty on the part of the participants in these *Proceedings,* let it be stated at the outset that much can be done to make the self-study process more effective and useful to the library, to its director, and to its staff; that the integration of the evaluation of libraries in the general accreditation process can be improved; and that there are opportunities for new directions and initiatives in the selection and training of librarian-evaluators, in the interaction between evaluators and evaluatees, and in the mechanics of accreditation team operations.

Accreditation in higher education is necessary and useful. It is necessary for a number of reasons, which have been expressed quite well in the *Policies and Procedures Handbook* of the Commission on Higher Education of the Middle States Association of Colleges and Secondary Schools. The purposes of accreditation at the postsecondary level have been identified as several:

(1) fostering excellence in postsecondary education through the development of criteria and guidelines for assessing educational effectiveness;

(2) encouraging institutional improvement of educational endeavors through continual self-study and evaluation; assuring the educational community, the general public, and other agencies or organizations that an institution has clearly defined and appropriate educational objectives, has established conditions under which their achievement can reasonably be expected, appears in fact to be accomplishing them substantially, and is so organized, staffed, and supported that it can be expected to do so;

(3) providing counsel and assistance to established and developing institutions;

(4) protecting institutions against encroachments which might jeopardize their educational effectiveness or academic freedom.

Accreditation is useful because it provides opportunities for generating change. Accreditation requires self-study, and self-study sharpens staff perceptions. Evaluation is an educational process for those being evaluated and for those on the accreditation team.

The evaluation of libraries within the accreditation process has a number of benefits to individual libraries, to the communities and institutions they serve, to the librarians involved, and to the library profession in general. For the libraries, accreditation offers a means for self-appraisal, for the identification of needs, and for the solution of problems. It presents an opportunity to measure the libraries' progress both against a statement of institutional objectives and within the

Jay K. Lucker is the director of the Massachusetts Institute of Technology Libraries.

framework of accepted national standards. Libraries are forced at least once every ten years to step back from their necessary concern with the immediate demands of collection development and library services to focus on long-range goals and objectives and on an assessment of how well the library responds to the educational, research, and recreational needs of its users. For the parent institution, the evaluation of a library presents an opportunity for an independent assessment of effectiveness without the expense of a consultant. In most academic institutions there is only one library, unlike academic departments of which there are usually many, thus the obvious need for external review. The potentiality to reinforce program and budget needs in this process is not insignificant. Faculty, staff, and students, who often tend to have a rather parochial view of their particular library, can be made more conscious of its strengths as well as its weaknesses through the evaluation. A strong element of staff development is involved in accreditation. The skills of observation, synthesis of information, analysis, and evaluation must be used by those who provide the internal assessment as well as by those who provide the outside appraisal. Finally, I have observed that the library profession benefits if for no other reason than that the inclusion of librarians on accreditation teams identifies them as equal partners with faculty and administrators in the improvement of the quality of higher education.

To be dealt with next are some of the specific areas in the accreditation process that involve libraries. In terms of the institution being evaluated, the process begins with the self-study. Except for larger universities and colleges, most self-studies cover the entire institution, and even where the college or university chooses to focus on particular topics, the analysis of educational resources is usually included. Regardless of the scope of the self-study, it is inconceivable that the library or learning resources center not be included. The director of the library or someone of relatively high rank in the library should be a member of the self-study team. The library's portion of the self-study should, in cases where selected areas are addressed, include information germane to those topics. For example, studies focusing on student life or undergraduate education should include significant coverage in the library section on services and collections aimed at undergraduates. This author recalls being a member of a team that visited a large research university that chose the selected topics approach. One of the major foci was graduate education, yet the library chapter of the institutional report failed to identify the achievements and problems connected with support of a wide range of graduate programs. The presence of the library director on the self-study team would ensure a high degree of correlation between the institutional emphasis and the library's contribution to the report.

There is at least one other good reason for having the library director or senior staff member on the self-study team. Inevitably other portions of the institutional report will make reference to library collections, services, and facilities, particularly but not exclusively those dealing with academic departments, facilities, finances, and governance. While it would be nice to believe that everyone on the campus knows what the library is about, this usually isn't the case. Verification of data prior to publication will minimize confusion on the part of the visiting team; it may also prevent post-evaluation squabbling at the host institution.

The conduct of the library's self-appraisal is the single most valuable and, therefore, the most important element of the entire process. The library chapter should not be a rehash of the past or two past annual reports of the librarian. It certainly should not be a summation of acquisition, cataloguing, circulation, and attendance statistics since the founding of the college or university. The report should not be, as it often is, a catalogue of all the needs the librarian has identified over the years that the president, or provost, or vice-president has failed to satisfy. Conversely, the report should not focus on "how we run our library good." Well then, what should the report include? The principal focus should be on relating the library's goals, objectives, programs, services, and collections to the institution that it serves. Here are some of the issues that a library self-study should address:

1. What are the library's long- and short-term goals and objectives? How were they identified? How often are they reviewed and by whom?
2. How are the library's collections and services evaluated?
3. What are the particular characteristics of this library and are they significant in terms of the special qualities of the college or university?
4. What are the strengths and weaknesses in the collections, services, and staff?
5. What are the perceived and actual roles of the library in the educational process? If they are not identical, why?
6. How does the library staff function within the college or university community?

The library self-study must, however, include descriptive information as well as statistical data. It is here that the standards that have been discussed would be particularly valuable. First of all, in terms of numbers it would mean librarians would all be counting the same things the same way. Second, following the outline provided by the standards would ensure that all pertinent information would be included. More important, however, the standards address issues like governance, personnel, facilities, policy determination, and so on, that are essential ingredients in the evaluation process.

The process of internal self-study in libraries associated with accreditation is arguably often less effective than it might be in terms of staff involvement. The report is often written by the director and a committee. The committee may or may not include non-library staff. There is generally, however, a failure to include all or most of the staff in the process. This seems to be a wasted opportunity. Despite the inevitable loss of what might be described by some as productive time, the benefits in terms of staff development are so advantageous that the sacrifice of items catalogued, books bound, or orders typed would be well worth the investment. After all, it does happen only once every ten years!

The next topic is the librarian as evaluator. By and large, the level of experience among those librarians who have served on evaluation teams is high. The process by which they are chosen and trained is quite effective. However, it might be useful to train new librarian-evaluators by having them accompany an experienced accreditor on a visit: good on-the-job training. While this may add somewhat to the cost of accreditation, the long-term benefits are obvious. While there is the model of the accreditation team associate, rarely if ever is the librarian seen in that role.

As a member of the evaluation team, the librarian must become more involved in the overall evaluation of the institution. Too often librarians look only at libraries. It is impossible to evaluate a library properly without having extensive contact with faculty, students, and administrators, or without having a sense of the community in which the library operates. Other members of the team should, of course, be involved in evaluation of the library. Faculty members should be requested to examine and evaluate collections and services with an emphasis on their subject areas but also with an eye toward the overall operation.

Based on experience, following are a few techniques that have been found useful.

1. Meet with as many staff as possible, both individually and in groups.
2. Tell the staff why you are there, what you are doing, and what the purpose of the visit is. In most cases you can be sure that the library director has not done this!
3. Do your homework! Read that which has been sent to you and make notes on those areas where you have questions or need more information.
4. If you don't have all the information you need, call the librarian and ask for it before you go to the campus.
5. Talk to faculty and students about the library. If there is a faculty/student library committee, ask to meet with them but talk to others who do not have a direct involvement with the library.
6. After you have completed your evaluation, spend some time alone with the library director, first to verify things about which you are unsure, and second, to provide an overview of your impressions.

The regional associations should adopt the standards and guidelines formulated by ACRL as "guidelines" for accreditation of libraries and learning resources centers. These are, after all, documents that libraries have been using for their own internal evaluations. Librarians and administrators are familiar with them and they have been carefully assembled and tested. When available, the evaluative checklists such as the one for college libraries should be used.

A second concern has to do with the orientation of evaluators by the accreditation agencies. There is an impressive quality and depth of information provided during orientation sessions for first-time evaluators and first-time team chairpersons. These sessions are excellent in terms of the process, the purposes, and the techniques that are involved. However, a presentation on academic libraries not aimed at the librarian evaluators but at the other members of the team should be added. The lack of awareness on the part of some of the team members with regard to the organization, technology, and problems of today's academic libraries is frustrating. Such topics as resource sharing, collection development policies, automation, networks, on-line bibliographic searching, and staff development are generally foreign to most professors, deans, financial vice-presidents, deans of student affairs, etc., yet they are expected to listen and, one hopes, understand what the librarian member of the team is talking about. Orientation sessions for first-time librarian team members should be made mandatory; these should be conducted by an experienced librarian-evaluator.

It is to be hoped that something can be done to improve the process by which groups that accredit professional education look at libraries. In general, these groups tend to underestimate the relevance of libraries to their respective disciplines. The most common approach is what would be characterized as "bean counting." This requires the itemization of what seems like an infinite number of categories of things that a library might be expected to own. These agencies seem to be concerned about such matters as how long the library is open, to whom the librarian reports, the subject degrees held by the library staff, the number of chairs, carrels, microfilm readers and listening stations, and the like. Little attention seems to be paid to quality of collections and services, evaluation, identification of institutional needs, and cooperative agreements with other libraries. It should be noted in passing that the issue of to whom the librarian reports has been a significant issue in at least one profession and has involved considerable correspondence with a major library association that shall remain nameless.

Somewhat along the same lines, we ought to spend more time worrying about quality and less time on quantity. The emphasis in the standards on quality of collections and quality of service and quality of staff is most impressive. While certain basic quantitative criteria have been established and should be enforced, it is the relevance of the collections and services to the institution that will, in the end, determine a library's effectiveness.

Self-study of libraries and the evaluation of these institutions should not be seen as ends unto themselves. There is a direct correlation between the amount of dust on the director's copy of the library portion of the study and the quality of the library. Quite simply, the evaluation process should be viewed as part of a continuum, not something done once every ten years. While the intensity of effort required for an accreditation is necessarily greater than normal, participation in the process should establish in the minds of library directors a continual need to evaluate, analyze, revise goals and objectives statements, and seek means for improving the integration of the library in the college or university.

Particular attention needs to be paid to the libraries of institutions undergoing initial accreditation. The complexity of modern library organization and technology and the costs inherent therein almost ensure that the library or learning resources center will be one of the most sensitive areas for evaluation. The directors of the regional accreditation agencies might be in the best position to judge whether it might be useful to have an experienced librarian go along on what is usually identified as an "assessment visit for candidate status."

Like our counterparts in two- and four-year colleges, the major research universities are re-evaluated every ten years. In most instances the library or library system is part of the review. In large universities, however, the evaluation is almost always of the special topics variety. It is also extremely unlikely that the question of reaccreditation will arise. What then should the nature of the evaluation of the research library be? The routine evaluation of collections and services, even in the context of institutional and library goals and objectives mentioned earlier, would be of little value and would, in fact, be a rather boring experience.

Insofar as possible, the research library should also use the opportunity of an accreditation visit for a special topics approach. The evaluation visit might focus on one of a number of subjects. In an institution such as MIT, for example, it would be highly useful to focus on one of the following: staff development; involvement in local, regional, and national networks; collection development policies and practices; communication with staff, faculty, and students; or organizational structure. While an overall review of the M.I.T. Libraries would be expected and welcome, the concentration on one particular area would be seen as highly useful not only to the director and to the staff but also to the visiting librarian.

Some personal views and ideas on how libraries and librarians can be more effectively integrated into the accreditation process have been offered. The value of accreditation is unquestionable. In a period where resources for the support of academic institutions are becoming increasingly scarce and when the relevance of programs must constantly be evaluated and justified, one has in the accreditation process an effective and comprehensive method for maintaining the quality of academic libraries. The cooperative efforts of librarians, academic administrators, and executives of accreditation agencies are excellent ways of maximizing the usefulness of this system.

Small Group Discussions
Julie Carroll Virgo

Participants at the Institute were split into small groups to discuss the material presented and to respond to the following questions:

1. How can the evaluation of libraries be made more effective in the accrediting process?
2. What steps, if any, should be taken and who should accomplish these?
3. What are the four or five most pressing actions that need to be taken?

The reports from these discussions were presented to the entire group for further discussion and comment. Points made by the groups included:

1) That there be developed measures of library effectiveness;
2) That regional associations should provide copies of ACRL standards as guidelines and checklists to team members and institutions undergoing self-studies;
3) That regional associations encourage institutions to use broadly based library self-study committees;
4) That information about the whole accreditation process be more widely communicated — particularly the purpose and process;
5) That there be more effective training of library evaluators and more training of non-librarian members;
6) That there be encouraged cooperation among regional accrediting associations to develop uniform procedures and information regarding library self-study;
7) That there be established a joint COPA/ACRL Accreditation Committee on the evaluation of libraries;
8) That as much should be done as possible to coordinate regional and specialized professional accrediting associations; e.g., in the areas of scheduling and procedures;
9) That it be urged that a way be sought to provide guidance from accrediting associations on the self-study process. Identify the librarian team members months in advance;
10) That better definition of library statistical terms for gathering information be encouraged;

The next set of concerns were discussed within the broad educational process. This includes library support for providing all kinds of educational opportunities. The recommendations which follow are not limited to the library at the exclusion of all other institutional and educational components of the total college/university educational process.

In light of this general frame of reference, one group made the following recommendations pertaining to the improvement of the evaluation of libraries as part of the accrediting process:

1) That the Standards and Accreditation Committee integrate all recommendations from the individual discussion groups as well as spe-

---

Julie Carroll Virgo is the executive director of the Association of College and Research Libraries.

cific recommendations presented in formal papers;

2) That wide dissemination of specific recommendations identified under #1 be promoted to librarians and personnel involved with the accrediting process, including academic administrators. Such dissemination may be in the form of:
    (A) Distribution of printed reports
    (B) Presentations at state and regional library association meetings
    (C) Presentations at such groups as ACE, AAHE, ASSCU
    (D) Release of news articles in such journals as *The Chronicle of Higher Education, Library Journal,* etc.;

3) Plan a follow-up institute in about 18 months to assess results of this institute.

4) Ask each of the accrediting agencies to improve its accrediting training programs for evaluators and institutions.

5) Accrediting agencies should assist librarians and institutions in assessing the integration of the library in the teaching and learning process through such means as:
    (A) Bibliographic instruction (individual and group)
    (B) Curriculum planning
    (C) Course and syllabi development
    (D) Testing and examination.

6) Encourage ACRL to place greter emphasis in the standards on integration of the library in the teaching process.

7) Faculty has a responsibility in evaluating the use and assessment of the library.

8) Librarians need to have a better way of participating in the self-study and accreditation process: that there be training to be team members.

9) Stress the need for an ongoing assessment of the library program as a part of the institutional planning process — not just at the time of an accreditation visit.

10) There needs to be a conduit for news about activities of accreditation associations activities through *C&RL News.*

11) ACRL should provide training information for non-librarian team members.

Another of the groups presented action recommendations according to the three agencies involved. These recommendations are:

I. *By the Individual Institutions*
    (A) Develop advanced awareness of the self-study at the campus so that preparation can be made ahead;
    (B) Use model self-study documents to integrate the self-study into normal campus planning procedure;
    (C) Develop a continuous planning process campus-wide, including libraries;
    (D) Obtain checklists of kinds of documents needed for self-study so such will be available;
    (E) Have department self-studies in advance of the normal accreditation self-study.

II. *By the Regional Accrediting Associations*

(A) Insist on continuous campus-wide planning, including libraries;
(B) Provide training for self-study by AV presentations for use on campus;
(C) Solicit comments on changing standards and on kinds of documents needed for self-study;
(D) Put campus chairman of planning and libraries on mailing lists of reference documents.

III. *By ACRL*

(A) Provide through *C&RL News* a conduit on activities of regional accrediting associations, especially those relating to libraries and learning resources;
(B) Develop help for non-librarians who become team members in looking at libraries;
(C) Develop more awareness by academic librarians of the accreditation process and its benefits.

Another group submitted the following recommendations:

1) That evaluation for accreditation emphasize accessibility to a full range of information resources and services in support of all academic programs, whether offered on campus or off, whether directed at traditional or non-traditional learners; in support of this recommendation, ACRL should prepare a checklist for the evaluation of library resources and services that support extension/off campus/continuing education/or other such programs. This checklist could accompany a revised set of guidelines for library support of extension students or be incorporated in the standards for various types of libraries; i.e., university, college, two year. Further, the standards of regional accrediting agencies should require that institutions demonstrate that accessibility to a full range of information resources and services is being provided to *all* students and faculty.

2) That the criteria of regional accrediting agencies for the evaluation of libraries and other learning resources be made more consistent;

This recommendation should be implemented by the regional accrediting agencies, perhaps with COPA coordination and support from ACRL.

3) That evaluation of libraries and other learning resources for the purposes of institutional accreditation involve a broad spectrum of the academic community; for example, institutional self-study teams for libraries and other learning resources should have non-librarian members and non-librarian members of regional accrediting teams should contribute to the evaluation of an institution's library and other learning resources;

ACRL, individual librarians, COPA, and the regional accrediting agencies can all help to implement this recommendation through both official; e.g., guidelines for self-study preparation, or unofficial communication channels; e.g., discussion with other team members during an institutional evaluation visit.

4) That a majority of regional teams have a librarian member; this is recommended because of the variety of programs, technical complexity, and financial impact which the provision of high quality

information services requires.

In support of this recommendation, ACRL should prepare a well thought out statement of rationale for distribution to the regional accrediting agencies, and individual librarians should nominate themselves or other qualified librarians for service on accrediting teams.

In the concluding session, the following points were made:

1. The library association should nominate librarians for accreditation teams to regional associations.

2. When sending vitae to regional accrediting associations, stress the librarians' generalist abilities — they are not any one subject discipline; they are used to dealing with large budgets; they have concerns that relate to student services, instruction and research; and they deal with the administration and its concerns.

3. The entire burden must not be placed on librarians alone to evaluate the library as a teaching instrument. Bring into standards the outcomes of demands made on the library; e.g., when a faculty member gives a librarian a reading list, the faculty member should then follow-up on the extent to which the students use those materials. On every campus, the library is generally the most underutilized resource.

4. ACRL should sponsor workshops on how libraries can approach the self-study process and on how librarians can be effective team members.

5. ACRL needs to be in communication with the regional accrediting associations and COPA. ACRL must act as a catalyst.

6. Publicize in *C&RL News* that the regional associations want to hear from librarians who are willing to serve on committees, participate in training sessions, or are willing to serve on a team.

7. Some regional accrediting associations (such as New England) would be happy to co-sponsor training workshops, as long as they do not need to spend money.

8. ACRL can work with regional accrediting associations through the ACRL chapter network. Chapters could work with regional accrediting associations disseminating information, being involved with training, and working with faculty.

9. The regional accrediting associations should communicate with their Boards about the librarians' concerns. ACRL can provide speakers to address the regional associations. ACRL can assist the regional associations with their training.

10. The self-study process must be seen as an integral part of the whole institutional planning process, including the library, and viewed as an on-going process.

Conclusion of ACRL/COPA Institute on Libraries and Accreditation in Institutions of Higher Education
James F. Bemis

Introduction. Reflecting upon the twelve substantive and informative papers delivered during the afternoon of the first day and the morning of the second day, one could hardly expect more of a relatively short institute. The speakers were well prepared, without exception, and delved into most of the current topics and issues on libraries and the accreditation of postsecondary institutions. Yet, the small discussion groups and reports from those groups, which followed the principal speakers, added significantly to the institute. The discussions not only served to reinforce many of the points made by the speakers, but highlighted the ways in which the institutional libraries and the regional accrediting agencies can improve for the benefit of each other and the institutions they serve. Since the text of each speaker's paper is included in the *Proceedings,* this conclusion will not recount those papers. The conclusion will attempt to state briefly from memory and hand-written notes, what was learned from the institute for possible application by those directly concerned. It is organized according to the four principals — the individual institutions, the regional accrediting commissions for higher education, the Association of College and Research Libraries, the Council on Postsecondary Accreditation.

Postsecondary Institutions. While library buildings, holdings and staff are important in judging library quality, data on the actual use of the campus libraries are frequently underutilized. Library assessment is too often limited to general circulation and acquisition figures. The opinions of students and teachers need to be assessed. An analysis of library usage should also be directly related to teaching methods and their effectiveness.

Library self-study, like institutional self-study, should be an ongoing process for purposes of improvement. Just as librarians need to be involved in the broad aspects of institutional self-study and planning, faculty have a responsibility for library assessment and planning. Too often the library portion of a comprehensive self-study is planned, conducted and written entirely by library professionals. In such cases the institution loses a golden opportunity to evaluate library resources and services as perceived by faculty and students, to set widely accepted institutional goals for the library, and to establish a firm foundation for planning efforts.

Better use should be made of the services and resources available for library self-study. Checklists, guidelines, standards, model self-studies, and other documents are readily available and should be utilized. It is not enough to rely solely on the publications of the regional accrediting commission.

Whether an institution is involved in self-study for institutional accreditation or recognition by one or more of the professional accrediting agencies, the library is usually significantly involved. Too often these evalutions are not articulated or coordinated; there is frequent overlapping and duplication among the agencies involved. Such overlapping and duplication places an unneces-

James F. Bemis is the executive director of the Northwest Association of Schools and Colleges.

sary burden on libraries as well as other institutional operations. An institution should insist that, whenever appropriate, the accrediting agencies with which it wishes to associate function cooperatively. Such cooperation should include one self-study to satisfy the agencies concerned, an articulated on-site evaluation, and a cooperative report of the evaluation.

Regional Accrediting Commissions of Higher Education. Despite the fact that the accreditation of institutions has been going on in four of the six regions since before the turn of the century, regional postsecondary accreditation is misunderstood in the educational community. Adequacy of the library in relation to accreditation is an area commonly misunderstood. Too many think that total number of volumes and back issues of scholarly journals are equated to library quality by the accrediting commissions. The regional commissions, unilaterally and through COPA, need to communicate more effectively the importance of library resources in relation to the educational programs, rather than numbers, and how the resources are used by faculty and students.

Through the papers presented and the discussions that followed, it was noted that regional commissions differ considerably in the use of librarians as evaluators on accreditation teams. Some assign a professional librarian to virtually every team, others make it a practice of using librarians primarily in the evaluation of more complex institutions, and one does not usually assign librarians but relies on generalists almost exclusively. A strong point was made that librarians on evaluation teams should be used as generalists as well as library specialists. Librarians are prepared in subject disciplines; they are used to dealing with large budgets; they have concerns that relate to student services, instruction, research; and they deal with the administration and its many concerns. In other words, the work of the librarian cuts across the entire educational enterprise. It seemed to be the sense of the participants that the regional accrediting agencies might reach a more common position on the assignment and use of professional librarians on evaluation teams.

Regional library standards for the accreditation of a postsecondary institution, although qualitative, vary considerably. Indeed, some prefer guidelines to standards or publish very general statements on library resources in applying the principle of judging an institution against its own purposes. In the 1970s revised library standards/guidelines were approved by the Association of College and Research Libraries for two-year institutions below the baccalaureate level, for colleges serving bachelors and masters levels, and for universities that emphasize graduate study, professional education, and research. Except for the need to place more emphasis on library usage in the standards/guidelines, the speakers and other institute participants were complimentary and supportive of the revisions. No longer do the ACRL standards/guidelines establish normative prescriptions for uniform application. They provide a general framework within which informed judgment can be applied to individual circumstances. There appeared to be agreement among the conferees that regional accrediting commissions might make better use of the ACRL standards/guidelines in revising their standards, and that library standards of the regionals might be more consistent. There appeared to be good support for the suggestion that evaluation teams be routinely provided appropriate ACRL statements and checklists for use during on-site visits.

The importance of institutional self-study in the accreditation process can hardly be overemphasized. Learning resources are a fundamental concern. Personal assistance and guidance from the accrediting agency to the institution involved in the self-study process is often directed to top level administrators and a few faculty who filter the information down to the lower echelons. Because of the importance of learning resources to self-study, the librarians urged accrediting associations to provide them with more guidance. They expressed a strong need for first hand, person-to-person relationships with agency representatives. The idea was presented, and received some support, that the accrediting agency might identify to the institution early in the self-study process the professional librarian who would serve on the evaluation team. This person would informally advise the institutional representatives in regard to library analysis and answer questions about the process prior to the on-site visit.

Help from the accrediting agencies was also requested in assisting librarians and institutions to assess the integration of the library in the teaching and learning process. This might be accomplished through such means as bibliographic instruction (individual and group), curriculum planning, course and syllabic development, and testing.

Association of College and Research Libraries. The revised standards for three types of institutions, as reported earlier, received good support from the institute participants. ACRL and its various committees were commended. There was a consensus, however, that ACRL should be encouraged to place greater emphasis in the standards on integration of the library in the teaching process.

ACRL through its publication, *C&RL News,* might provide a conduit on activities of the regional accrediting commissions which are related especially to libraries and learning resources. Proposed revisions of regional library standards could be published and suggestions solicited for consideration by the agencies. Articles in *C&RL News* could serve to develop an awareness by academic librarians of the accreditation process and its benefits.

During an institutional evaluation for accreditation, most team members share in the responsibility of evaluating the library. ACRL might assist the regionals in developing information and materials for non-librarians who review learning resources. The Evaluative Checklist for Reviewing a College Library Program was cited as a good example of the help ACRL might provide. Particular attention was directed to the problem of evaluating library resources and services that support continuing education and the variety of off campus educational activities. A revised set of guidelines for these activities might be incorporated in the standards for various types of libraries, i.e., university, college, two-year, and a checklist could accompany each set.

There was general support for the position that a majority of regional evaluation teams should include a librarian because of the variety of programs usually offered, the technical complexity of providing adequate library services, and the financial resources needed for high quality information services. In support of this position, ACRL should prepare a statement of rationale for distribution to the regional accrediting commissions. ACRL should also encourage individual librarians to nominate themselves or other qualified librarians for service on evaluating teams.

ACRL might take a more active interest in institutional self-study and the accreditation process without usurping the responsibility of the regionals. Need was expressed for ACRL to sponsor workshops on how libraries can approach the self-study, library standards/guidelines, and how a librarian might function most effectively as a member of an evaluation team.

Council on Postsecondary Accreditation. As the national organization that brings together recognized accrediting agencies in postsecondary education, COPA is in a key position to assist the regionals and to serve as a catalyst for the improvement of nongovernmental accreditation. While each regional commission is responsible for developing its own standards, COPA could serve to formulate and coordinate a review of regional library standards directed toward more consistency and overall improvement. A starting point might be an ACRL/COPA Library Committee which was recommended and appeared to have good support.

COPA, while aware that accreditation is misunderstood by educators as well as laypersons, needs to continue and enhance its efforts in achieving a general understanding of educational accreditation. Being national in scope and representing fifty-two accrediting agencies, COPA is considered to be in the best position to develop informational materials to help create broader understanding of the accrediting process.

COPA is also keenly aware of the overlapping and duplication problem in the accrediting role of various agencies. Institutions will be more successful in their efforts to have accrediting agencies articulate and coordinate their evaluations by having COPA as a resolute partner in the endeavor.

Follow Up. Because the institute was so well received by the participants, there was strong support for follow-up activities. Wide distribution of the *Proceedings* was encouraged. Oral presentations on the institute were suggested at state and regional association meetings, at appropriate meetings of accrediting agencies, to the COPA Board, to the Assembly of Institutional Accrediting Bodies, and before such groups as ACE, AAHE, and ASSCU. News articles were suggested for such journals as *The Chronicle of Higher Education, Library Journal, Educational Record,* etc. Finally, it was considered important that a follow-up institute be planned by ACRL/COPA in about eighteen months to assess the results of the June 1980 institute.

Appendix A

Summary Analyses of the Regional Accrediting Commissions' Guidelines and ACRL Standards on the Evaluation of Libraries

A1   Middle States Association of Colleges and Schools Commission on Higher Education

A2   New England Association of Schools and Colleges Commission on Institutions of Higher Education

A3   New England Association of Schools and Colleges Commission on Vocational, Technical, Career Institutions

A4   North Central Association of Colleges and Schools Commission on Institutions of Higher Education

A5   Northwest Association of Schools and Colleges Commission on Colleges

A6   Southern Association of Colleges and Schools Commission on Colleges

A7   Southern Association of Colleges and Schools Commission on Occupational Educational Institutions

A8   Western Association of Schools and Colleges Accrediting Commission for Senior Colleges and Universities

A9   Western Association of Schools and Colleges Accrediting Commission for Community and Junior Colleges

A10 ACRL Standards for University Libraries

A11 ACRL Standards for College Libraries

A12 ACRL Guidelines for Two-Year College Learning Resources Programs

A13 ACRL Guidelines for Library Services to Extension Students

Middle States Association of Colleges and Schools
Commission on Higher Education
Evaluation of Libraries

Comments on the evaluation of libraries are found in *Policies and Procedures,* beginning on page 21, and in the *Self-Study Handbook,* under G, page 20.

Middle States Commission's concerns are: Does the library undergird programs? Is the library used? Do professors encourage library time by giving projects that require library time? Middle States is working to determine the amount allocated by institutions from operating budgets toward the operation of the library. New criteria for measuring quality and effectiveness are needed. (Kirkwood, Heindel)

Library consortia are encouraged. There is no specific answer to the question of how many books make an adequate library. In some cases, Middle States has found that small institutions may have too many unused periodical subscriptions.

Policies and Procedures—Library/Learning Center (pages 21-23)

This narrative stresses that the effectiveness of the library as a learning center is of paramount importance. Its collections should be appropriate and adequate to support the instructional program, and they should be widely used by both students and faculty. The quality of a library's holdings, their direct relevance to the institution's educational programs, and the extent of their utilization, are more important than merely the number of volumes catalogued or shelved.

Selected statements:

Faculty and staff need to work closely together in planning the development

and employment of library resources to achieve their educational objectives ...
The director and staff must demonstrate the competence and be given sufficient
responsibility and funds to facilitate the optimum functioning of the library as a
learning center. Status and privileges of library staff should be commensurate
with the significance and responsibilities of their positions.

The library/learning resources center is the chief resource of any faculty and
student body ...

The principles on which a library/learning resource center's adequacy can be
tested are clear. It should support all the subjects the institution offers, containing or having ready access to important source materials and a truly representative selection of secondary works and special studies covering each field from a
variety of significant points of view ...

Any library/learning resources center should be largely self-contained. Also encouraged are ... cultural and specialized information on tape, records, and film
... possibilities ... for linking up with data retrieval and computer systems which
can increase the library's value and dimensions as an information and learning
center. Cooperative arrangements with neighboring libraries and networks are encouraged as means of greatly enhancing an institution's resources.

Use of the library is stressed, and the physical adequacy of the library is emphasized.

The Handbook for Institutional Self-Study notes that effectiveness of the li-
brary/learning resources center is of primary importance, as is effective use of the
library, availability of materials, development of materials, and interaction between faculty and librarians. (page 20)

New England Association of Schools and Colleges, Inc.
Commission on Institutions of Higher Education
Evaluation of Libraries
New England's Commission on Institutions of Higher Education includes in its
Standards for Accreditation the following standard on *Library and Learning Re-
sources* (page 6):

The institution should provide those learning resources necessary to support
the educational program and the intellectual and cultural development of faculty
and students.

The institution should have its own library or collection of learning resources.
Collections of print and non-print materials should be appropriate to the range
and complexity of the educational program, to each curriculum of studies, and to
student enrollment. Materials should be housed in convenient locations and readily accessible to students.

Adequate study space should be provided. The collection should be administered by a professionally qualified and numerically adequate staff.

The exchange of materials and services with other academic or local libraries
and within library networks is encouraged.

In its *Guidelines for Institutions on Initiation, Modification, or Expansion of
Off-Campus Educational Activities,* the Commission includes an extensive statement on *Library and other Learning Resources.* Acknowledging the difficulty of
providing library, laboratory, and other learning resources adequate to support
off-campus programs, the Commission places heavy emphasis on the demonstrated adequacy of these resources. Here are excerpts:

Before an off-campus program is initiated, there should be a careful, written evaluation by the appropriate on-campus administrative and academic personnel of the library, laboratory and other resources needed for the program ... A determination should then be made concerning the availability of the needed resources in the area ...

Written agreements with adjacent libraries or laboratories should then be executed, specifying the conditions under which off-campus students will have access to these facilities, collections, and services. In addition to relying on other libraries, the institution should establish a collection of basic learning materials to which students will have easy access at times convenient to them. Provision for borrowing books from the institutional main library should be made.

Adequate and inviting study space and facilities should be provided ... the institution should make certain that competent personnel are available to answer student questions, advise them on library use, and direct and supervise the institutional collection ... the library and learning resources should be constantly evaluated by appropriate institutional on- and off-campus personnel ... The off-campus libraries should be under the overall supervision and direction of the person in charge of the institution's main library and learning resources center.

In its *Self-Study Guide,* New England's Commission on Institutions of Higher Education repeats its standard. Institutions are requested to make available in the team's workroom brochures describing for students the library and other learning resource facilities, hours, and services; information on staff; and information on library utilization.

The institution is directed to include specific information on the library/learning resource services in its Self-Study Report, including: the philosophy utilized in providing library, laboratory, and other learning resources adequate to support off-campus programs, the Commission places heavy emphasis on the utilization, circulation, holdings, and acquisitions (by books and periodicals), non-print (audiovisual) materials, interlibrary loans, and other aspects of library use. Expenditures of the institution over each of the past three years for books, periodicals, non-print materials, supplies and equipment, binding, and library salaries (professional and clerical) are requested. The institution is asked to indicate the percentage of the institution's educational and general budget spent for these resources for each of the three years. The institution is asked, "To what extent and how are faculty and students involved in the formulation and implementation of library policies and procedures? In selection of books and materials? In improving library service?"

A projection is also requested: "In appraising the institution with respect to the standard on *Library and Learning Resources,* what weaknesses have been identified? What strengths? What plans are in operation or contemplated to remedy weaknesses or implement changes?"

William J. MacLeod, Director of Evaluation for the Commission, believes that two things should be emphasized with regard to the evaluation of libraries. "One is the fact that availability of resources is not the only or major problem, but the use of resources is ... Another is the importance of cooperation. This means going beyond networks which are essentially concerned with physical arrangements necessary for the movement of resources among a group of institutions. Agreements for cooperative processing, and formal acquisition agreements in a variety of media represent two possibilities." MacLeod cautions, "The growth of cooperation always runs afoul of the fact that local autonomy and local choice seem threatened. On the other hand, my own judgment is that the 80's will see more questions asked of institutions about the possibility of cooperative arrangements, and justly so. Library staff better have some answers."

New England Association of Schools and Colleges, Inc.
Commission on Vocational, Technical, Career Institutions
Evaluation of Libraries

In its Standards of Membership for Specialized Institutions of Higher Education awarding an Associate Degree at the Technical or Career Level, the Commission on Vocational, Technical, Career Institutions includes this standard on the *Library:*

The quality of the library facilities and collections and the degree to which the library is used by the students and faculty are particularly important. The library should be professionally staffed and should be strong enough to support all parts of the curriculum. The faculty, students, and library staff should cooperate in developing the collection as an integral part of the instructional program.

The Commission's Self-Study Outline for its institutions includes seven questions about *Learning Centers:*

1. What are the institution's current figures with respect to library: (a) attendance, (b) circulation, (c) holdings and acquisitions (by books and periodicals), (d) inter-library loans, and (e) other information relating to library use?

2. What were the institution's expenditures during each of the past three years for (a) books, periodicals, bindings, and supplies and equipment, and (b) library salaries (professional, clerical)? (c) In what areas are the institution's present library holdings most satisfactory? (d) If the library holdings are believed to be inadequate or weak, estimate the cost of remedying deficiencies in each area and within the total collection. (e) What are the institution's plans for remedying the deficiencies?

3. (a) Does the library (or other facility) serve as a learning center for other audio and visual media? (b) What learning resources of these types are currently available?

4. Describe the library staff organization and record the training and experience of each member. (a) Is each professional staff member accorded the rank and status appropriate to qualifications and position? (b) Is the library adequately staffed with qualified professional, semi-professional, technical, and clerical personnel to provide appropriate services in resources as identified by the goals and objectives of the library?

5. (a) To what extent and how are faculty and students involved in the formulation and implementation of library policies and procedures? (b) Who selects and who approves library purchases? (c) What is the faculty and student evaluation of the library, including its strengths, needs, and holdings?

6. (a) How adequate are library facilities in reading space, equipment, hours available, and reference help? (b) What improvements are planned during the next five years?

7. On the basis of the self-study analysis and the Commission's Standard on *Library* identify the following: (a) strengths, (b) weaknesses, and (c) if appropriate,

recommendations for improvement.

North Central Association of Colleges and Schools
Commission on Institutions of Higher Education
Evaluation of Libraries
The Commission's *Handbook on Accreditation* is currently being revised.

With the publication of its *1978 Statements,* the Commission specifies that each institution, to be accredited, must meet the following criteria:

1. have clear and publicly stated purposes appropriate to a postsecondary educational institution;
2. have established conditions and procedures under which these purposes can be realized;
3. appear after evaluation by the Commission to be accomplishing its purposes substantially;
4. is organized, staffed, and supported so that it can be expected to continue to accomplish its purposes;
5. fully meet the criteria of eligibility for consideration for accreditation and fulfill the obligations of membership through the Commission.

In its directions to institutions preparing for evaluation, the Commission asks the institutions to go beyond description to provide assessment, evidence of effectiveness, and plans for the future.

Library and learning resources are considered a major component of an institution. In the current handbook, on page 67, the Commission states:

Library and other learning resources. Learning resources adequate to support the educational program and adequately staffed should be readily accessible to students on campus and during periods of study or other activities away from campus. Learning resources are a significant component of an educational program only if they are used. This is largely the responsibility of the instructional staff. In its list of information needed about off-campus programs, the Commission includes this question:

11. What physical resources are needed for the off-campus programs (classrooms, laboratories and other special purpose rooms, library and other learning resources, computers, etc.)? What arrangements have been made to provide these resources? How does the quality of these resources compare with that on campus? What assurances does the institution have that these resources will be available for as long as they are needed for the off-campus programs?

The Commission's *Basic Institutional Data* form, which all institutions are required to submit as a part of their self-study report for evaluation, includes a section on libraries.

V. Data Form E—LIBRARY/LEARNING RESOURCE CENTER 17-18
Part 1 requests information on the past two years and the current year on selected elements of the collection and transactions:

1. Number of book titles
2. Number of physical units of microforms, especially microfiche and microfilm.
3. Number of titles of catalogued non-print media, i.e., films, film-loops, etc.
4. Number of periodical titles
5. Number of newspapers
6. Number of other (non-periodical) serial titles

7. Student use of book collection—number of books in circulation annually among students divided by the number of students enrolled. (FTE)
8. Student use of reserved books—number of books in circulation annually among students divided by number of students enrolled. (FTE)
9. Student use of non-print materials—number of non-print media units (film-strips, tapes, etc.) used annually (in the library/center or outside if checked out) by students divided by number of students enrolled. (FTE)
10. Faculty use of book collection—number of books in circulation annually among faculty divided by the number of faculty. (FTE)

Part 2 deals with library/learning resource center expenditures over a three-year period. Institutions are requested to present data where applicable or to sub-stitute the proper HEGIS form and to report from current budget and actual expenditures for the previous two years and for this campus only.

Operating expenditures:
1. Total salaries, before deductions, of regular center staff
2. Salary equivalents of contributed-service staff
3. Total wages paid to students and other hourly assistants
4. Expenditures for purchase of books and other printed library materials
5. Expenditures for non-print media
6. Expenditures for binding and rebinding
7. Expenditures for on-site production of materials
8. Other operating expenditures (INCLUDING replacement of equipment and furnishings but EXCLUDING all capital outlay)
9. TOTAL

Estimated cost of items which, though not charged to library/center accouts, constitute library/center materials and services
10. Binding
11. Automation Services
12. Other (specify)

Student and other hourly assistance
13. Annual total number of hours of student assistance
14. Annual total number of hours of other hourly assistance

While the Commission has no extended statement on library and learning resource centers or on other areas generally, the information provided in the *Basic Institutional Data* forms provides explicit data which supplements the information provided in the self-study report by the institution undergoing evaluation.

Comments of Thurston Manning, Director of the NCA Commission on Institutions of Higher Education:

The basic point is that libraries cannot be judged apart from their relationship to the purposes of the institution. In the case of libraries, these purposes may include services to the educational programs, undergraduate and graduate; research purposes, and archival resources, the maintenance of records and information against possible future use. Another important area is that of general public usage for cultural and recreational purposes.

A second comment is that most of the standards of the various library associations are process-resource criteria rather than outcome criteria. By their nature, such standards are not purposive; that is, they do not relate to the institution's purposes in an obvious way. In the best sense, these process-resource criteria may describe the resources necessary to achieve purposes although it is very difficult to demonstrate necessity, especially in quantitative terms. A good set of process-resource standards will describe a particular pattern of resources and processes which may be very good, but they are not the only pattern that would enable an institution to accomplish its purposes; therefore, they may be unnecessarily restrictive. (A good example is the ABA requirement that a law librarian must report to the dean of the law school rather than to the director of libraries in an institution.)

It is important to distinguish between a *necessary* level and a *sufficient* level. A true minimum is difficult to establish. Most of the quantitative standards of the library associations really describe a sufficient level. The difference is obvious. If a minimum of 85,000 volumes is required, is a library with 84,999 volumes not acceptable? No one can really know what the necessity line is, although many can judge what a sufficient level might be.

My experience is that library information in a self-study report often offers too much in the way of certain kinds of statistics and too little in the way of other sorts of analysis that would be very useful in making a determination of the library's effectiveness. This is because libraries are easy sources of some kinds of statistics: the number of volumes, expenditures, and books that go in and out. Staffs are trained to gather these data. Because these statistics are easily available, they are also the ones used in library self-studies determine whether the library's resources meet the standards of the associations. Some lack even face validity—for example, the number of volumes in an institution without regard to their variety and appropriateness.

On the other hand, libraries in general have not collected some statistics that would be quite useful: circulation patterns over time; the number and nature of book circulations to freshmen as opposed to upperclassmen or faculty. The nature and use of books within the library when books are not checked out is another area of interest. In-library usage of open-shelf areas or core libraries may be very important information; but it is difficult to come by. Finally, the actual usage of the library for a number of purposes beyond direct use of the library's material is important and revealing—the library's use as a study hall, or for recreational reading, or for social purposes. It is important to know how much of the usage of the library's resources goes in these varied directions, and to what effect.

Northwest Association of Schools and Colleges
Commission on Colleges
Evaluation of Libraries
This information is taken from the 1978 Edition of the Commission on Colleges' Accreditation Standards.

IV. *Library* (page 6)
Standard

The library is a vital instrument of instruction. It serves as an indispensable agent not only in general education but also in the cultural development of students, faculty, and the community it serves.

Libraries are increasingly becoming not only repositories for books and periodicals, but also student and faculty service centers. As an indispensable part of the complete instructional program, many libraries are assuming the responsibility for audio-visual equipment and materials, music recordings, and art collections.

The library should be administered as part of the instructional program by a well trained professional staff with representatives of the teaching faculty acting in an advisory capacity. Services should be evaluated regularly to observe the library's effectiveness through the nature and extent of its use.

The library holdings should, by quality, size, and nature, support and stimulate the entire educational program. Substantially stronger holdings should be required for graduate and research programs. The collections should be housed in a well-lighted, ventilated, and adequately equipped building, with sufficient seating capacity to accommodate the needs of the students and faculty. The library should be open adequate and appropriate hours with the materials organized for easy access, use, and proper presentation.

The Northwest Association considers the standards of the American Library Association for two-year, college, or university libraries useful guidelines.

The delegate assembly of the Northwest Association at its annual business meeting on December 4, 1979, approved additions to three standards, including the Library standard, for the accreditation of postsecondary institutions, which become effective September 1, 1980. This is the addition to Standard IV, *Library*:

> Occasionally an institution will make library services available to students and faculty through specific arrangements with another institution or other agencies where the holdings and service are adequate to support the programs and capable of maintaining an adequate level of support. In such cases, it is incumbent upon the institution to demonstrate that these arrangements are capable of sustaining an adequate level of support in the foreseeable future and meeting the needs of prospective program changes and additions. All institutions that extend programs off campus must demonstrate that library services fully adequate to the programs are conveniently available and are in fact used by students and faculty.

Southern Association of Colleges and Schools
Commission on Colleges
Evaluation of Libraries

The Standards of the College Delegate Assembly of the SACS Commission on Colleges includes an extensive standard on the evaluation of libraries. Standard Six, *Library* (pages 24-26), begins with an overall statement of expectations concerning the library, and contains subsections on Staff, Budget, Resources, Services, and Institutional Relationships.

The introductory statement:

The library is important in the achievement of educational goals of students and faculty. To serve the user well, each library must have basic resources to support the institution's purposes and programs. Such resources should be available in a well-equipped facility which will encourage maximum utilization by the campus community. Moreover, to facilitate use of such resources, both on and off campus, a competent professional staff should be available to assist the users. In determining the priorities for resources and services, the chief library administrator should actively seek the advice of the administration, faculty, students, and library staff. It is important that the collections of print and non-print materials be organized for easy access and that adequate hours be maintained.

Educational institutions exist with a diversity of educational programs and objectives. Each institution must develop for its library a statement of mission and objectives appropriate to the institution. Such statements should be developed with the active involvement of the administration, faculty, students, and library staff so that each can accept these statements and relate them to their everyday tasks and needs. Because objectives change, the library should be evaluated regularly and systematically to be sure it is meeting the needs of its users and supporting the programs and objectives of the institution. (page 24)

The Commission's Standard Nine, *Special Activities,* includes the expectation that adequate resources (including library resources) will be available for the activity offered.

Bennett J. Hudson, Associate Executive Director of the Commission, identifies four concerns as those most commonly identified in the evaluation of libraries:

1. Inadequate number of support and paraprofessional staff.
2. Faculty status for professional library staff.
3. Deficiencies in both total numbers and in balance in the book collection.
4. The need for greater faculty involvement in library development and greater encouragement and/or insistence by faculty that students make use of library resources.

Hudson finds the need for greater faculty involvement in library development and greater encouragement of students to use library resources to be an increasingly common (and probably valid) concern. He finds a disturbing tendency among evaluators to cite specific minimum numbers of books as being required for certain levels of institutions, although teams are admonished not to cite specific numbers in the written report. "The justifications for these quantitative minimums are not readily forthcoming but, rather, are apparently some kind of 'conventional wisdom.' I think this area needs attention by both the regionals and professional learning resources people. I'm certainly willing to defer to the professional judgments of these people but they should be able to articulate some sort of rationale."

Southern Association of Colleges and Schools
The Commission on Occupational Educational Institutions
Evaluation of Learning Resource Centers

The Southern Association Commission on Occupational Educational Institutions has information about the evaluation of Learning Resource Centers in three publications:

1. *The COEI Self-Study Manual,* intended as a general guide for institutions undertaking self-study for the purpose of accreditation, has a five-page section on its *Standard 6: Learning Resource Center(s).* The section begins with seven questions related to the center. The institution is asked to provide specific information about the expenditures of the LRC for the past two years; to provide numbers about the availability of resource materials; and to provide an analysis of resources. Learning resource materials for resources in separate departments are also required, as is a listing of multi-media equipment and facilities. The institution must complete a table with regard to availability and use of multi-media materials. The section on the LRC concludes with a request for a summary evaluation of the strengths, weaknesses, or limitations as perceived by the institution and the institution's plan for resolving identified weaknesses. (pages 31-36)

2. *The Policies and Standards of Delegate Assembly of the Commission on Occupational Education Institutions* has its Standard Six: Learning Resource Center(s) (page 28), which indicates that:

> Learning resource center(s) must be provided by the institution. This requirement may be met in any one or any combination of the following ways: (1) within the individual classrooms, (2) within the individual laboratories, (3) within individual shops, or (4) in a schoolwide learning resource center. Provision must be made in the budget for supplies, maintenance, and repair of equipment.

The Standard includes specific requirements in these areas: facilities, budget, staff, records, service, and evaluation.

3. The *Procedures Handbook for Visiting Team Leader* provides a checklist for Standard Six (page 18) so that the team can determine whether the standards for each of the six elements of Standard Six are met in a satisfactory fashion.

Western Association of Schools and Colleges
Accrediting Commission for Senior Colleges and Universities
Evaluation of Libraries

WASC's Accrediting Commission for Senior Colleges and Universities has an extensive standard on the evaluation of libraries in its *Handbook of Accreditation,* January 1980 (pages 27-30). Here is a summary of that standard.

STANDARD FIVE: LIBRARY AND OTHER LEARNING RESOURCES

Standard 5.A.

Library holdings and other learning resources are sufficient in quantity, depth, diversity, and currentness to support all of the institution's academic offerings at appropriate levels.

Standard 5.B.

Teaching faculty are involved in selection and evaluation of library and learning resource materials.

Standard 5.C.

Library and learning resources are readily available and used by the institution's academic community, both on and off campus.

Standard 5.D.

A professional staff with pertinent expertise is available to assist users of library and other learning resources.

Under each standard, components of the standard are listed as examples of what is expected of an institution.

The standard stresses that all resources of a college or university exist to implement the educational program and thereby accomplish institutional purposes. Learning resources include facilities, equipment, materials, persons, and software which augment the curricular offerings, such as: the library facility with its collections, equipment, service personnel, and other resources; the instructional technology program of the institution including traditional audiovisual distribution services, materials, and equipment, and the more modern electronic design/production/distribution of curricular support information; tele-communications including radio and microwave; and the computer support system. Learning resources encompass instructional development functions as well as direct instructional service.

For most colleges and universities, learning resources are a central support to the total educational program. Both collection requirements and the service program will differ depending on the mission and program of the institution. An institution offering graduate work, especially doctoral study, is expected to have major holdings available, including serials, in all of its graduate areas.

The Commission is also concerned about library resources for non-traditional and off-campus programs, especially where those are at the graduate level. Included in its *Standard Nine: Special Educational Programs* is Standard 9.A.10:

Learning resources, including library facilities, laboratories, classrooms, study areas, offices, and other equipment and facilities, are adequate to support the programs and courses offered at each off-campus site. The institution documents the availability of these resources to students. (page 38)

In its detailed statement on *Accreditation of Graduate Work* (pages 137-143) the Commission includes the caveat that ...

Generally, institutions should rarely undertake offering the Ph. D. without extensive and guaranteed ready access to relevant library holdings, laboratory facilities, and, where appropriate, to clinical or service situations. (page 140)

The Commission also expresses its concern for the adequacy of learning resources in its statement on *Innovative and Nontraditional Programs* (pages 144-145) and its statement on *Postsecondary Educational Programs Conducted by Accredited or Candidate Institutions on Military Bases* (pages 146-151).

The Commission advises teams not to cite specialized accreditation requirements in team reports; but Kay J. Andersen, Executive Director, indicates that librarians "will and should draw upon their familiarity with ALA standards." He also notes, "I have a little problem with librarians on teams because of the mass of material they present to the chairperson."

Western Association of Schools and Colleges
Accrediting Commission for Community and Junior Colleges
Evaluation of Learning Resources

WASC's Accrediting Commission for Community and Junior Colleges has an extensive statement on learning resources (pages 42-45) in its 1978 *Handbook*.

According to Executive Director Robert E. Swenson, this commission's teams are particularly concerned about:

1. the involvement of staff in the selection of materials;
2. the adequacy of facilities, staffing, and materials to support the institutional mission;
3. evidence of use;
4. evaluation of materials and services by the users.

The Guidelines define the term learning resources to include library, audio-visual facilities, telecommunications, and the like; it encompasses instructional system components.

The library is central to the total educational program. Collection requirements will differ depending on the variety, depth, and level of offerings. An institution is expected to have major holdings in all areas it attempts to cover. While neighboring and available libraries may augment resources, no institution should rely exclusively, or even largely, on resources it does not control or to which it does not have irrevocable access and effective use.

The guidelines stress the need for a variety of learning resources related to the curriculum and developed with close cooperation between professional library personnel and faculty; resources related to the institution's mission and departmental needs; adequate and attractive facilities; effective utilization of learning resources; and a resource collection adequate for the scope and purpose of the curriculum, methods of instruction, number of students and faculty, use of the center by students and faculty, and the availability of other library resources.

The guidelines require a description of the learning resources in seven specific areas and appraisal according to a suggested list of questions; plans for the future are also requested. The institution is asked to supply a selected list of materials in the evaluation team room or another convenient location: leaflets or brochures that describe the learning resource facilities, hours, and services; information on staff; information on library utilization; financial data; and the percentage of the total current budget of the institution expended during each of the last three years on library and other learning resource items.

Standards For University Libraries

Draft prepared by a joint committee established by the Association of Research Libraries and the Association of College and Research Libraries; draft appeared in April 1978 issue of *College & Research Libraries News.* Revised in August 1978 by joint ARL-ACRL Committee on University Library Standards; on October 26, 1978, the ARL membership unanimously endorsed the revised statement. At ALA Midwinter meeting in January 1979, the ACRL Board also voted to ratify the revised statement; published in final form in April 1979 issue of *College and Research Libraries News.*

Introduction.
The fundamental assumption of these standards is that the library has a central and critical importance in a university. 101

A. *SERVICES.* Three standards . . . services offered by university library shall promote and facilitate effective use of recorded information in all formats by all the university's clientele . . . maintain records which are complete, consistent, and in conformity with national bibliographical standards and requirements . . . provide maximum access to its collections for all its clientele. 102

B. *COLLECTIONS.* Three standards . . . collections of sufficient size and scope to support university's total instructional needs and to facilitate the university's research programs . . . collections developed systematically and consistently within the terms of explicit and detailed policies . . . contain all of the varied forms of recorded information. 102-103

C. *PERSONNEL.* Two standards . . . sufficient number and variety of personnel to develop, organize, and maintain such collections and to provide such reference and information services as will meet the university's needs . . . personnel practices based on sound, contemporary administrative practice and consistent with personnel practices within the university as well as goals and purposes of the library. 104

D. *FACILITIES.* Two standards . . . library shall have facilities which meet present and anticipated future requirements of university and its programs . . . located so that the university community will have convenient access to them. 104-105

E. *ADMINISTRATION AND GOVERNANCE.* Four standards . . . place of library within administrative and governance structure of university shall be clearly identified, and responsibilities and authority of library administration and its chief administrative officer defined . . . library's own governance structure shall be clearly specified and consonant with governance structure of university as well as with the particular needs and requirements of the library . . . close administrative relationship among all libraries within university so users may make full and effective use of library resources and services . . . library's major policies shall be clearly defined and regularly reviewed. 105

F. *FINANCE.* Two standards . . . Budgetary support for library shall be sufficient to enable it to fulfill its obligations and responsibilities as identified in the preceding standards . . . library budget shall be a distinct part of the university's budget, and it shall be developed and managed by the chief administrative officer of the university library. 106

There is commentary on each standard. There is also an appendix, "Quantitative Analytical Techniques for University Libraries." (107) The caveat is offered that it is difficult, if not impossible, to devise a common statistical measure which could be applied to all libraries . . . "but" simple inspection of ARL data, aided by rankings, ranges, averages, and medians, does provide useful insights for the experienced library manager . . . 107 Examples are given.

Standards For College Libraries

Adopted by the Association of College and Research Libraries, a division of the American Library Association, July 3, 1975.

Introduction.
Since the beginning of colleges, libraries have been considered an essential part of advanced learning. Their role has ever been to provide access to the human records needed by members of the higher education community for the successful pursuit of academic programs.

The Standards . . . describe a realistic set of conditions which, if fulfilled, will provide an adequate library program in a college . . . intended to apply to libraries serving academic programs at the bachelors and masters degree levels . . . to libraries serving universities which grant fewer than ten doctoral degrees per year . . . not designed for use in two-year colleges, larger universities, independent professional schools, specialized programs or other typical institutions. 3

These Standards are organized on the basis of the major functions and components of library organizations and services.

STANDARD 1: OBJECTIVES OF THE LIBRARY. The college library shall develop an explicit statement of its objectives in accord with the goals and purposes of the college . . . development of objectives the responsibility of library staff, in consultation with students, faculty, administrative officers . . . statement of objectives shall be reviewed periodically and revised as needed. 3

STANDARD 2: THE COLLECTIONS. The library's collections shall comprise all corpuses of recorded information owned by the college for educational, inspirational, and recreational purposes, including multi-dimensional, aural, pictorial, and print materials . . . library shall provide quickly a high percentage of such materials needed by its patrons . . . amount of materials to be provided shall be determined by a formula (Formula A, page 4) which takes into account the nature and extent of the academic programs of the institution, its enrollment, and the size of its teaching faculty. (Basic collection: 85,000 volumes) (Grades according to how quickly library can provide what percent of its volumes as are called for: A to D.) 5

STANDARD 3: ORGANIZATION OF MATERIALS. Library collections shall be organized by nationally approved conventions and arranged for efficient retrieval at time of need ... a union catalog of holdings that permits identification of items, regardless of format, by author, title, subject ... catalog may be developed either by single library or jointly among several ... catalog in format that can be consulted by a number of people concurrently ... also requisite subordinate files ... except for certain categories of material which are for convenience best segregated by form, library materials shall be arranged on the shelves by subject ... patrons shall have direct access to library materials on shelves. 6

STANDARD 4: STAFF. The library shall be of adequate size and quality to meet agreed-upon objectives ... staff shall comprise qualified librarians, skilled supportive personnel, and part-time assistants serving on an hourly basis ... marks of librarian shall include a graduate library degree from an ALA-accredited program, responsibility for duties of a professional nature, and participation in library professional affairs beyond local campus ... librarians organized as an academic department or school and shall administer themselves in accord with ACRL "Standards for Faculty Status for College and University Librarians." Number of librarians shall be determined by a formula (Formula B, page 7). . . . appropriate balance of effort among librarians, supportive personnel, and part-time assistants . . . using ability of all individuals. 7 (1 librarian for each 500 FTE . . .)

STANDARD 5: DELIVERY OF SERVICE. The college library shall establish and maintain a range and quality of services that will promote the academic program of the institution and encourage optimal library use. Four standards re: provision of materials, their copying, availability, etc. 5.4. Where academic programs are offered away from a campus, library services shall be provided in accord with ACRL's "Guidelines for Library Services to Extension Students." 8

STANDARD 6: FACILITIES. The college shall provide a library building containing secure facilities for housing its resources, adequate space for administration of those resources by staff, and comfortable quarters and furnishings for their utilization by patrons. Size determined by formula (Formula C, page 10); shape and internal distribution determined by function ... except in unusual circumstances, the collections and services shall be administered within a single structure. 9 (Formula C ... size calculated on basis of formula which considers size of student body, requisite administrative space, and number of physical volumes in collections.)

STANDARD 7: ADMINISTRATION. The college library shall be administered in a manner which permits and encourages the fullest and most effective use of available library resources. Statutory or legal foundation for library's activities shall be recognized in writing ... librarian a member of library faculty reporting to president or chief academic officer of institution ... responsibilities and authority of librarian and procedures for appointment defined in writing ... standing advisory committee of students and faculty serving as main channel of formal communication between library and its user community. Library shall maintain written policies and procedure manuals covering internal library governance and operational activities . . . maintain systematic and continuous program for evaluating performance and identifying needed improvements . . . develop statistics not only for purposes of planning and control but also to aid in preparation of reports designed to inform its publics of its accomplishments and problems . . . library shall develop, seek out, and utilize cooperative programs for purposes of either reducing its operating costs or enhancing its services, so long as such programs create no unreimbursed or unreciprocated costs for other libraries or organizations . . . shall be administered in accord with the spirit of the ALA "Library Bill of Rights." 10-11

STANDARD 8: BUDGET. The college librarian shall have the responsibility for preparing, defending, and administering the library budget in accord with agreed-upon objectives . . . amount of library appropriation shall express a relationship to the total institutional budget for educational and general purposes . . . librarian shall have sole authority to apportion funds and initiate expenditures within the library approved budget, in accord with institutional policy . . . library shall maintain such internal accounts as are necessary for approving its invoices for payment, monitoring its encumbrances, and evaluating flow of expenditures. 11

AN EVALUATIVE CHECKLIST FOR REVIEWING A COLLEGE LIBRARY PROGRAM

At the ALA Annual Conference in June 1979 the ACRL Board of Directors approved the recommendation of the Standards and Accreditation Committee that "An Evaluative Checklist for Reviewing a College Library Program" be adopted as a supplement to "Standards for College Libraries." The checklist was developed by the Committee, field-tested, and published for information of ACRL members. "When properly applied it will discriminate among the several levels of quality in library programs." It follows the organization of the standards. Formulae are cited. "It is acknowledged that it would be desirable to include more precise measures. . . However, there is no consensus among academic librarians for their preparation at this time." 305

Guidelines for Two-Year College Learning Resources Programs
Approved by the ACRL Board of Directors on June 29, 1972.

Two-year college. Any institution of higher education which offers less than a baccalaureate degree . . . comprehensive community colleges, public and private junior colleges, and technical institutes . . .

Learning resources. Includes library, audiovisual and telecommunications and encompasses instructional development and functions and instrucational systems components. 305

Introduction. Describes role of two-year colleges, role of learning resources program, and offers a glossary of terms.

I. OBJECTIVES AND PURPOSES

A. The college makes provision for a Learning Resources Program. 307

B. Learning Resources Programs have a statement of defined purpose and objectives. 308

II. ORGANIZATION AND ADMINISTRATION

A. The responsibilities and functions of LRP within the institutional structure and the status of the chief administrator and heads of Learning Resource Units are clearly defined. 308

B. The relationship of a LRP to the total academic program necessitates involvement of the professional staff in all areas and levels of academic planning. 308

C. Advisory committees composed of faculty and students are essential for the evaluation and extension of services.

D. The chief administrator is responsible for the administration of the Learning Resources Program . . . carried out by . . . established lines of authority, definition of responsibilities, and channels of communication through heads of Learning Resources Units as defined in writing. 309

E. Internal administration of a LRP is based on staff participation in policy, procedural, and personnel decisions. 309

F. Budget planning and implementation of a LRP is the responsibility of the chief administrator.

G. The accumulation of pertinent statistics and maintenance of adequate records is a management responsibility.

H. Adequate management includes the preparation and dissemination of information to administration, faculty, and students concerning activities, services, and materials.

I. Responsibilities for all learning resources and services should be assigned to a central administrative unit. 309

J. Multicampus districts take advantage of the opportunity for close cooperation, exchange of resources, and shared technical processes while providing full resources and services for every campus. 310

III. BUDGET

A. Learning Resources Program budget is a function of program planning. It is designed to implement the realization of institutional and instructional program objectives. B-J further elaboration. 310-11

IV. INSTRUCTIONAL SYSTEM COMPONENTS 311

A. Staff. Ten points relating to staff.

B. Facilities. Eight points relating to physical facilities, arrangements.

C. Instructional Equipment. Three points.

D. Materials. Fifteen points.

V. SERVICES 315

A. Users of Learning Resources have the right to expect:

1. That facilities, materials, and services are available to meet demonstrated instructional needs for their use;

2. That an atmosphere be provided which allows sensitive and responsive attention to their requirements;

3. That professional staff be readily available for interpretation of materials and services and for consultation on instructional development;

4. That physical facilities be maintained to make use comfortable and orderly;

5. That requests for scheduling, circulation, distribution, and utilization of materials and related equipment be handled expeditiously;

6. That acquisition, production, and organization of materials meet their

instructional and personal needs.

VI. INTERAGENCY COOPERATIVE ACTIVITIES 315

A. Cooperative arrangements for sharing of resources are developed with other institutions and agencies in the community, region, state, and nation.

B. The institution is willing to consider participation in cooperative projects, such as shared cataloging, computer use, and other services which may be mutually beneficial to all participants.

C. Responsibility for the collection and preservation of community history and for the accumulation of other local and statistical data is shared with other institutions and is coordinated with them.

(Reprinted from December 1972 *College and Research Libraries News,* No. 11. ACRL News Issue (B) of College & Research Libraries, Vol. 33, No. 7, pages 305-315)

STATEMENT ON QUANTITATIVE STANDARDS FOR TWO-YEAR LEARNING RESOURCES PROGRAMS
Approved by ACRL Board in June 1979.

This document is designed as a supplement to the Guidelines, to meet recurring requests for suggested quantitative figures for help in planning and evaluating programs. "No absolutes are presented here . . . no conclusive research provides quantitative measures of some factors. In such cases the professional judgment and extensive experience of the members of the committee have been the basis for the recommendations."

Adherence to every single element in the LRP is not considered essential . . . the significant variable accepted for most elements is enrollment expressed as FTE students. The standards that are quantitative are not expected to remain constant; there is a recommendation for review every three years.

STAFF
BUDGET
COLLECTION SIZE
ANNUAL ACCESSIONS
SPACE REQUIREMENTS
EQUIPMENT FOR DISTRIBUTION
PRODUCTION
Specific checks are given in all these areas.

Guidelines for Library Services to Extension Students
These guidelines reprinted from the ALA Bulletin, January 1967, are currently under review. George V. Hodowanec, member of the Standards and Accreditation Committee of ACRL, has developed proposed revised guidelines for library services to extension students with a summary of relevant literature and a survey of academic librarians. (June 1980) The rationale for this review is that both institutions and off-campus programs, and the clientele for off-campus programs, have changed a great deal in the thirteen years since the first guidelines were published.

Introduction. Whatever the circumstances under which the extension courses are taught, library resources should be as important to the successful conduct of the course as would be the case for the same course being taught in the regular university program.

The following assumptions are basic to any guidelines for library services to extension students:

1. Because of the increased and continuing demand for higher education by persons in full-time positions in communities beyond easy commuting distance from the university, the need for university classes to be taught off campus will continue and offerings will continue and offerings will undoubtedly increase.

2. It is the desire of the university and the reasonable expectation of the student that a course taught through extension should not suffer in quality because it is not taught as a part of the university on-campus program.

3. If library resources are essential to a particular course taught on campus, they are equally essential if that course is taught through extension.

4. The ratio of graduate courses to undergraduate courses taught for credit through extension, which is already high, will continue to increase significantly.

The following are offered as guidelines for the improvement of library services for the extension student.

1. Library services for extension purposes should be financed on a regular basis.

2. A professional librarian should be given the specific responsibility for handling library materials and services for extension classes.

3. Before approving the teaching of a course off campus, the appropriate officer in the extension division, the instructor, and the librarian in charge of library materials and services for extension should consider jointly what the library needs are for the course and the extent to which these can be supplied locally or through the university library.

4. Special attention should be given to the availability of library resources taught at the graduate level.

5. The use of the university library should be encouraged and, where feasible, required.

6. Essential journal materials and indexes should be provided despite the understandable problems invoved in making them available.

The . . . "guidelines" are not meant to be used as "standards" in evaluating library services to extension students . . . but to serve only as a guide to an institution concerned about its own program.

ALA BULLETIN, January 1967, pages 50-55

APPENDIX B

Library Standards of the Association of
College and Research Libraries

Standards for University Libraries

FOREWORD

The following statement of university library standards has been prepared by a joint committee established by the Association of Research Libraries and the Association of College and Research Libraries. A draft of the statement appeared in the April 1978 issue of *College & Research Libraries News*.

In August 1978, the Joint ARL-ACRL Committee on University Library Standards revised this draft. On October 26, 1978, the ARL membership unanimously endorsed the statement as revised. At the ALA Midwinter Meeting in January 1979, the ACRL Board also voted to ratify the revised statement. "Standards for University Libraries" is being published in its final form in this issue of *C&RL News* for the information of ACRL members.

STANDARDS
FOR UNIVERSITY LIBRARIES

Prepared by a joint committee of the Association of Research Libraries and the Association of College and Research Libraries, a division of the American Library Association.

Introduction

These standards have been prepared to assist faculty, university administrators, librarians, accrediting agencies, and others in the evaluation and improvement of university library services and resources. These statements are intended to apply only to those institutions of higher education which have been characterized by the Carnegie Commission on Higher Education as "doctoral granting institutions."[1] All of these institutions emphasize graduate study, professional education, and research. Despite these basic similarities, university libraries are also characterized by a high degree of individuality, particularly with respect to policies, programs, responsibilities, and traditions. Hence, these standards are not intended to establish normative prescriptions for uniform application. Rather, they are meant to provide a general framework within which informed judgment can be applied to individual circumstances.

The fundamental assumption of these standards is that the library has a central and critical importance in a university. This importance has been recognized repeatedly by analysts of higher education. In his 1966 report to the American Council on Education, Allan M. Cartter, for example, stated:

"The library is the heart of the university; no other single non-human factor is as closely related

to the quality of graduate education. A few universities with poor library resources have achieved considerable strength in several departments, in some cases because laboratory facilities may be more important in a particular field than the library, and in other cases because the universities are located close to other great library collections such as the Library of Congress and the New York Public Library. But institutions that are strong in all areas invariably have major national research libraries."[2]

As with all institutions, universities and their libraries have experienced considerable change over time. Further changes are taking place now, and others clearly lie ahead. Particularly noteworthy is the increasing sense of interdependence and commitment to coordination among universities generally. With regard to university libraries, the following developments are particularly important: the growth of interlibrary cooperation, especially resource sharing; the strengthening and expansion of service programs, such as bibliographic instruction; the increasing importance of recorded information in nonprint formats; the application of automated systems to library operations and the growth of machine-readable data bases; the closer interaction between librarians and faculty and the improved status of librarians within the university; increased stress on the effectiveness and efficiency of operations. A recognition of such trends and their importance is fundamental to these standards.

Recognizing the increasing interdependence of universities in developing and maintaining scholarly resources, these standards are intended to provide guidance in identifying that level of library self-sufficiency which is essential to the health and vigor of a university and its academic programs. The general assumption is that the primary obligation of a university library is to meet the instructional and research needs of the students and faculty at that university. However, no university library can acquire all of the recorded information that its clientele may find useful. An attempt is made, therefore, to recognize the mechanisms being developed to promote cooperative access to scholarly information, to identify the current limitations of interdependence, and to enumerate the factors which are essential in maintaining an environment in which instruction and research can flourish.

Care has been taken to limit the standards to succinct statements focusing on the elements judged to be most critical in determining the adequacy of a university library. Amplification of the principles identified in the standards is provided in the form of commentary.

Standard A.1

In order to support the instructional, research, and public service programs of the university, the services offered by a university library shall promote and facilitate effective use of recorded information in all formats by all of the library's clientele.

Commentary on Standard A.1

In developing and implementing its program of service, a university library should give priority to the needs of the students, faculty, and other academic staff of the university, who may be said to constitute the library's "primary clientele." While it may also have obligations or commitments to other clienteles or constituencies, the library should recognize that these are secondary.

A university library should provide the following services: reference and information services which are available at adequately identified and designated points during established service hours; specialized and in-depth assistance to individuals in the use of the library's resources; bibliographic instruction programs; services which will facilitate access to nonprint media and machine-readable data bases; and services which will facilitate access to recorded information in other library collections.

These services should be designed to meet effectively the whole range of different informational and bibliographical needs that arise in the various academic areas and in all other parts of the university.

While universities should place great emphasis on meeting the intensive library needs of graduate students and faculty, they should be careful to provide adequately for the needs of undergraduate students.

Finally, university libraries should recognize that, to one degree or another, they share a responsibility with all research libraries to support higher education in general and each other in particular through cooperative efforts.

Standard A.2

In order to ensure maximum access to its collections and their contents, a university library shall maintain records of its collections which are complete, consistent, and in conformity with national bibliographical standards and requirements.

Commentary on Standard A.2

The extent of bibliographical coverage that must be provided in a particular library will depend on many factors, such as whether or not the library has open or closed access stacks, the extent and nature of the library's specialized collections, the history and traditions of the library and of the university, and the nature of specific cooperative arrangements that the library may have entered into with other libraries and library consortia.

To ensure effective access to its collections as well as to increase its operational efficiency, a university library's bibliographic records should conform to recognized standards of cataloging and classification, and its bibliographic apparatus should be internally consistent. Its bibliographic records should be adjusted in conjunction with periodic inventories of the collections. Every multi-unit university library should have a union catalog of its cataloged holdings.

Standard A.3

Within the limits of the university's particular responsibilities and priorities, a university library shall provide maximum access to its collections for all of its clientele.

Commentary on Standard A.3

Various factors are involved in providing access to a library's collections, such as circulation policies and procedures, service hours, security arrangements, and actual operating efficiency. While practices vary significantly from library to library, certain principles should be followed in each library. Most items in the library collections should be readily available both for consultation in the library and for circulation to authorized clientele. Access to and circulation of rare, fragile, and high-demand materials should be appropriately controlled and restricted. To ensure maximum availability of the collections to those authorized to use them, terms of loan should be carefully set and should generally be similar for all user categories.

Adequate precautions should be taken to control loss of or damage to the library's collections. The prompt return in good condition of all circulated materials should be effectively enforced for all borrowers.

Circulation procedures and stack maintenance operations in a university library should be effective and efficient. There should be a regular and continuing program of shelf reading. Library service hours should be responsive to high- and low-use periods, to the number of branch, departmental, and other special libraries in the system as well as to the availability of alternative study space.

Standard B.1

A university library's collections shall be of sufficient size and scope to support the university's total instructional needs and to facilitate the university's research programs.

Commentary on Standard B.1

A university library should provide all of the resources that are necessary for direct support of the university's full instructional programs at both the undergraduate and the graduate levels. If these resources are not readily available in the library, the instructional programs cannot be carried out successfully. These resources include required and assigned readings, reference and bibliographical materials, basic journals and serials, as well as any other library materials that undergraduate or graduate students are expected to be able to consult readily in their courses of study, or in the preparation of theses and dissertations.

Weak collections can hamper research. The accumulation and preservation of substantial collections and the implementation of comprehensive acquisition programs must be recognized as providing a resource whose presence within a university is essential to the conditions under which knowledge is effectively increased and transmitted. It is clear that no university library can be expected to possess in its collections all of the recorded information which faculty or doctoral students may need to consult as they pursue their research. Nevertheless, it is essential that collections be of such size, scope, and quality that they promote rather than restrict research. While every library should take care to develop collections whose areas of concentration reflect and support the academic priorities and strengths within the university, interlibrary arrangements, which have long been established for the mutual support of exceptional research needs, must continue to be relied upon to supplement even the most comprehensive research collections.

The continued rapid growth of scholarly literature and the costs of providing access to this literature for those in the university community have necessitated formal and informal arrangements among libraries to ensure maximum access to this literature. Common methods of sharing resources and improving access have been loans between libraries, provision of visiting privileges for scholars, agreements on the acquisitions of materials, and sharing of bibliographic information.

While interlibrary cooperation, as presently practiced, may not promise large cost savings in the immediate future, significant improved methods of supplementing local resources are in the active planning stages. University libraries must participate in the development of these new access mechanisms to ensure that local, regional, national, and international interests are effectively served.

Attempts have been made to identify precise quantitative measures of adequate collection size and growth rates for a university library. No such formula has yet been developed which can be generally applied. At present, such formulas as exist can only yield approximations which indicate a general level of need. If they are applied arbitrarily and mechanically, they can distort the realities of a given situation. Nevertheless, quantitative measures are increasingly important in guiding the qualitative judgment that must ultimately be applied to university libraries and their collections. One technique is the use of regression analysis to facilitate the comparison of similar libraries to one another;[3] another of some general applicability is the "index of quality" developed by the American Council on Education for relating library collection size to graduate program quality.[4]

Standard B.2

A university library's collections shall be developed systematically and consistently within the terms of explicit and detailed policies.

Commentary on Standard B.2

Given the great breadth of university library collections and the wide variations in depth of collections among subjects held, it is essential that there be a collections development policy to guide the selection and acquisition of materials.

By establishing such a policy, librarians seek to ensure that the library's collections are planned and developed in relation to the university's academic, research, and service goals and priorities and within the limits of resources available.

Working in close consultation with faculty and administration, librarians, particularly subject specialists, should assume the responsibility for drafting and implementing this policy.

Recognizing the inherent difficulties in collection development, it is imperative that the library have full and continuous access to information about all developments, actual and planned, in the academic, research, and service programs of the university and its components which affect the library.

Once codified, the library's collection development policy should be made known to and endorsed by the university faculty and administration. To ensure that this policy reflects changes within the university, the policy should be regularly and carefully reviewed.

Standard B.3

A university library's collections shall contain all of the varied forms of recorded information.

Commentary on Standard B.3

The university library has traditionally been recognized as the repository within the university for the printed information needed to support the university's instructional and research programs. As recorded information becomes increasingly available in a variety of nonprint formats, such as films, sound recordings, and video tapes, it is appropriate that this material, except where needed exclusively for classroom use, also be acquired, organized, and made available through the university library.[5]

SECTION C: PERSONNEL

Standard C.1

A university library shall have a sufficient number and variety of personnel to develop, organize, and maintain such collections and to provide such reference and information services as will meet the university's needs.

Commentary on Standard C.1

The size of a university library's staff is determined by many factors, including the number of physically separate library units, the number of service points requiring staff, the number of service hours provided, the number and special characteristics of items processed annually, the nature and quality of the processing to which they are subjected, the size of the collections, and the rate of circulation of the collections. Interinstitutional cooperative arrangements may also affect staff size. As such factors vary widely from one institution to another, no single model or formula can be provided for developing an optimum staff size.

A university library should have on its staff a variety of personnel: professional, clerical, and student-assistant staff. The librarians should perform the core academic and professional functions of the library: collection development, reference and information services, and substantive activities related to the bibliographic control of materials. All categories of personnel should have appropriate education and experience, including, when necessary, graduate or professional degrees in their particular specialties. The recognized terminal degree for librarians is the master's degree from an American Library Association accredited library school program, although additional graduate degrees may sometimes be desirable.

The deployment of personnel within a specific university library is related to the range of operations and services provided by that library and to its total workload requirements.

Standard C.2

Personnel practices within a university library shall be based on sound, contemporary administrative practice and shall be consistent with personnel practices within the university as well as the goals and purposes of the library.

Commentary on Standard C.2

The terms and conditions of employment of the several categories of staff in a university library should be consonant with the established terms and conditions of employment of staff in related categories elsewhere within the university. Terms and conditions of employment for librarians, for example, should parallel those of the rest of the university's academic staff, just as terms and conditions of employment for the library's clerical and student staff should parallel those of similar employees within the university as a whole.

A comprehensive university library personnel management program should address recruitment, appointment, promotion, tenure, dismissal, appeal, definition of position responsibilities, classification and pay plans, orientation and training programs, review of employee performance, staff development, and counseling.

More specific guidance on these matters is provided in the following documents: "Statement on Faculty Status of College and University Librarians"[6] and "Library Education and Personnel Utilization."[7]

SECTION D: FACILITIES

Standard D.1

A university library shall have facilities which meet the present and anticipated future requirements of the university and its programs.

Commentary on Standard D.1

A university library's buildings should be of sufficient size and quality to house the collections and to provide sufficient space for their use by students, faculty, and other clientele. There should also be adequate space for the library operations necessary for the provision of its services. Adequacy of facilities cannot be determined simply on the basis of present requirements. The size and composition of the university's enrollment, the nature of its instructional and research programs, the form and publication rate of library materials strongly influence library requirements, and it is necessary that these requirements be subject to continuous evaluation and planning.

A university library should be attractive, inviting, and carefully designed to promote operational efficiency and effectiveness of use. Specific factors relevant here include general environmental features that affect clientele, staff, and collections (light, ventilation, temperature and humidity control, vertical and horizontal transportation, safety features, etc.), layout of the stacks, number and variety of reader stations, relationship between stacks and reader stations, relationship among service points, effective flow of materials, and adequacy of space for staff and operations.

The fundamental consideration in designing a library building should be its function. Since the nature of collections, services, operations, and the needs of a library's clientele can change significantly over time, present and future flexibility is an important element in library design. Although the architectural style and traditions of a university may dictate certain design features for a library building, such factors should not be allowed to compromise basic functional considerations.[8]

Standard D.2

Libraries shall be so located that the university community will have convenient access to them.

Commentary on Standard D.2

The requirements of interdisciplinary studies and research, recognition of the needs of undergraduate students, the urgency of achieving operating economies—these and other factors have revived interest in centralizing physically dispersed library units in order to improve access to resources and avoid costly duplication in the development and maintenance of collections. There are circumstances, however, such as campus geography, intensity of use, and size of collections which may continue to justify the maintenance of multiple library units. Remote storage facilities may also be established in attempting to deal with space inadequacies although this usually inhibits convenience of access. Where the pattern of decentralization persists in any form, it is important that libraries be located so as to minimize inconvenience to all library users.[9]

SECTION E: ADMINISTRATION AND GOVERNANCE

Standard E.1

The place of the university library within the administrative and governance structure of the university shall be clearly identified, and the responsibilities and authority of the library administration and its chief administrative officer shall be defined.

Commentary on Standard E.1

If there is ambiguity within the university community as to the particular place occupied by the library within the administrative and governance structure of the university, and if the authority and responsibilities of the library's chief administrative officer are not clearly identified, misunderstanding, conflict, and confusion can sometimes result to the detriment of both the university and its library. Because it is closely related to instruction and research, the university library should be formally recognized as one of the major academic units within the university, and its chief administrative officer should participate regularly and directly in university-wide academic planning and decision making. For similar reasons, this person should report directly to the chief academic officer of the university.

The long-recognized need in institutions of higher education to involve faculty in library matters has led to the institutionalization of the advisory library committee. Because of the fundamental importance of the library to instruction and research and the consequent need for close, continuing interaction between the faculty and the library, the existence of the library committee is

valuable. The committee should be advisory, and its responsibilities should be clearly delineated.

Standard E.2

The university library's own administrative and governance structure shall be clearly specified and shall be consonant with the governance structure of the university as well as with the particular needs and requirements of the library.

Commentary on Standard E.2

In order to facilitate effective organizational activity and decision making, it is essential that the administrative and governance structure of the university library itself be clearly specified. This will involve identifying the roles and responsibilities of all categories of library personnel in the governance of the library. It is essential that library governance reflect the principles and practice followed elsewhere within the university, although they should be modified as necessary to embody those conditions and issues peculiar to an academic library.

Standard E.3

There shall be a close administrative relationship among all libraries within the university to the end that library users may make full and effective use of library resources and services.

Commentary on Standard E.3

No single pattern of library administration will serve all universities equally well, but whatever pattern an institution chooses should have as its principal purpose the equitable distribution of library resources and services. The needs of scholars differ from discipline to discipline and often the needs of students differ from those of faculty. These competing interests cannot always be reconciled, but one important task of library administration is to achieve as much balance as possible in the provision of services to all groups.

However administrative relationships among library units within a university are determined, it is essential that adequate coordinating mechanisms be established and enforced to ensure that service policies are in reasonable harmony, that costs related to duplication are controlled, and that access to all library collections is maximized.

Standard E.4

A university library's major policies and procedures shall be clearly defined and regularly reviewed.

Commentary on Standard E.4

In order to ensure that it is effective internally and understood externally, a university library should clearly define its major policies and procedures and record them in written form. The written statements of policy should be readily available to all members of the library staff, and policies which have external relevance (such as the library's collection development policy or circulation policy) should be accessible to the library's clientele and to others who may need or desire to consult them. These policies, as well as the practices that implement them, should be regularly reviewed to ensure that they continue to be appropriate.

SECTION F: FINANCE

Standard F.1

Budgetary support for the university library shall be sufficient to enable it to fulfill its obligations and responsibilities as identified in the preceding standards.

Commentary on Standard F.1

The total budgetary needs of a university library can be determined only in relation to its responsibilities. Many attempts have been made to develop formulas or other "objective" measures for determining the budgetary requirements of a university library. These measures range from matching funding with student enrollment to defining a minimum percentage of the total university G and E budget which should be devoted to the library. Such "objective" approaches to budget determination do not always take cognizance of the range and complexity of demands which any university library must meet, as well as the significantly different library needs of different universities.

These conditions also make it impossible to identify a viable model that can be applied to all university libraries for allocating their budgets by major category (salaries and wages, acquisitions, binding, miscellaneous supplies, and other expense). Allocation ultimately depends on local requirements and priorities. For example, if a university library is expected to operate a substantial number of discrete units with parallel and duplicative activities, its expenditures for salaries and wages will be higher than if this were not the case.

Under any circumstances, it is essential that a university library be provided with sufficient funding to enable it to develop appropriate collections, provide appropriate services, carry out necessary operations, and satisfy identified expectations and requirements. If funding is less than is necessary to fulfill these obligations, the library will be unable to meet university needs.

A university library should be expected to operate on a sound financial basis. To do this, the library and its administration must be able to identify and support its fiscal request effectively and to report adequately on expenditure of funds.

Standard F.2

The university library budget shall be a distinct part of the university's budget, and it shall

be developed and managed by the chief administrative officer of the university library.

Commentary on Standard F.2

The authority to prepare, submit, defend, and administer the university library budget should be delegated clearly and explicitly to the chief administrative officer of the university library. He or she should have full responsibility for managing this budget as well as the authority necessary to maximize the use of the library's total resources. He or she should have the same degree of latitude and responsibility that is exercised by other major administrative officers within the university. The library should be responsible for preparing adequate and regular reports on expenditures throughout the year. These reports should conform to the university's requirements and, where necessary, to its standardized procedures and practices.

Because of the importance of the library within the university and the need that it respond effectively to changing demands, priorities, and academic programs, it is essential that the library budget be developed in relationship to and with full cognizance of the total university budget-planning process, and that the library's chief administrative officer be directly and significantly involved in this process.

REFERENCES

1. Carnegie Commission on Higher Education, *A Classification of Institutions of Higher Education* (Berkeley, Calif.: The Commission, 1973), p.1–2, 9–22. This publication identifies 173 "doctoral granting institutions."

2. Allan M. Cartter, *An Assessment of Quality in Graduate Education* (Washington, D.C.: American Council on Education, 1966), p.114.

3. William J. Baumol and Matityahu Marcus, *Economics of Academic Libraries* (Washington, D.C.: American Council on Education, 1973).

4. Cartter, *An Assessment of Quality in Graduate Education*, p.114.

5. The best recent discussion of the importance of nonprint media for higher education is Carnegie Commission on Higher Education, *The Fourth Revolution: Instructional Technology in Higher Education* (New York: McGraw-Hill, 1972).

6. In *Faculty Status for Academic Librarians: A History and Policy Statement* (Chicago: American Library Assn., 1975), p.35–38.

7. "Library Education and Personnel Utilization" (Chicago: American Library Assn., 1976).

8. Considerable valuable information is available in several publications, the best of which remains Keyes D. Metcalf, *Planning Academic and Research Library Buildings* (New York: McGraw-Hill, 1965).

9. This issue has been the subject of considerable

analysis. See, particularly, Ralph E. Ellsworth, *The Economics of Book Storage in Academic Libraries* (Metuchen, N.J.: The Association of Research Libraries and the Scarecrow Press, 1969). Also useful is Jeffrey A. Raffel and Robert Shishko, *Systematic Analysis of University Libraries* (Cambridge, Mass.: MIT Press, 1969).

APPENDIX

QUANTITATIVE ANALYTICAL TECHNIQUES FOR UNIVERSITY LIBRARIES

The university libraries[1] to which quantitative measures might be applied are so complex, so diverse in the programs they support, and so different from each other that it is extremely difficult, if not impossible, to devise a common statistical measure which could be applied to all of them. This problem is further complicated by the character and inadequacy of the currently available data. Herman Fussler, for example, observes that: "libraries, like universities, tend to have very inadequate analytical data on their own operations and performance. Such data, especially as they relate to costs and system responses to user needs, are critically important in any effort to improve a library's efficiency and responsiveness."[2] Fritz Machlup, in the course of his recent efforts to measure the holdings and acquisitions of libraries on a broad scale, has complained about the lack of adequate data.[3] Other observers have challenged the utility of present library data collection.[4] They focus on perceived failures to measure performance or effectiveness. Nevertheless, academic institutions do compete for faculty and students, and one of the elements in this competition is the adequacy of library services and collections. Comparative judgments about academic libraries are made, and these comparisons can be aided by quantitative measures.

Unfortunately, much of the data which are needed to actually make interinstitutional comparisons is not easily available, although some useful data can be obtained from ARL statistics. The LIBGIS and HEGIS surveys also supply data, but these are usually too old for current needs or in a form which is difficult to use. Consequently, the analyst is compelled to rely on what is available: ARL statistics, authorities who have written on the subject, and such limited surveys as he or she can make. All of these methods have varying degrees of utility, but with the possible exception of the ARL data, none provide the raw data on which empirically derived measures can be based. Certain "common" practices can be discerned, and the advice of authorities can be weighed, but these, however valuable, do not constitute quantitative measures in an empirically derivable, logically justifiable sense. To have reliable quantitative measures, the categories to be measured must be defined,

and a mechanism for gathering the necessary data must be developed.

In the absence of either of these necessary conditions, it is difficult to do more than perform what analyses can be performed on ARL data. Briefly, these fall into three categories: (a) insights obtained by simple inspection of the data; (b) the construction of ratios which reduce the quantity of data to be comprehended and facilitate comparison; and (c) regression analysis which performs roughly the same function from the analyst's point of view as the construction of ratios but also requires an effort on the part of the analyst to group like institutions together and gives the analyst some indication of how well this has been accomplished (coefficient of determination).

Simple inspection of ARL data, aided by rankings, ranges, averages, and medians, does provide useful insights for the experienced library manager who can mentally discount obvious discrepancies and differences between institutions and can restrict comparisons to a homogeneous group. However, to read, for example, that in 1976–77 the number of volumes in ARL libraries ranged between Harvard's 9,547,576 and McMaster's 906,741, that the average library held 2,127,047, and the median was 1,653,000 may give the reader a sense of perspective, which is valuable, but it is of limited use in drawing comparisons between rather different institutions.

A reduction of data can be achieved by the use of ratios or percentages, as is shown in the example of ratio analysis below. Some of those which can be generated from existing data include:

1. The ratio of professional to nonprofessional staff

2. Expenditure for library materials as a percent of total library operating expenditure

3. Ratio of salary expenditures to library material expenditures

This kind of data reduction aids analysis by making the data more comprehensible. For example, among ARL libraries in 1976–77, the ratio of professional to nonprofessional staff ranged from 1.08 to 0.24; the average was 0.51 and the median 0.49. The overwhelming majority of libraries tended toward a pattern of one professional to two nonprofessionals. Among ARL libraries in 1976–77, expenditures for library materials as a percent of total library expenditures ranged from 19.14 percent for Toronto to 50.61 percent for Houston. The average was 31.46 percent and the median 30.09 percent. The vast majority of ARL libraries tended to spend 30 percent of their budgets on acquisitions. The obverse of materials expenditure for libraries is salary expenditure. Expressed as a ratio of salary to materials it ranged from 3.6 in the case of Toronto, to 0.8 in the case of Houston, with the median 1.9 and the average 1.93.

From ratios such as these, a deeper insight into

library operations can be obtained, but it would be rash to conclude that all libraries should spend 30 percent of their budgets for books and 60 percent for salaries or that the ratio of professional to nonprofessional should always be 1:2. Local conditions dictate differing policies. A library with many branches may require a higher ratio of professionals to nonprofessionals. Conversely, differing operating conditions, different types of staffing may dictate different ratios. An example of a more extended kind of ratio analysis is that of Allan Cartter's Library Resources Index, which is described in a following section. Yet, even this kind of ratio should be viewed cautiously. At best, ratio analysis can serve only as a background against which local conditions may be evaluated.

Regression analysis also provides a form of data reduction, but it compels the analyst to attempt to group like institutions together. Baumol and Marcus provide a guide to its use in library data analysis.[5] The concluding section of this appendix gives an example of its application. But the same caveats about drawing inferences that apply to ratio analysis apply to regression analysis.

In addition to these, there is a growing literature on performance evaluation of libraries which is expressed in various ways. F. W. Lancaster summarizes some of the possible approaches:

"1. The ability of the library to deliver a particular item when it is needed.

"2. The ability of the catalog and the shelf arrangement to disclose the holdings of particular items or of materials on particular subjects.

"3. The ability of reference staff to answer questions completely and accurately.

"4. The speed with which a particular item can be located when needed.

"5. The speed with which a reference inquiry can be answered or a literature search conducted and the results presented to the library user.

"6. The amount of effort that the user must himself expend in exploiting the services of the library (including factors of physical accessibility of the library and its collections, the size and quality of the library staff, and the way in which the collections are cataloged, indexed, shelved and signposted."[6]

Performance measures are, however, still in the early stages of their development. They may eventually prove to be extremely important to libraries, but they are likely to be most useful in making intrainstitutional rather than interinstitutional decisions. In sum, there are no simple solutions, no ready panaceas, no easily available substitutes for intelligent analysis of available data.

Example of Ratio Analysis

Table 1 below demonstrates the application of ratio analysis to library materials expenditures as a percentage of total library operating expenditures. It is based on the latest (1976–77) ARL data. For the sake of brevity and because this is simply used as an example, only twenty of the total applicable ninety-three institutions have been included.

The Library Resources Index

The Library Resources Index is a specialized index devised by Allan M. Cartter and published

TABLE 1
LIBRARY MATERIALS EXPENDITURES AS A PERCENTAGE
OF TOTAL LIBRARY OPERATING EXPENDITURES (VALUE)
FOR TWENTY UNIVERSITY LIBRARIES, 1976–77

Rank Order Number	Institution Number	Institution Name	Value
1	31	Houston	50.61
2	3	Arizona	44.63
3	82	Texas A & M	44.05
4	87	VPI & SU	42.84
5	81	Texas	42.69
6	28	Georgia	42.21
7	35	Iowa	42.15
8	71	South Carolina	42.08
9	68	Rice	41.67
10	42	Louisiana State	40.19
11	20	Connecticut	40.04
12	60	Oklahoma State	39.51
13	53	Nebraska	39.30
14	80	Tennessee	39.22
15	52	Missouri	38.93
16	4	Arizona State	38.62
17	22	Dartmouth	38.30
18	24	Emory	38.23
19	1	Alabama	38.08
20	57	Notre Dame	37.87

Rank Order Overall Index	Institution Name	Total Volume Index	Volumes Added Index	Serials Index	Overall Library Resources Index
1	Harvard	4.49	2.25	3.89	3.54
2	Illinois	2.74	1.95	3.43	2.71
3	Yale	3.24	2.40	2.44	2.69
4	Calif., Berkeley	2.31	1.75	3.90	2.65
5	Texas	1.91	2.87	2.41	2.39
6	Indiana	2.07	2.39	1.71	2.05
7	Columbia	2.22	1.57	2.31	2.03
8	Michigan	2.31	1.81	1.92	2.02
9	Stanford	2.05	1.67	2.13	1.95
10	Toronto	1.87	2.15	1.66	1.90
11	Calif., Los Angeles	1.84	1.44	2.26	1.84
12	Washington	1.52	2.16	1.64	1.77
13	Cornell	1.87	1.33	2.08	1.76
14	Chicago	1.83	1.60	1.76	1.73
15	Wisconsin	1.52	1.30	1.92	1.58
16	Ohio State	1.53	1.50	1.15	1.39
17	Minnesota	1.58	0.93	1.48	1.33
18	Duke	1.35	1.28	1.33	1.32
19	Princeton	1.37	1.18	1.25	1.27
20	Pennsylvania	1.31	1.08	1.10	1.16

in his *An Assessment of Quality in Graduate Education.*[7] It is an average of three indexes and is computed in the following way. First, the pool of institutions to be compared is determined. (In the example, shown as table 2, this pool is all ARL libraries and the data are for 1976–77). Second, three variables are isolated: (a) total volumes; (b) volumes added; and (c) periodicals received. A separate index is formed for each variable by finding the average for each variable and dividing the average value into the value for each institution.

For example, assume that the average number of periodicals held in ARL libraries is 15,000, and three institutions have totals respectively of 60,000, 15,000, and 7,500. Dividing the average, 15,000, into each of these figures yields index values of 4, 1, and .5. Similarly, values are found for each institution for the other two variables: volumes added and total volumes. Then the three index values for each institution are summed, divided by three, and sorted into descending order. For example, refer to institution number 8 in table 2. It is Michigan. It has index values of 2.31, 1.81, and 1.92. The sum of these is 6.04. Dividing this by 3 yields 2.01, the overall library resources index.

Mr. Cartter's index was based on 1963–64 data. His general conclusion at that time was: "Those libraries which fall below .5 are probably too weak to support quality graduate programs in a wide range of fields, although they may be adequate for an institution that specializes in technology or in advanced work in a very limited number of areas."[8]

Table 2 demonstrates an application of the Li-

brary Resources Index to twenty ARL libraries, using 1976–77 ARL data.

Regression Analysis Tables Using ARL Data, 1975–76

In analyzing data from ARL libraries, the strongest statistical relationships are found to exist when these libraries are categorized in some way. Therefore, by way of example, ARL libraries may be grouped in four different ways:

1. All ARL academic libraries.
2. All private ARL academic libraries in the U.S.
3. All public ARL academic libraries in the U.S.
4. All Canadian ARL academic libraries.

Further, for each group additional tables may be developed that predict the values of certain different (dependent) variables based upon the value of other (independent) variables. Six variables, for example, which can be examined are:

1. Professional staff
2. Total staff
3. Gross volumes added
4. Expenditures for library materials
5. Total library expenditures
6. Current periodicals held

For each library in each of the four groups noted above, the following predictions then can be made:

1. Number of professional staff based on number of volumes held
2. Number of total staff based on number of volumes held
3. Number of gross volumes added based on volumes held

TABLE 3
EXAMPLE OF REGRESSION ANALYSIS APPLIED
TO SIZE OF PROFESSIONAL STAFF (Y)

Institution	Y Value	Y Estimate	Residual	Display		
Library A	37	39	−2	X		
Library B	52	48	+4		X	
Library C	63	55	+8			X
Library D	60	72	−12	X		
					least squares line normalized	

4. Expenditures for library materials based on gross volumes added and volumes held

5. Total expenditures based on volumes held, gross volumes added, and total staff

6. Number of current serials based on number of volumes held

Thus, for each table there can be plotted a display of variables, together with observations for each institution, and which include for each dependent variable its actual value, its estimated value, and the residual, which is the difference between the actual and the estimated value. For example, assume we have the display shown above as table 3, which predicts the number of professional staff a library is expected to have based upon the number of volumes held.

The first column identifies each institution; the second shows the actual value for each variable; the third shows the expected value based on the regression equation computation which has been done; the fourth is the difference between columns two and three; and the fifth is a plot of the data.

Looking at Library A, we see that it has thirty-seven professional staff, but based on the other libraries in its comparison class, it would be expected to have thirty-nine. The actual value is two fewer than expected, so its position on the graph is plotted to the left of the least squares line. (See any standard textbook on statistics for detailed explanation of this technique.) Libraries B and C have more professionals than would be expected, so they are plotted to the right of the line. Consequently, by inspection, the library

manager can note any obvious anomalies between his or her institution and others.

REFERENCES FOR APPENDIX

1. Doctoral granting institutions in Carnegie Commission on Higher Education. *A Classification of Institutions of Higher Education* (Berkeley, Calif.: The Commission, 1973). p.1–2, 9–22.

2. Herman H. Fussler, *Research Libraries and Technology, A Report to the Sloan Foundation* (Chicago: Univ. of Chicago Press, 1973), p.61.

3. Fritz Machlup, "Our Libraries: Can We Measure Their Holdings and Acquisitions," *AAUP Bulletin* 62:303–7 (Oct. 1976).

4. See, for example, Morris Hamburg and others, *Library Planning and Decision Making Systems* (Cambridge, Mass.: MIT Press, 1974).

5. William J. Baumol and Matityahu Marcus, *Economics of Academic Libraries* (Washington, D.C.: American Council on Education, 1973).

6. F. W. Lancaster, *The Measurement and Evaluation of Library Services* (Washington, D.C.: Information Resources, 1977), p.323.

7. Allan M. Cartter, *An Assessment of Quality in Graduate Education* (Washington, D.C.: American Council on Education, 1966).

8. *Ibid.*, p.114.

Editor's Note: Members may order single copies by sending a self-addressed label to the ACRL office. Nonmembers should include $1.00 with their order. ■■

Standards for College Libraries

Approved as policy by the Board of Directors of the Association of College and Research Libraries, on July 3, 1975. These Standards supersede and replace the 1959 "Standards for College Libraries" (College & Research Libraries, July 1959, p.274–80).

Introduction

Since the beginning of colleges libraries have been considered an essential part of advanced learning. Their role has ever been to provide access to the human records needed by members of the higher education community for the successful pursuit of academic programs. Total fulfillment of this role, however, is an ideal which has never been and probably never will be attained. Libraries can therefore be judged only by the degree to which they approach this ideal. Expectations moreover of the degree of total success that they should attain are widely various, differing from institution to institution, from individual to individual, from constituency to constituency. It is this diversity of expectations that prompts the need for standards.

The Standards hereinafter presented do not prescribe this unattainable ideal. They rather describe a realistic set of conditions which, if fulfilled, will provide an adequate library program in a college. They attempt to synthesize and articulate the aggregate experience and judgment of the academic library profession as to adequacy in library resources, services, and facilities for a college community. They are intended to apply to libraries serving academic programs at the bachelors and masters degree levels. They may be applied also to libraries serving universities which grant fewer than ten doctoral degrees per year,* They are not designed for use in two-year colleges, larger universities, independent professional schools, specialized programs or other atypical institutions.

These Standards are organized on the basis of the major functions and components of library organization and services and are arranged as follows:

1. Objectives
2. Collections
3. Organization of Materials
4. Staff
5. Delivery of Service

* Specifically these Standards address themselves to institutions defined by the Carnegie Commission on Higher Education as Liberal Arts Colleges I and II and Comprehensive Universities and Colleges I and II, in *A Classification of Institutions of Higher Education* (Berkeley, Cal., 1973).

6. Facilities
7. Administration
8. Budget

A brief explanatory exegesis is appended to each Standard, citing the reasons for its inclusion and providing suggestions and comments upon its implementation. Complete background considerations for these commentaries may be found in the literature of librarianship.

There are a number of additional areas wherein standards are felt to be desirable when it is possible to prepare them, but for which no consensus among librarians is apparent at this time. These include measures of library effectiveness and productivity, the requisite extent and configuration of non-print resources and services, and methods for program evaluation. Research and experimentation should make it possible, however, to prepare standards for them at some future time.

STANDARD 1:
OBJECTIVES OF THE LIBRARY

1   *The college library shall develop an explicit statement of its objectives in accord with the goals and purposes of the college.*
1.1 *The development of library objectives shall be the responsibility of the library staff, in consultation with students, members of the teaching faculty, and administrative officers.*
1.2 *The statement of library objectives shall be reviewed periodically and revised as needed.*

Commentary on Standard 1

The administration and faculty of every college have a responsibility to examine from time to time their education programs and to define the purposes and goals of the institution. Members of the library faculty share in this exercise, and they have thereafter the responsibility to promote library service consistent with institutional aims and methods. Successful fulfillment of this latter responsibility can best be attained when a clear and explicit statement of derivative library objectives is prepared and promulgated so that all members of the college community can understand and evaluate the appropriateness and effectiveness of library activities.

Preparation of library objectives is an obligation of the library faculty with the assistance of the rest of the library staff. In this effort, however, the library should seek in a formal or structured way the advice and guidance of students, of members of the teaching faculty, and of administrative officers. Library objectives should be kept current through periodic review and revision as needed.

In preparing its statement of objectives, the library staff should consider the evolution in recent decades of new roles for the American college library. Although the college library continues as in the past to serve as the repository for the printed information needed by its patrons, its resources have now been extended to embrace new forms of recorded information, and its proper purpose has been enlarged through changes in the scope of the curriculum and by new concepts of instruction. Thus it now serves also as a complementary academic capability which affords to students the opportunity to augment their classroom experience with an independent avenue for learning beyond the course offerings of the institution. Even this instructional objective of the library, however, must be conceived and formulated within the overall academic purpose of the college.

STANDARD 2:
THE COLLECTIONS

2   *The library's collections shall comprise all corpuses of recorded information owned by the college for educational, inspirational, and recreational purposes, including multi-dimensional, aural, pictorial, and print materials.*

2.1   *The library shall provide quickly a high percentage of such materials needed by its patrons.*

2.1.1   *The amount of print materials to be thus provided shall be determined by a formula (See Formula A) which takes into account the nature and extent of the academic program of the institution, its enrollment, and the size of its teaching faculty.*

Commentary on Standard 2

The records of intellectual endeavor appear in a wide range of formats. Books represent extended reports of scholarly investigation, compilations of findings, creative works, and summaries prepared for educational purposes. The journal has become the common medium for scientific communication and usually represents more recent information. Scientific reports in near-print form are becoming an even faster means of research communication. Documents represent compilations of information prepared by governmental agencies, and newspapers contain the systematic recording of daily activities throughout the world.

Many kinds of communication can be better and sometimes faster accomplished through such non-print media as films, slides, tapes, radio and television recordings, and realia. Mi-

---

FORMULA A—

The formula for calculating the number of relevant print volumes (or microform volume-equivalents) to which the library should provide prompt access is as follows (to be calculated cumulatively):

1. Basic Collection . . . . 85,000 vols.
2. Allowance per FTE Faculty Member . . . . . 100 vols.
3. Allowance per FTE Student . . . . 15 vols.
4. Allowance per Undergraduate Major or Minor Field° . . . . . 350 vols.
5. Allowance per Masters Field, When No Higher Degree is Offered in the Field° . . . . 6,000 vols.
6. Allowance per Masters Field, When a Higher Degree is Offered in the Field° . . . . 3,000 vols.
7. Allowance per 6th-year Specialist Degree Field° . . . . 6,000 vols.
8. Allowance per Doctoral Field° . . . . 25,000 vols.

A "volume" is defined as a physical unit of any printed, typewritten, handwritten, mimeographed, or processed work contained in one binding or portfolio, hardbound or paperbound, which has been cataloged, classified, and/or otherwise prepared for use. For purposes of this calculation microform holdings should be included by converting them to volume-equivalents. The number of volume-equivalents held in microform should be determined either by actual count or by an averaging formula which considers each reel of microform as one, and five pieces of any other microformat as one volume-equivalent.

Libraries which can provide promptly 100 percent as many volumes or volume-equivalents as are called for in this formula shall, in the matter of quantity, be graded A. From 80-99 percent shall be graded B; from 65-79 percent shall be graded C; and from 50-64 percent shall be graded D.

   ° See Appendix I, "List of Fields."

crophotography is an accepted means of compacting many kinds of records for preservation and storage. Recorded information may also come in the form of manuscripts, archives, and machine-readable data bases. Each medium of communication provides unique dimensions for the transmission of information, and each tends to complement the others.

This inherent unity of recorded information, and the fundamental commonality of its social utility, require that regardless of format, all kinds of recorded information needed for academic purposes by an institution be selected, acquired, organized, stored, and delivered for use within the library. In this way the institution's information resources can best be articulated and balanced for the greatest benefit of the entire community.

It is less important that a college hold legal title to the quantity of library materials called for in Formula A than it be able to supply the amount quickly—say within fifteen minutes—as by contract with an adjacent institution or by some other means. An institution which arranges to meet all or part of its library responsibilities in this way, however, must take care that in doing so it not create supernumerary or unreimbursed costs for another institution and that the materials so made available are relevant to its own students' needs.

Since a library book collection once developed, and then allowed to languish, loses its utility very rapidly, continuity of collection development is essential. Experience has shown that even after collections have attained sizes required by this Standard, they can seldom retain their requisite utility without sustaining annual gross growth rates, before withdrawals, of at least five percent.

Higher education has thus far had too little experience with non-print library materials to permit tenable generalizations to be made about their quantitative requirements. Since consensus has not yet been attained among educators as to the range, extent, and configuration of non-print services which it is appropriate for college libraries to offer, no generally applicable formulas are possible here. It is assumed, however, that every college library should have non-print resources appropriate to institutional needs.

The goal of college library collection development should be quality rather than quantity. A collection may be said to have quality for its purpose only to the degree that it possesses a portion of the bibliography of each discipline taught, appropriate in quantity both to the level at which each is taught and to the number of students and faculty members who use it. Quality and quantity are separable only in theory: it is possible to have quantity without quality; it is not possible to have quality without quantity defined in relation to the purposes of the institution. No easily applicable criteria have been developed, however, for measuring quality in library collections.

The best way to assure quality in a college library collection is to gain it at point of input. Thus rigorous discrimination in the selection of materials to be added to the library's holdings, whether as purchases or gifts, is of considerable importance. Care should be exerted to select a substantial portion of the titles listed in the standard, scholarly bibliographies reflecting the curriculum areas of the college and supporting general fields of knowledge. A number of such subjects lists for college libraries have been prepared by learned associations. Among general bibliographies *Books for College Libraries* is useful especially for purposes of identifying important retrospective titles. For current additions, provision should be made to acquire a majority of the significant new publications reviewed in *Choice*. Generous attention should be given also to standard works of reference and to bibliographical tools which provide access to the broad range of scholarly sources as listed in Winchell's *Guide to Reference Books*. Institutional needs vary so widely for periodical holdings that quantitative standards cannot be written for them at this time, but in general it is good practice for a library to own any title that is needed more than six times per year. Several good handlists have been prepared of periodical titles appropriate for college collections.

College library collections should be evaluated continuously against standard bibliographies and against records of their use, for purposes both of adding to the collections and identifying titles for prompt withdrawal once they have outlived their usefulness to the college program. No book should be retained in a college library for which a clear purpose is not evident in terms of the institution's current or anticipated academic program; when such clear purpose is lacking, a book should be retired from the collections.

Although in the last analysis the library staff must be responsible for the scope and content of the collections, it can best fulfill this responsibility with substantial help and consultation from the teaching faculty and from students. Of greatest benefit to the library is continuing faculty assistance in defining the literature requirements of the courses in the curriculum, definitions which should take the form of written selection policies. In addition, members of the teaching faculty may participate in the selection of individual titles to be obtained. If this latter activity, however, is carried out largely by the library, then the teaching faculty should review the books acquired both for their appropriateness and the quality of their contents.

STANDARD 3:
ORGANIZATION OF MATERIALS

3 *Library collections shall be organized by nationally approved conventions and arranged for efficient retrieval at time of need.*

3.1 *There shall be a union catalog of the library's holdings that permits identification of items, regardless of format, by author, title, and subject.*

3.1.1 *The catalog may be developed either by a single library or jointly among several libraries.*

3.1.2 *The catalog shall be in a format that can be consulted by a number of people concurrently and at time of need.*

3.1.3 *In addition to the catalog there shall also be requisite subordinate files, such as serial records, shelf lists, authority files, and indexes to nonmonographic materials.*

3.2 *Except for certain categories of material which are for convenience best segregated by form, library materials shall be arranged on the shelves by subject.*

3.2.1 *Patrons shall have direct access to library materials on the shelves.*

Commentary on Standard 3

The acquisition alone of library materials comprises only part of the task of providing access to them. Collections must be indexed and systematically arranged on the shelves before their efficient identification and retrieval at time of need, which is an important test of a good library, can be assured. For most library materials this indexing can best be accomplished through the development of a union catalog with items entered in accord with established national or international bibliographical conventions, such as rules for entry, descriptive cataloging, filing, classification, and subject headings.

Opportunities of several kinds exist for the cooperative development of the library's catalog, through which economy can be gained in its preparation. These include the use of centralized cataloging by the Library of Congress and the joint compilation of catalogs by a number of libraries. Joint catalogs can take the form of card files, book catalogs, or computer files. Catalogs jointly developed, regardless of format, can satisfy this Standard provided that they can be consulted—under author, title, or subject—by a number of library patrons concurrently at their time of need. Catalogs should be subject to continual editing to keep them abreast of modern terminology, current technology, and contemporary practice.

Proper organization of the collections will also require the maintenance of a number of subordinate files, such as authority files and shelf lists, and of complementary catalogs, such as serial records. Information contained in these files should also be available to library users. In addition, some library materials such as journals, documents, and microforms are often indexed centrally by commercial or quasi-commercial agencies, and in such cases access should be provided to those indexes as needed, whether they be in published or computer-based format.

Materials should be arranged on the shelves by subject matter so that related information can be consulted together. Some kinds of materials, however, such as maps, microforms, and non-print holdings, may be awkward to integrate physically because of form and may be segregated from the main collection. Other materials, such as rarities and manuscripts or archives, may be segregated for purposes of security. Materials in exceptionally active use, such as bibliographies, works of reference, and assigned readings, may be kept separate to facilitate access to them. Except in such cases, however, the bulk of the collections should be classified and shelved by subject in open stack areas so as to permit and encourage browsing.

STANDARD 4:
STAFF

4 *The library staff shall be of adequate size and quality to meet agreed-upon objectives.*

4.1 *The staff shall comprise qualified librarians, skilled supportive personnel, and part-time assistants serving on an hourly basis.*

4.2 *The marks of a librarian shall include a graduate library degree from an ALA-accredited program, responsibility for duties of a professional nature, and participation in professional library affairs beyond the local campus.*

4.2.1 *The librarians of a college shall be organized as an academic department—or, in the case of a university, as a school—and shall administer themselves in accord with ACRL "Standards for Faculty Status for College and University Librarians" (See Appendix II).*

4.3 *The number of librarians required shall be determined by a formula (Formula B, below) which takes into account the enrollment of the college and the size and growth rate of the collections.*

4.3.1 *There shall be an appropriate balance of effort among librarians, supportive personnel, and part-time assistants, so that every staff member is employed as nearly as possible commensurate with his library training, experience, and capability.*

4.4 *Library policies and procedures concerning staff shall be in accord with sound personnel management practice.*

Commentary on Standard 4

The college library will need a staff comprising librarians, supportive personnel, and part-time assistants to carry out its stated objectives. The librarian has acquired through training in a graduate library school an understanding of the principles and theories of selection, acquisition, organization, interpretation, and administration of library resources. Supportive staff members have normally received specialized or on-the-job training for particular assignments within the library; such assignments can range in complexity from relatively routine or business functions to highly technical activities often requiring university degrees in fields other than librarianship. Well managed college libraries also utilize some part-time assistants, many of whom are students. Although they must often perform repetitive and more perfunctory work, given good training and adequate experience such assistants can often perform at relatively skilled levels and constitute an important segment of the library team.

Work assignments, both to these several levels and to individuals, should be carefully conceived and allocated so that all members of the library staff are employed as nearly as possible commensurate with their library training, experience, and capability. This will mean that the librarians will seldom comprise more than 25–35 percent of the total FTE library staff.

The librarians of a college comprise the faculty of the library and should organize and administer themselves as any other departmental faculty in the college (or in the case of the university, the library faculty is equivalent to a school faculty, and should govern itself accordingly). In either case, however, the status, responsibilities, perquisites, and governance of the library faculty shall be fully recognized and supported by the parent institution, and it shall function in accord with the ACRL "Standards for Faculty Status for College and University Librarians."

The staff represents one of the library's most important assets in support of the instructional program of the college. Careful attention is therefore required to proper personnel management policies and procedures. Whether administered centrally for the college as a whole or separately within the library, these policies and practices must be based upon sound, contemporary management understanding consistent with the goals and purposes of the institution. This will mean that:

1. Recruitment methods should be based upon a careful definition of positions to be filled, utilization of a wide range of sources, qualifications based upon job requirements, and objective evaluation of credentials.

2. Written procedures should be followed in matters of appointment, promotion, tenure, dismissal, and appeal.

3. Every staff member should be informed in writing as to the scope of his responsibilities and the individual to whom he is responsible.

4. Classification and pay plans should give recognition to the nature of the duties performed, training and experience required, and rates of pay and benefits of other positions requiring equivalent background.

5. There should be provided a structured program for the orientation and training of new staff members and opportunities for the continuing education of existing staff.

6. Supervisory staff should be selected on the basis of job knowledge and human relations skills and provide training in these responsibilities as needed.

7. Systems should be maintained for periodic review of employee performance and for recognition of achievement.

8. Career opportunities and counseling should be made available to library staff members at all levels and in all departments.

FORMULA B—

The number of librarians required by the college shall be computed as follows (to be calculated cumulatively):

For each 500, or fraction thereof, FTE students up to 10,000	1 librarian
For each 1,000 or fraction thereof, FTE students above 10,000	1 librarian
For each 100,000 volumes, or fraction thereof, in the collection	1 librarian
For each 5,000 volumes, or fraction thereof, added per year	1 librarian

Libraries which provide 100 percent of these formula requirements can, when they are supported by sufficient other staff members, consider themselves at the A level in terms of staff size; those that provide 75–99 percent of these requirements may rate themselves as B; those with 55–74 percent of requirements qualify for a C; and those with 40–54 percent of requirements warrant a D.

STANDARD 5:
DELIVERY OF SERVICE

'5   *The college library shall establish and maintain a range and quality of services that will promote the academic program of the institution and encourage optimal library use.*

5.1   *Proper service shall include: the provision of continuing instruction to patrons in the effective exploitation of libraries; the guidance of patrons to the library materials they need; and the provision of information to patrons as appropriate.*

5.2   *Library materials shall be circulated to qualified patrons under equitable policies and for as long periods as possible without jeopardizing their availability to others.*

5.2.1   *The availability of reading materials shall be extended wherever possible by the provision of inexpensive means of photocopying.*

5.2.2   *The quality of the collections available locally to patrons shall be enhanced through the use of "National Interlibrary Loan Code 1968"* (See Appendix II) *and other cooperative agreements which provide reciprocal access to multi-library resources.*

5.3   *The hours of public access to the materials on the shelves, to the study facilities of the library, and to the library staff, shall be consistent with reasonable demand, both during the normal study week and during weekends and vacation periods.*

5.4   *Where academic programs are offered away from a campus, library services shall be provided in accord with ACRL's "Guidelines for Library Services to Extension Students"* (See Appendix II).

Commentary on Standard 5

The primary purpose of college library service is to promote the academic program of the parent institution. The successful fulfillment of this purpose will require that librarians work closely with teaching faculty to gain an intimate knowledge of their educational objectives and methods and to impart to them an understanding of the services which the library can render. Both skill in library use and ease of access to materials can encourage library use, but the major stimulus for students to use the library has always been, and likely always will be, the instructional methods used in the classroom. Thus close cooperation between librarians and classroom instructors is essential.

Such cooperation does not come about fortuitously; it must be a planned and structured activity, and it must be assiduously sought. It will require not only that librarians participate in the academic planning councils of the institution but also that they assist teaching faculty in appraising the actual and potential library resources available, work closely with them in developing library services for new courses and new pedagogical techniques, and keep them informed of new library capabilities.

A key service of a college library is the introduction and interpretation of library materials to patrons. This activity takes several forms. The first form is instruction in bibliography and in the use of information tools. It will also familiarize patrons with the physical facilities of the library, its services and collections, and the policies and conditions which govern their use. Bibliographic instruction and orientation may be given at many levels of sophistication and may use a variety of instructional methods and materials, including course-related instruction, separate courses with or without credit, group or individualized instruction, utilizing print or non-print materials.

The second basic form which interpretation will take is conventional reference work wherein individual patrons are guided by librarians in their appraisal of the range and extent of the library resources available to them for learning and research, in the most effective marshalling of that material, and in the optimal utilization of libraries. Most library interpretative work is of this kind.

The third major genre of library interpretation is the delivery of information itself. Although obviously inappropriate in the case of student searches which are purposeful segments of classroom assignments, the actual delivery of information—as distinct from guidance to it—is a reasonable library service in almost all other conceivable situations.

As regards the circulation of library materials, the general trend in recent years has been toward longer loan periods, but these periods must be determined by local conditions which will include size of the collections, the number of copies of a book held, and the extent of the user community. Circulation should be for as long periods as are reasonable without jeopardizing access to materials by other qualified patrons. This overall goal may prompt some institutions to establish variant or unique loan periods for different titles or classes of titles. Whatever loan policy is used, however, it should be equitably and uniformly administered to all qualified categories of patrons.

Locally-held library resources should be extended and enhanced in every way possible for the benefit of library patrons. Both the quantity and the accessibility of reading materials can be extended through the provision of inexpensive means of photocopying within the laws regarding copyright. Local resources should aso be extended through the provision and encouragement of reciprocal arrangements with other libraries as through the "National Interlibrary Loan Code 1968" and joint-access consortia. Beyond its own local constituency every library also has a responsibility to make its holdings available to other students and scholars in at least three ways—in-house consultation, photocopy, and through interlibrary loan.

The number of hours per week that library services should be available will vary, depending upon such factors as whether the college is in an urban or rural setting, teaching methods used, conditions in the dormitories, and whether the student body is primarily resident or commuting. In any case, library scheduling should be responsive to reasonable local need, not only during term-time week-days but also on weekends, and, especially where graduate work is offered, during vacation periods. In many institutions readers may need access to study facilities and to the collections during more hours of the week than they require the personal services of librarians. The public's need for access to librarians may range upward to one hundred hours per week, whereas around-the-clock access to the library's collections and/or facilities may in some cases be warranted.

Special library problems exist for colleges that provide off-campus instructional programs. Students in such programs must be provided with library services in accord with ACRL's "Guidelines for Library Services to Extension Students." These Guidelines require that such services be financed on a regular basis, that a librarian be specifically charged with the delivery of such services, that the library implications of such programs be considered before program approval, and that courses so taught encourage library use. Such services, which are especially important at the graduate level, must be furnished despite their obvious logistical problems.

STANDARD 6:
FACILITIES

6 *The college shall provide a library building containing secure facilities for housing its resources, adequate space for administration of those resources by staff, and comfortable quarters and furnishings for their utilization by patrons.*

6.1 *The size of the library building shall be determined by a formula* (See Formula C) *which takes into account the enrollment of the college, the extent and nature of its collections, and the size of its staff.*

6.2 *The shape of the library building and the internal distribution of its facilities and services shall be determined by function.*

6.3 *Except in unusual circumstances, the college library's collections and services shall be administered within a single structure.*

Commentary on Standard 6

Successful library service presupposes an adequate library building. Although the type of building provided will depend upon the character and the aims of the institution, it should in all cases present secure facilities for housing the library's resources, sufficient space for their administration by staff, and comfortable quarters and furnishings for their utilization by the public, all integrated into a functional and esthetic whole. The college library building should represent a conscious planning effort, involving the librarian, the college administration, and the architect, with the librarian responsible for the preparation of the building program. The needs of handicapped patrons should receive special attention in the designing of the library building.

Many factors will enter into a determination of the quality of a library building. They will include such esthetic considerations as its location on the campus, the grace with which it relates to its site and to neighboring structures, and the degree to which it contributes esthetically to the desired ambience of the campus. They will also include such internal characteristics as the diversity and appropriateness of its accommodations and furnishings, the functional distribution and interrelationships of its spaces, and the simplicity and economy with which it can be utilized by patrons and operated by staff. They will include moreover such physical characteristics as the adequacy of its acoustical treatment and lighting, the effectiveness of its heating and cooling plant, and the selection of its movable equipment.

Decentralized library facilities in a college have some virtues, and they present some difficulties. Primary among their virtues is their adjacency to the laboratories and offices of some teaching faculty members within their service purview. Primary among their weaknesses are their fragmentation of unity of knowledge, their relative isolation from library users (other than aforementioned faculty), the fact that they can seldom command the attention of qualified staff over either long hours during a week or over a sustained period of time, and the excessive costs of creating duplicate catalogs, periodical lists, circulation services, and attendant study facilities. Where decentralized library facilities are being considered, these costs and benefits must be carefully compared. In general, experience has shown that except where long distances are involved, decentralized library facilities are at the present time unlikely to be in the best pedagogical or economic interests of a college.

7 *The college library shall be administered in a manner which permits and encourages the fullest and most effective use of available library resources.*

7.1 *The statutory or legal foundation for the library's activities shall be recognized in writing.*

7.2 *The college librarian shall be a member of the library faculty and shall report to the president or the chief academic officer of the institution.*

7.2.1 *The responsibilities and authority of the college librarian and procedures for his appointment shall be defined in writing.*

7.3 *There shall be a standing advisory committee comprising students and members of the teaching faculty which shall serve as the main channel of formal communication between the library and its user community.*

7.4 *The library shall maintain written policies and procedure manuals covering internal library governance and operational activities.*

7.4.1 *The library shall maintain a systematic and continuous program for evaluating its performance and for identifying needed improvements.*

7.4.2 *The library shall develop statistics not only for purposes of planning and control but also to aid in the preparation of reports designed to inform its publics of its accomplishments and problems.*

7.5 *The library shall develop, seek out, and utilize cooperative programs for purposes of either reducing its operating costs or enhancing its services, so long as such programs create no unreimbursed or unreciprocated costs for other libraries or organizations.*

FORMULA C—

The size of the college library building shall be calculated on the basis of a formula which takes into consideration the size of the student body, requisite administrative space, and the number of physical volumes held in the collections. In the absence of consensus among librarians and other educators as to the range of non-book services which it is appropriate for libraries to offer, no generally applicable formulas have been developed for calculating space for them. Thus, space required for a college library's non-book services and materials must be added to the following calculations:

a. *Space for readers.* The seating requirement for the library of a college wherein less than fifty percent of the FTE enrollment resides on campus shall be one for each five FTE students; the seating requirement for the typical residential college library shall be one for each four FTE students; and the seating requirements for the library in the strong, liberal arts, honors-oriented college shall be one for each three FTE students. In any case, each library seat shall be assumed to require twenty-five square feet of floor space.

b. *Space for books.* Space required for books depends in part upon the overall size of the book collection, and is calculated cumulatively as follows:

	Square Feet/Volume
For the first 150,000 volumes	0.10
For the next 150,000 volumes	0.09
For the next 300,000 volumes	0.08
For holdings above 600,000 volumes	0.07

c. *Space for administration.* Space required for such library administrative activities as acquisition, cataloging, staff offices, catalogs, and files shall be one-fourth of the sum of the spaces needed for readers and books as calculated under (a) and (b) above.

This tripartite formula indicates the net assignable area necessary for all library services except for non-book services. (For definition of "net assignable area" see "The Measurement and Comparison of Physical Facilities for Libraries," produced by ALA's Library Administration Division. See Appendix II.) Libraries which provide 100 percent as much net assignable area as is called for by the formula shall qualify for an A rating as regards quantity; 75-99 percent shall warrant a B; 60-74 percent shall be due a C; and 50-59 percent shall warrant a D.

7.6 *The library shall be administered in accord with the spirit of the ALA "Library Bill of Rights."* (See Appendix II.)

Commentary on Standard 7

Much of the commentary on general administration of the college library is gathered under the several other Standards. Matters of personnel administration, for example, are discussed under Standard 4, and fiscal administration is glossed under Standard 8. Some important aspects of library management, however, must be considered apart from the other Standards.

Primary among administrative considerations which are not part of other Standards is the matter of the responsibilities and authority both of the library as an organization and of the college librarian as a college officer. No clear set of library objectives, no tenable program of collection development, no defensible library personnel policy can be developed unless there is first an articulated and widespread understanding within the college as to the statutory, legal or other basis under which the library is to function. This may be a college bylaw, or a trustee minute, or a public law which shows the responsibility and flow of authority under which the library is empowered to act. There must also be a derivative document defining the responsibility and authority vested in the office of the college librarian. This document may also be statutorily based and should spell out, in addition to the scope and nature of his duties and powers, the procedures for his appointment and the focus of his reporting responsibility. Experience has shown that, for the closest coordination of library activities with the instructional program, the college librarian should report either to the president or to the chief officer in charge of the academic affairs of the institution.

Although the successful college library must strive for excellence in all of its communications, especially those of an informal nature, it must also have the benefit of an advisory committee representing its user community. This committee—of which the college librarian should be an *ex officio* member—should serve as the main channel of formal communication between the library and its publics and should be used to convey both an awareness to the library of its patrons' concerns, perceptions, and needs, and an understanding to patrons of the library's capabilities and problems. The charge to the committee should be specific, and it should be in writing.

Many of the precepts of college library administration are the same as those for the administration of any other similar enterprise. The writing down of policies and the preparation of procedures manuals, for example, are required for best management of any organization so as to assure uniformity and consistency of action, to aid in training of staff, and to contribute to public understanding. Likewise sound public relations are essential to almost any successful service organization. Although often observed in their omission, structured programs of performance evaluation and quality control are equally necessary. All of these administrative practices are important in a well managed library.

Some interlibrary cooperative efforts have tended in local libraries to enhance the quality of service or reduce operating costs. Labor-sharing, for example, through cooperative processing programs has been beneficial to many libraries, and participation in the pooled ownership of seldom-used materials has relieved pressure on some campuses for such materials to be collected locally. The potential values of meaningful cooperation among libraries are sufficient to require that libraries actively search out and avail themselves of cooperative programs that will work in their interests. Care should be taken, however, to assure that a recipient library reimburse, either in money or in kind, the full costs of any other institution that supplies its service, unless of course the supplying institution is specifically charged and funded so to make its services available.

College libraries should be impervious to the pressures or efforts of any special interest groups or individuals to shape their collections and services in accord with special pleadings. This principle, first postulated by the American Library Association in 1939 as the "Library Bill of Rights," should govern the administration of every college library and be given the full protection of all parent institutions.

STANDARD 8:
BUDGET

8 *The college librarian shall have the responsibility for preparing, defending, and administering the library budget in accord with agreed-upon objectives.*

8.1 *The amount of the library appropriation shall express a relationship to the total institutional budget for educational and general purposes.*

8.2 *The librarian shall have sole authority to apportion funds and initiate expenditures within the library approved budget, in accord with institutional policy.*

8.3 *The library shall maintain such internal accounts as are necessary for approving its invoices for payment, monitoring its encumberances, and evaluating the flow of its expenditures.*

Commentary on Standard 8

The library budget is a function of program planning and tends to define the library's objectives in fiscal terms and for a stated interval of time. Once agreed to by the college administration, the objectives formulated under Standard 1 should constitute the base upon which the library's budget is developed. The degree to which the college is able to fund the library in accord with its objectives is reflected in the relationship of the library appropriation to the total educational and general budget of the college. Experience has shown that library budgets, exclusive of capital costs and the costs of physical maintenance, which fall below six percent of the college's total educational and general expenditures are seldom able to sustain the range of library programs required by the institution. This percentage moreover will run considerably higher during periods when the library is attempting to overcome past deficiencies, to raise its "grade" on collections and staff as defined elsewhere in these Standards, or to meet the information needs of new academic programs.

The adoption of formulas for preparation of budget estimates and for prediction of library expenditures over periods of time are relatively common, especially among public institutions. Since such formulas can often provide a gross approximation of needs, they are useful for purposes of long-range planning, but they frequently fail to take into account local cost variables, and they are seldom able to respond promptly to unanticipated market inflation or changes in enrollment. Thus they should not be used, except as indicators, in definitive budget development.

Among the variables which should be considered in estimating a library's budget requirements are the following:

1. The scope, nature, and level of the college curriculum;

2. Instructional methods used, especially as they relate to independent study;

3. The adequacy of existing collections and the publishing rate in fields pertinent to the curriculum;

4. The size, or anticipated size, of the student body and teaching faculty;

5. The adequacy and availability of other library resources in the locality to which the library has contracted access;

6. The range of services offered by the library, the number of service points maintained, the number of hours per week that service is provided, etc.;

7. The extent to which the library already meets the Standards defined in these pages.

Procedures for the preparation and defense of budget estimates, policies on budget approval, and regulations concerning accounting and expenditures may vary from one institution or jurisdiction to another, and the college librarian must know and conform to local practice. In any circumstance, however, sound prac-

tices of planning and control require that the librarian have sole responsibility and authority for the allocation—and within college policy, the reallocation—of the library budget and the initiation of expenditures against it. Depending upon local factors, between 35 and 45 percent of the library's budget is normally allocated to the purchase of materials, and between 50 and 60 percent is expended for personnel.

The preparation of budget estimates may be made on the basis of past expenditures and anticipated needs, comparison with similar libraries, or statistical norms and standards. More sophisticated techniques for detailed analysis of costs by library productivity, function, or program—as distinct from items of expenditure —have been attempted in some libraries. Such procedures require that the library develop quantitative methods by which to prepare estimates, analyze performance, and determine the relative priority of services rendered. Although this kind of budgeting, once refined, may lead to more effective fiscal control and greater accountability, libraries generally have thus far had too limited experience with program budgeting or input-output analysis to permit their widespread adoption at this time.

APPENDIX I
List of Fields
(Count each line as one program)

Advertising
Afro-American/Black Studies
Agriculture & Natural Resources
   Agricultural Biology
   Agricultural Business
   Agricultural Chemistry
   Agricultural Economics
   Agricultural Education
   Agricultural Engineering:
     See Engineering
   Agriculture
   Agronomy
   Animal Science
   Crop Science: See Agronomy
   Dairy Science
   Fisheries
   Food Industries
   Forestry
   Fruit Science and Industry
   International Agriculture
   Mechanized Agriculture
   National Resources Management
   Ornamental Horticulture
   Poultry Industry
   Range Management
   Soil Science
   Veterinary, Pre-
   Watershed Management
   Wildlife Management
American Studies
Anthropology
Architecture (See also City Plg.; Engr.; Landscape Arch)

Art
Art History
Asian Studies (See also East Asian)
Astronomy
Behavioral Sciences
Bilingual Studies
Biochemistry
Biology, Biological Sciences (See also Botany,
    Microbiology, etc.)
Biology and Mathematics
Black Studies: See Afro-American
Botany
Business Administration
  Accounting
  Business Administration
  Business Economics
  Business Education
  Business, Special interest
  Business Statistics
  Data Processing
  Finance
  Hotel and Restaurant Management
  Industrial Relations
  Information Systems: Listed alphabetically
    under "I"
  Insurance
  International (World) Business
  Management (Business)
  Marketing (Management)
  Office Administration
  Operations Research
    (Management Science)
  Personnel Management
  Production/Operations Management
  Public Relations
  Quantitative Methods
  Real Estate
  Secretarial Studies
  Transportation Management
Cell Biology
Chemical Physics
Chemistry
Chinese
City/Regional/Urban Planning
Classics
Communications
Communicative Disorders
    See Speech Pathology
Comparative Literature
Computer Science
Corrections: See Criminal Justice
Creative Writing
Crime, Law and Society
Criminalistics (Forensic Science)
Criminal Justice Administration
Criminal Justice—Corrections
Criminal Justice—Security
Criminology
Cybernetic Systems
Dance
Dietetics and Food Administration
Drama (Theater Arts)
Earth Sciences
East Asian Studies
Ecology/Environmental Biology
    (See also Environmental Studies)
Economics

Education
  Adult Secondary
  Child Development
  Counseling/Guidance
  Curriculum and Instruction
  Culturally Disadvantaged
  Deaf
  Education
  Educational Administration
  Educational Foundations and Theory
  Educational Psychology
  Educational Research
  Educational Supervision
  Elementary Education
  Gifted
  Health and Safety
  Instructional Media
    (Audio-Visual)
  Learning Disabilities
    (Handicapped)
  Mentally Retarded
  Orthopedically Handicapped
  Reading Instruction
  School Psychology: See Psychology
  Secondary Education
  Special Education
  Special Education Supervision
  Special Interest
  Visually Handicapped
  Visually Handicapped:
    Orientation and Mobility
Engineering
  Aeronautical Engineering, Aerospace and
    Maintenance
  Aeronautics (Operations)
  Agricultural
  Air Conditioning, Air Pollution:
    See Environmental Engineering
  Architectural
  Biomedical Engineering
  Chemical
  Civil
  Computer
  Construction
  Electrical
  Electrical/Electronic
  Electronic
  Engineering
  Engineering Materials
  Engineering Mechanics
  Engineering Science
  Engineering Technology
  Environmental
  Environmental Resources
  Industrial Administration
  Industrial Engineering
  Measurement Science
  Mechanical
  Metallurgical
  Nuclear
  Ocean
  Structural
  Surveying and Photogrammetry
  Systems
  Transportation
  Water Pollution: See Environmental
  Water Resources

English
English as a Second Language
Entomology
Environmental Studies
Ethnic Studies (See also Afro-American and Mexican-American)
European Studies
Expressive Arts: See Fine and Creative Arts
Film
Fine and Creative Arts
Foods and Nutrition: See Dietetics
French
Genetics
Geography
Geology
German
Government: See Political Science
Government—Journalism
Graphic Communications (Printing)
Graphic Design
Health and Safety: See Education
Health, Public (Environmental)
Health Science
History
Home Economics
Hotel Management: See Business
Humanities
Human Development
Human Services
Hutchins School
India Studies
Industrial Arts
Industrial Design
Industrial Technology
Information Systems
Interior Design
International Relations
Italian
Japanese
Journalism (see also Communications)
Landscape Architecture
Language Arts
Latin American Studies
Law Enforcement: See Criminal Justice
Liberal Studies
Library Science
Linguistics
Literature (See also English)
Marine Biology
Marriage and Family Counseling
Mass Communications: See Communications
Mathematics
Mathematics, Applied
Medical Biology: See Medical Laboratory Technology
Medical Laboratory Technology (Clinical Science)
Meteorology
Mexican-American/La Raza Studies
Microbiology
Music Education
Music (Liberal Arts)
Music (Performing)
Natural Resources: See Agriculture
Natural Science
Nursing (See also Health Sciences)
Occupational Therapy

Oceanography
Park Administration
Philosophy
Philosophy and Religion
Physical Education
  (Men)
  (Women)
Physical Science
Physical Therapy
Physics
Physiology
Police Science: See Criminal Justice
Political Science
Psychology
  Clinical
  College Teaching
  Developmental
  Educational: See Education
  Industrial
  Physiological
  Psychology
  Research
  School
  Social
Public Administration
Public Relations: See Business category or Communications degrees
Radiological and Health Physics
Radio—Television (Telecommunications)
Recreation Administration
Rehabilitation Counseling
Religious Studies
Russian
Russian Area Studies
Social Sciences (See also Anthropology, Sociology, etc.)
Social Welfare and Services
Sociology
Spanish
Special Major
Speech and Drama
Speech Communication
Speech Pathology and Audiology
  Communicative Disorders
Statistics
Theater Arts: See Drama
Urban Planning: See City Planning
Urban Studies
Vocational Education
Zoology

APPENDIX II
Other Works Cited

"[ACRL] Standards for Faculty Status for College and University Librarians." *College and Research Libraries News* (September 1972), 33:210–12.

"[ACRL] Guidelines for Library Services to Extension Students." *ALA Bulletin* (January 1967), 61:50–55.

"The Measurement and Comparison of Physical Facilities for Libraries"; typescript. Chicago: American Library Association, Library Administration Division, 1969. 17pp.

"Library Bill of Rights." *ALA Handbook of Organization 1974–1975*, p.93.

"National Interlibrary Loan Code, 1968." Chicago: American Library Association, Reference and Adult Services Division. 4pp.

The "Standards for College Libraries" were first prepared by a committee of ACRL and promulgated in 1959. The present 1975 revision was prepared by the ACRL Ad Hoc Committee to Revise the 1959 Standards. Members were Johnnie Givens, Austin Peay State University (Chairman); David Kaser, Graduate Library School, Indiana University (Project Director and Editor); Arthur Monke, Bowdoin College; David L. Perkins, California State University, Northridge; James W. Pirie, Lewis & Clark College; Jasper G. Schad, Wichita State University; and Herman L. Totten, School of Librarianship, University of Oregon.

The effort was supported by a J. Morris Jones—World Book Encyclopedia—ALA Goals Award.

Copies of these Standards are available, upon request, from the ACRL Office, 50 E. Huron St., Chicago, IL 60611.　■■

An Evaluative Checklist for Reviewing a College Library Program

Editor's Note: At the ALA Annual Conference in June 1979 the ACRL Board of Directors approved the recommendation of the Standards and Accreditation Committee that "An Evaluative Checklist for Reviewing a College Library Program" be adopted as a supplement to "Standards for College Libraries." The Standards and Accreditation Committee developed the checklist and then evaluated it by asking a representative sample of fifty college libraries to test it in the field. The checklist appears in this issue of C&RL News for the information of ACRL members.

INTRODUCTION

The Evaluative Checklist is based on the 1975 "Standards for College Libraries" developed by the Association of College and Research Libraries, a division of the American Library Association. The standards "describe a realistic set of conditions which, if fulfilled, will provide an adequate library program in a college. They attempt to synthesize and articulate the aggregate experience and judgment of the academic library profession as to adequacy in library resources, services, and facilities for a college community."[1] The standards cover libraries serving academic programs at the bachelor's and master's degree levels as defined by the Carnegie Commission on Higher Education as Liberal Arts Colleges I and II and Comprehensive Universities and Colleges I and II.[2,3] The checklist has been validated and field-tested. When properly applied it will discriminate among the several levels of quality in library programs.

The status of a library program is not likely to be known without periodic evaluation. Before

1. "Standards for College Libraries," *College & Research Libraries News* 36:277 (Oct. 1975).
2. Carnegie Foundation for the Advancement of Teaching, *A Classification of Institutions of Higher Education* (Berkeley, Calif.: The Foundation, 1973).
3. Libraries serving junior and community colleges should consult: "AAJC-ACRL Guidelines for Two-Year College Library Learning Resource Centers," *College & Research Libraries News* 33:305–15 (Dec. 1972).
   Recently developed University Library Standards cover libraries serving comprehensive universities: ARL/ACRL Joint Committee on University Library Standards, "University Library Standards," *College & Research Libraries News* 40:101–10 (April 1979).

completing the checklist, the evaluator should review the Application Procedures and Directions for Use that precede the checklist. He or she may also wish to study the text of the "Standards for College Libraries" covered by the checklist.

The checklist follows the organization of the standards stated at the head of the following sections:

1. Objectives
2. Collections
3. Organization of Materials
4. Staff
5. Delivery of Service
6. Facilities
7. Administration
8. Budget

It is acknowledged that it would be desirable to include more precise measures of library effectiveness and productivity, nonprint resources and services, and program evaluation in the checklist. However, there is no consensus among academic librarians for their preparation at this time.

APPLICATION PROCEDURES

Evaluation in general is a process, a complex of tools, used to produce a picture of what's happening, with some further goals in mind. The primary concern of the checklist is with evaluating how well a college library is performing some of its key functions to enable it to chart a course for improvement. The collection of checklist scores without providing the evaluators with operational information, analyzing accurately the results, and formulating appropriate recommendations will result in a simplistic comparison rather than producing a framework for improving library services. To accomplish its purpose, the checklist should be the instrument of an evaluating process which includes the following components—

1. Widespread participation and input of the total college community in the evaluation of library programs, and the review of the results.
2. The evaluators' review and understanding of the broad goals and specific objectives of the college and its library.
3. The use of the Evaluative Checklist in recording judgments concerning levels of library services.
4. The collection of information not furnished by the checklist which describes program effectiveness in terms of the objectives set forth.

5. The interpretation of the results and drawing of conclusions which furnish information about the growth, progress, and effectiveness of the library's programs.
6. The formulation of recommendations that will support revised objectives and improve library services.

The college community and its library evaluators should be aware of the limitations of any evaluating process. These include the coverage of the evaluating instrument (the checklist does not pretend to cover everything), and the objectivity of the evaluation process. Judgmental decisions are involved throughout all phases of the evaluation as the participants adjust their activities in terms of the feedback received. An alert evaluator is aware of the influence of his or her own experience, the impact of personalities, and potential errors in methodology, data collection, and interpretation. The community itself, and the library in particular, are in the best position to evaluate what the study means, and to utilize it in improving library programs.

DIRECTIONS FOR USE

Circle *one* of the numbers at the left of the statement that most accurately represents conditions in the library you are evaluating. If a statement accurately describes the library, circle the middle number (2, 5, 8, or 11) at the left of that statement. If you think conditions are below what is described, circle the higher number (3, 6, 9, or 12). If the conditions at the library are above, circle one of the lower numbers (1, 4, 7, or 10). Circle *only one* of the numbers in the 1 to 12 grouping.

EXAMPLE

Standard 5: Delivery of Service

A. Library Instruction

1 2 3	Librarians routinely work closely with the teaching faculty in identifying instructional needs and teach the use of library resources and services to meet these needs.
4 5 6	Librarians are regularly called on for consultative assistance and instruction in the use of library resources and services.
7 8 9	Librarians provide consultative assistance in the use of library resources and services when requested and free from other duties.
10 11 12	Librarians are rarely available to provide library instruction services.

Directions for use and interpretation of the Profile graph accompany the Profile on pages 313–15.

EVALUATIVE CHECKLIST

Standard 1: Objectives of the Library

1 The college library shall develop an explicit statement of its objectives in accord with the goals and purposes of the college.

1.1 The development of library objectives shall be the responsibility of the library staff, in consultation with students, members of the teaching faculty, and administrative officers.

1.2 The statement of library objectives shall be reviewed periodically and revised as needed.

(Circle only one of the twelve numbers)

1 2 3	The college library's statement of objectives is conceived and formulated within the overall academic purpose of the college, is recognized by the college community as supporting its educational goals and instructional needs, and is kept current through periodic reviews and revisions by the library faculty, teaching faculty, and administrative staff.
4 5 6	The library's statement of objectives generally conforms with the overall academic purpose of the college, but requires minor revisions or better dissemination so that all members of the college community can understand and evaluate the appropriateness and effectiveness of library services.
7 8 9	The college library's statement of objectives requires substantial revision and updating to coordinate it with the educational goals and instructional needs of the college.
10 11 12	The college library does not have a statement of objectives conceived and formulated within the overall academic purpose of the college and consistent with the institution's educational goals and instructional needs.

Standard 2: The Collections

2 The library's collections shall comprise all corpora of recorded information owned by the college for educational, inspirational, and recreational purposes, including multi-dimensional, aural, pictorial, and print materials.

2.1 The library shall provide quickly a high percentage of such material needed by its patrons.

2.1.1 The amount of print materials to be thus provided shall be determined by Formula A (see Appendix) which takes into account the nature and extent of the academic program of the institution, its enrollment, and the size of its teaching faculty.

A. Availability of Library Materials*

1 2 3   The library acquires, organizes, stores, and delivers for use within, or circulation from, the library all college-owned forms of recorded information required to support the college's educational programs and interests.

4 5 6   The library acquires and organizes most college-owned recorded information, but the delivery of this information is somewhat restricted by storage and access conditions at the library or other campus locations.

7 8 9   College-owned materials required to support several curriculum areas of the college are not acquired and organized by the library, and delivered through its services.

10 11 12   A substantial corpus of college-owned recorded information is not acquired, organized, stored, and delivered for use within, or circulated from, the library.

B. Accessibility of Library Materials*

1 2 3   The library is able to deliver, from its own collection or via interlibrary systems, a substantial quantity of materials satisfying the user's needs and assignment schedules.

4 5 6   The library is frequently able to deliver, from its own collection or via interlibrary systems, a sufficient quantity of materials satisfying the user's needs and assignment schedules.

7 8 9   The quantity/quality of available library materials is uneven, thereby limiting the library's ability to supply materials requested, or to deliver them without significant delays.

10 11 12   The quantity/quality of library materials is so limited that the library is unable to supply many materials requested, or deliver them without intolerable delays.

C. Selection of Materials*

1 2 3   The library selects an adequate portion of the bibliography of the disciplines represented by the curriculum, appropriate in quantity to both the level of instruction and to the number of students and faculty who use it. The collection's annual growth rate, before withdrawals, exceeds 5 percent.

4 5 6   The library collection generally supports the college's curriculum and interests except for the need to improve coverage in a few subject areas. The annual growth rate approaches 5 percent.

7 8 9   The library collection is uneven in its support of the college's curriculum and interests. Basic collections should be developed for several disciplines.

10 11 12   The library collection is generally inadequate in its support of the college's academic program. A substantial portion of titles listed in standard, scholarly bibliographies, or considered by the faculty as supporting their instructional needs, are not represented in the library collection.

D. Withdrawal of Materials*

1 2 3   Continuous evaluation of the collection provides for the withdrawal of materials which do not contribute to the college's current or anticipated academic programs.

4 5 6   The collection is periodically evaluated to identify outdated or nonsupportive materials. More frequent reviews are required in a few subject areas.

7 8 9   Several subject collections contain much material which should be withdrawn because it is outdated or nonsupportive of current or anticipated academic programs.

10 11 12   The collection generally contains material which has outlived its usefulness to the college's programs.

E. Quantity of Materials*

    Using Formula A (see Appendix) for calculating the number of relevant print volumes (or microform volume-equivalents) to which the library should provide prompt access—

1 2 3   The library can provide promptly 90–100 percent called for.

4 5 6   The library can provide promptly 80–90 percent called for.

7 8 9   The library can provide promptly 65–70 percent called for.

10 11 12   The library can provide promptly 50–64 percent called for.

Standard 3: Organization of Materials

3   Library collections shall be organized by nationally approved conventions and arranged for efficient retrieval at time of need.

*Circle only one of the twelve numbers.

3.1 There shall be a union catalog of the library's holdings that permits identification of items, regardless of format, by author, title, and subject.

3.1.1 The catalog may be developed either by a single library or jointly among several libraries.

3.1.2 The catalog shall be in a format that can be consulted by a number of people concurrently and at time of need.

3.1.3 In addition to the catalog there shall also be requisite subordinate files, such as serial records, shelf lists, authority files, and indexes to nonmonographic materials.

3.2 Except for certain categories of material which are for convenience best segregated by form, library materials shall be arranged on the shelves by subject.

3.2.1 Patrons shall have direct access to library materials on the shelves.

A. Indexing of Library Materials*

1 2 3 The library has a bibliographic control system for the classification, bibliographic identification, location, and retrieval of all library materials which conforms to national conventions and includes author, title, and subject entries.

4 5 6 The library has a bibliographic control system that is adequate most of the time, but excludes some materials according to form or location.

7 8 9 The college community reports some difficulties in identifying, locating, and retrieving specific library materials because of deficiencies in the organization and coverage of the bibliographic control system.

10 11 12 Library materials are consistently difficult to identify, locate, and retrieve because the bibliographic control system requires major reorganization.

B. Arrangement of Library Materials*

1 2 3 Most library materials are arranged on the shelves by subject and the college community locates, browses, and selects these materials with ease.

4 5 6 Library materials are generally arranged on open shelves by subject, although the complexities of classification or storage arrangements of some materials reduce easy access to them.

7 8 9 The complexities or disorganization of the arrangement of library materials discourage the college community from using the materials.

10 11 12 Library materials are very difficult

*Circle only one of the twelve numbers.

to locate and retrieve, and their inaccessibility seriously deters their optimum use.

Standard 4: Staff

4 The library staff shall be of adequate size and quality to meet agreed-upon objectives.

4.1 The staff shall comprise qualified librarians, skilled supportive personnel, and part-time assistants serving on an hourly basis.

4.2 The marks of a librarian shall include a graduate library degree from an ALA-accredited program, responsibility for duties of a professional nature, and participation in professional library affairs beyond the local campus.

4.2.1 The librarians of a college shall be organized as an academic department—or, in the case of a university, as a school—and shall administer themselves in accord with ACRL "Standards for Faculty Status for College and University Librarians" (see Appendix II [of "Standards for College Libraries"]).

4.3 The number of librarians required shall be determined by a formula (Formula B, [Appendix]) which takes into account the enrollment of the college and the size and growth rate of the collections.

4.3.1 There shall be an appropriate balance of effort among librarians, supportive personnel, and part-time assistants, so that every staff member is employed as nearly as possible commensurate with his library training, experience, and capability.

4.4 Library policies and procedures concerning staff shall be in accord with sound personnel management practice.

A. Staff Size*

1 2 3 The library has sufficient professional, technical, and clerical staff to provide satisfactory services meeting the library's objectives. Using Formula B (see Appendix) for calculating the number of librarians, the library provides 90–100 percent of the requirements.

4 5 6 Using Formula B for calculating the number of librarians, the library provides 75–90 percent of the requirements.

7 8 9 Using Formula B for calculating the number of librarians, the library provides 55–74 percent of the requirements.

10 11 12 Using Formula B for calculating the number of librarians, the library provides 40–54 percent of the requirements.

B. Professional Responsibilities*

1 2 3   Leadership and instructional and consultative services are provided by qualified librarians who have faculty status and administer themselves in accord with the ACRL "Standards for Faculty Status for College and University Librarians."

4 5 6   The administration and delivery of library services are provided by qualified librarians recognized and supported by the college, but without full coverage of the ACRL "Standards for Faculty Status."

7 8 9   The responsibility for library services is delegated to librarians without professional status and departmental organization.

10 11 12   The responsibility for administering library services is assigned to institutional staff members not qualified as librarians.

C. Support Staff*

1 2 3   The qualified clerical and technical staff is sufficient in number, with assignment of responsibilities commensurate with job requirements, training, and experience.

4 5 6   Clerical and technical assistance is usually sufficient. Mismatching of job assignments among clerical and professional staff infrequently occurs.

7 8 9   Clerical and technical assistance is available, but there are frequent shortages or mismatching of job assignments among support and professional staff.

10 11 12   Clerical and technical assistance is generally not available.

D. Personnel Management*

1 2 3   Written policies and procedures consistent with the goals and responsibilities of the college direct the recruiting, appointment, training, evaluation, promotion and tenure, or dismissal of the library staff.

4 5 6   Library personnel policies are consistent with the goals and responsibilities of the college, although several procedures require revision and updating.

7 8 9   Library personnel policies are frequently inconsistent with the goals and responsibilities of the college. Policy and procedural improvements are necessary.

10 11 12   Major revisions are required in library personnel policies and procedures to establish sound management practices.

Standard 5: Delivery of Service

5   The college library shall establish and maintain a range and quality of services that will promote the academic program of the institution and encourage optimal library use.

5.1   Proper service shall include: the provision of continuing instruction to patrons in the effective exploitation of libraries; the guidance of patrons to the library materials they need; and the provision of information to patrons as appropriate.

5.2   Library materials shall be circulated to qualified patrons under equitable policies and for as long periods as possible without jeopardizing their availability to others.

5.2.1   The availability of reading materials shall be extended wherever possible by the provision of inexpensive means of photocopying.

5.2.2   The quality of the collections available locally to patrons shall be enhanced through the use of "National Interlibrary Loan Code, 1968" (see Appendix II [of "Standards for College Libraries"]) and other cooperative agreements which provide reciprocal access to multi-library resources.

5.3   The hours of public access to the materials on the shelves, to the study facilities of the library, and to the library staff shall be consistent with reasonable demand, both during the normal study week and during weekends and vacation periods.

5.4   Where academic programs are offered away from a campus, library services shall be provided in accord with ACRL's "Guidelines for Library Services to Extension Students" (see Appendix II [of "Standards for College Libraries"]).

A. Library Instruction*

1 2 3   Librarians routinely work closely with the teaching faculty in identifying instructional needs and teach the use of library resources and services to meet these needs.

4 5 6   Librarians are regularly called on for consultative assistance and instruction in the use of library resources and services.

7 8 9   Librarians provide consultative assistance in the use of library resources and services when requested and free from other duties.

10 11 12   Librarians are rarely available to provide library instruction services.

*Circle only one of the twelve numbers.

B. Information Services*

1 2 3 The library staff provides a variety of information, instruction, and interpretative services, and meets most of its community's demands for these services.

4 5 6 The library staff provides a variety of information, instruction, and interpretative services, but is unable to meet some demands for these services.

7 8 9 Limited information services are available to the college community, and may be restricted to certain clientele.

10 11 12 Information services are not available to the college community.

C. Circulation*

1 2 3 Uniformly administered circulation policies regulate use of library materials for periods that are reasonable without jeopardizing the college community's access to materials.

4 5 6 Circulation policies regulate the use of library materials for periods that are usually acceptable. A review of the policies is desirable to correct minor problems.

7 8 9 Circulation policies are frequently restrictive without cause. Regulations are confusing and inconsistently administered.

10 11 12 Circulation policies do not facilitate access to library materials, and are poorly administered.

D. Access to Multi-Library Resources*

1 2 3 The library efficiently delivers materials and services provided by local, state, and national libraries via interlibrary loan codes and joint access consortia to students, faculty, and staff.

4 5 6 The library delivers materials and services provided by other libraries to students, faculty, and staff, but delays and/or access difficulties sometimes restrict service effectiveness.

7 8 9 The library delivers materials and services provided by other libraries only to selected individuals or groups in the academic community.

10 11 12 The library seldom provides its college community with access to the materials and services of other libraries.

E. Hours*

1 2 3 The number of hours per week that

*Circle only one of the twelve numbers.

library services and facilities are available meets the study and research needs of the college community.

4 5 6 Library hours are usually responsive to the community's needs for library services and facilities. There are requests for minor changes in these hours.

7 8 9 There are periods during the week (e.g., evenings, weekends) and the academic year (e.g., vacations, exams) when library hours are not responsive to the community's needs.

10 11 12 An insufficient number of library hours seriously deters the college community from achieving its educational goals.

Standard 6: Facilities

6 The college shall provide a library building containing secure facilities for housing its resources, adequate space for administration of those resources by staff, and comfortable quarters and furnishings for their utilization by patrons.

6.1 The size of the library building shall be determined by a formula (see Formula C [Appendix]) which takes into account the enrollment of the college, the extent and nature of its collections, and the size of its staff.

6.2 The shape of the library building and the internal distribution of its facilities and services shall be determined by function.

6.3 Except in unusual circumstances, the college library's collections and services shall be administered within a single structure.

A. The Building*

1 2 3 The building housing the library collection and services is fully equipped to support a quality program, functional in arrangement, accommodating to users and staff, and flexible in accommodating growth needs.

4 5 6 The design and arrangement of the library building generally supports service, storage, and growth requirements, but would be improved by renovations, expansions, or rearrangement.

7 8 9 The library building has a number of deficiencies which limit its contribution to and support of library services.

10 11 12 The library building is deficient in several critical areas, e.g., storage space, security, service, facilities, efficient design. These deficiencies seriously handicap the library in its delivery of service to the community.

B. Building Size*

Using Formula C (see Appendix) for calculating the net assignable area necessary for all library services except non-book services—

1 2 3   The library's facilities provide 90–100 percent of the space called for.

4 5 6   The library's facilities provide 75–90 percent of the space called for.

7 8 9   The library's facilities provide 60–74 percent of the space called for.

10 11 12   The library's facilities provide 50–59 percent of the space called for.

Standard 7: Administration

7   The college library shall be administered in a manner which permits and encourages the fullest and most effective use of available library resources.

7.1   The statutory or legal foundation for the library's activities shall be recognized in writing.

7.2   The college librarian shall be a member of the library faculty and shall report to the president or the chief academic officer of the institution.

7.2.1   The responsibilities and authority of the college librarian and procedures for his appointment shall be defined in writing.

7.3   There shall be a standing advisory committee comprising students and members of the teaching faculty which shall serve as the main channel of formal communication between the library and its user community.

7.4   The library shall maintain written policies and procedure manuals covering internal library governance and operational activities.

7.4.1   The library shall maintain a systematic and continuous program for evaluating its performance and for identifying needed improvements.

7.4.2   The library shall develop statistics not only for purposes of planning and control but also to aid in the preparation of reports designed to inform its publics of its accomplishments and problems.

7.5   The library shall develop, seek out, and utilize cooperative programs for purposes of either reducing its operating costs or enhancing its services, so long as such programs create no unreimbursed or unreciprocated costs for other libraries or organizations.

7.6   The library shall be administered in accord

*Circle only one of the twelve numbers.

with the spirit of the ALA "Library Bill of Rights" (see Appendix II [of "Standards for College Libraries"]).

A. Administration of the Library*

1 2 3   The library program is directed by a well-qualified librarian with faculty appointment who administers library services which support the full range of the college's educational program.

4 5 6   The library program is directed by a well-qualified librarian; a better orientation of library services to the college's educational program is desirable.

7 8 9   The library director does not attend to the full range of the library's responsibilities, and a review of the causes should be initiated.

10 11 12   The college community generally believes the library is not serving its educational program, and a major reorganization appears desirable.

B. Organization Authority*

1 2 3   The library's responsibilities and flow of authority under which it is empowered to act are described in official college documents such as bylaws, trustee documents, or public laws.

4 5 6   The library's responsibilities and flow of authority under which it is empowered to act are described in official college documents such as organizational charts, reporting structure diagrams, and job descriptions.

7 8 9   The library's responsibilities and flow of authority are inadequately covered by official college and administrative documents.

10 11 12   The library's responsibilities and flow of authority are not covered in official college and administrative documents.

C. Librarian's Authority*

1 2 3   The scope and nature of the college librarian's duties and powers, the procedures for his appointment, and the focus of his reporting responsibilities are defined in writing.

4 5 6   Some of the college librarian's duties and powers, appointment procedures, and reporting responsibilities are defined in writing.

7 8 9   The written description of the responsibilities and authority of the college librarian is generally inadequate and incomplete.

10 11 12   There is a minimal or no written description of the responsibilities and authority of the college librarian.

D. Reporting Structure*

1 2 3 The college librarian reports to either the president or the chief officer in charge of academic affairs of the college.

4 5 6 The college librarian reports to the office of academic affairs, but does not always review reports and recommendations with the chief academic officer.

7 8 9 The college librarian reports to a learning resources director or dean who reports to the chief academic officer.

10 11 12 No person has been given the administrative responsibility for receiving reports from the college librarian.

E. Library Committee*

1 2 3 A committee composed of representatives of the college community meets regularly to advise the librarian on matters of policy, user needs, and concerns, and effectively assists the community in understanding the library's capabilities and problems.

4 5 6 A committee composed of representatives of the college community advises the librarian on policy matters, user needs, and concerns, and conveys library information to the community. Its effectiveness could be improved.

7 8 9 A committee meets to advise the librarian on policy matters, user needs, and concerns, but is frequently ineffective as a channel of communication between the library and its community.

10 11 12 There is no committee or representative group to advise the librarian and channel communications between the library and its community.

F. Policy and Procedure Records*

1 2 3 Written policies and procedure manuals assuring uniformity and consistency of action and aiding staff training cover most of the library's technical and reader service operations.

4 5 6 Written policies and procedure manuals cover many of the library's operations, but several require revision and updating to incorporate policy and procedural changes.

7 8 9 A number of library operations require written policies and procedure manuals to assist administrative and training activities.

*Circle only one of the twelve numbers.

10 11 12 Generally the library does not have written policies and procedure manuals.

G. Evaluation of Services*

1 2 3 The library staff is continually involved in monitoring and evaluating the productivity, use of, and needs for library services, and uses this information to revise and develop library programs.

4 5 6 The library periodically monitors and evaluates its services and reviews user needs, and uses this information in program revisions and development.

7 8 9 The library conducts evaluations of its services and reviews user needs only in response to critical problems, or to provide data for reports.

10 11 12 Evaluations of library services and user needs are rarely conducted by the library, or used in program planning.

H. Public Relations*

1 2 3 Information concerning library service accomplishments and problems is regularly disseminated to the faculty, students, and administration. The forms of this information include news releases, reports, handbooks, brochures, reading lists, and displays.

4 5 6 Information concerning library services is occasionally disseminated to faculty, students, and staff or by request.

7 8 9 Information concerning library services is seldom disseminated to the community, but is sometimes supplied upon request.

10 11 12 Information concerning library services is rarely disseminated to the community or provided upon request.

I. Interlibrary Cooperation*

1 2 3 The library engages in and seeks interlibrary cooperative activities which enhance the qualities of its services and benefit its interests. The costs of these services are equitably distributed among the cooperating institutions.

4 5 6 The library engages in interlibrary cooperative activities which enhance the quality of its services and benefit its interests. However, the benefits of these services do not always balance their costs.

7 8 9 The library engages in interlibrary cooperative activities, but should improve its use of these services, and/or their cost-effectiveness.

10 11 12   The library does not seek or engage in interlibrary activities although services are available which would enhance the quality of its services and benefit its interests.

J. Bill of Rights*

1 2 3   The library is not restricted by partisan or doctrinal disapprovals in its selection of library materials, upholds the user's right of access to information, and has college support for the "Library Bill of Rights."

4 5 6   Partisan or doctrinal disapprovals seldom affect the selection of library materials or the user's access to information. Usually the "Library Bill of Rights" is supported by the library and the college.

7 8 9   The library supports the provisions of the "Library Bill of Rights," but the college does not always support these rights.

10 11 12   The library excludes materials or restricts access to information contrary to the provisions of the "Library Bill of Rights," and does not seek college support of the policy.

Standard 8: Budget

8   The college librarian shall have the responsibility for preparing, defending, and administering the library budget in accord with agreed-upon objectives.

8.1   The amount of the library appropriation shall express a relationship to the total institutional budget for educational and general purposes.

8.2   The librarian shall have sole authority to apportion funds and initiate expenditures within the library approved budget, in accord with institutional policy.

8.3   The library shall maintain such internal accounts as are necessary for approving its invoices for payment, monitoring its encumbrances, and evaluating the flow of its expenditures.

A. Budget Contents*

1 2 3   The budget of the library program developed by the librarian in consultation with library staff and college administrators reflects the library's priorities and objectives.

4 5 6   The budget of the library program developed by the librarian generally reflects most of the library's objec-

*Circle only one of the twelve numbers.

tives. Several allotments do not conform to program priorities.

7 8 9   The library budget partially reflects the library's objectives and priorities. The budgeting process requires revision.

10 11 12   The library budget is based on an arbitrary or undefined allotment of funds with minimal reference to the library's objectives and priorities. The budgeting process requires major revision.

B. Financial Support Requirements*

1 2 3   The library's annual appropriation, exclusive of capital and physical maintenance costs, is at least 6 percent of the college's total educational and general expenditures.

4 5 6   The library's annual appropriation, exclusive of capital and physical maintenance costs, is 5 to 6 percent of the college's total educational and general expenditures.

7 8 9   The library's annual appropriation, exclusive of capital and physical maintenance costs, is 4 to 5 percent of the college's total educational and general expenditures.

10 11 12   The library's annual appropriation, exclusive of capital and physical maintenance costs, is below 4 percent of the college's total educational and general expenditures.

C. Fiscal Accountability*

1 2 3   Regular reports reflect the status of allocations, encumbrances, and expenditures, and support sound practices of planning and control.

4 5 6   Reports reflecting the status of library accounts are issued periodically, but could be improved in scope, content, or frequency to support the administrative process.

7 8 9   Reports reflecting the status of library accounts are inadequate in scope and content, and/or issued too irregularly to provide accountability and support the administrative process.

10 11 12   There are few or no reports reflecting the status of library accounts, or those that exist fail the test of fiscal accountability.

PROFILE SHEET

This chart [fig. 1] is provided to tabulate and summarize the judgments recorded on the Evaluative Checklist. To develop a profile, transfer the marks from each item of the checklist to this sheet. Connect the marked circles by straight

	Strong ⟵									⟶ Weak		
Objectives												
	Mark only one of the twelve boxes											
Standard 1	1	2	3	4	5	6	7	8	9	10	11	12
Standard 2 Item A	1	2	3	4	5	6	7	8	9	10	11	12
Item B	1	2	3	4	5	6	7	8	9	10	11	12
Item C	1	2	3	4	5	6	7	8	9	10	11	12
Item D	1	2	3	4	5	6	7	8	9	10	11	12
Item E	1	2	3	4	5	6	7	8	9	10	11	12
Standard 3 Item A	1	2	3	4	5	6	7	8	9	10	11	12
Item B	1	2	3	4	5	6	7	8	9	10	11	12
Standard 4 Item A	1	2	3	4	5	6	7	8	9	10	11	12
Item B	1	2	3	4	5	6	7	8	9	10	11	12
Item C	1	2	3	4	5	6	7	8	9	10	11	12
Item D	1	2	3	4	5	6	7	8	9	10	11	12
Standard 5 Item A	1	2	3	4	5	6	7	8	9	10	11	12
Item B	1	2	3	4	5	6	7	8	9	10	11	12
Item C	1	2	3	4	5	6	7	8	9	10	11	12
Item D	1	2	3	4	5	6	7	8	9	10	11	12
Item E	1	2	3	4	5	6	7	8	9	10	11	12
Standard 6 Item A	1	2	3	4	5	6	7	8	9	10	11	12
Item B	1	2	3	4	5	6	7	8	9	10	11	12
Standard 7 Item A	1	2	3	4	5	6	7	8	9	10	11	12
Item B	1	2	3	4	5	6	7	8	9	10	11	12
Item C	1	2	3	4	5	6	7	8	9	10	11	12
Item D	1	2	3	4	5	6	7	8	9	10	11	12
Item E	1	2	3	4	5	6	7	8	9	10	11	12
Item F	1	2	3	4	5	6	7	8	9	10	11	12
Item G	1	2	3	4	5	6	7	8	9	10	11	12
Item H	1	2	3	4	5	6	7	8	9	10	11	12
Item I	1	2	3	4	5	6	7	8	9	10	11	12
Item J	1	2	3	4	5	6	7	8	9	10	11	12
Standard 8 Item A	1	2	3	4	5	6	7	8	9	10	11	12
Item B	1	2	3	4	5	6	7	8	9	10	11	12
Item C	1	2	3	4	5	6	7	8	9	10	11	12

Side labels (left margin): Objectives, Collections, Organization of Materials, Staff, Delivery of Service, Facilities, Administration, Budget

Fig. 1
Profile Sheet

lines. Then turn the sheet to a horizontal position to observe the resulting graph. Interpretive guidelines are provided [below].

USE OF THE PROFILE SHEET

Interpreting evaluations recorded on one profile sheet is a relatively simple task; summarizing and describing a number of profile sheets requires the application of regular frequency distributions. To construct such a distribution—

1. List every score value in the first column (denoted by symbol X) with the lowest number at the top.
2. Note the frequency (denoted by symbol f) of each score (the number of times a given score was obtained) to the right of the score in the second column of the table.

The table reveals at a glance how often each score was obtained; modalities, groupings, and skewings are easily identified. The scores could also be recorded in a grouped frequency distribution, using interval sizes of 4, although loss of information will occur with such groupings since they will not provide the exact value of each score.

EXAMPLE

Standard 1	Score (X)	Frequency (f)
	1	0
	2	0
	3	1
	4	3
	5	3
	6	4
	7	1
	8	0
	9	1
	10	0
	11	0
	12	0

The number of evaluations in this sample was 13.

Computations of central tendencies (means, medians, modes) are not advised because an evaluation cannot be described by a single number. After all scores are tabulated, trends and interrelationships should be observed to identify areas in which services might be improved, or new goals developed.

APPENDIX

Editor's Note: Appendix I, referred to in Formula A, and Appendix II, in Formula C, are published in the 1975 "Standards for College Libraries" (College & Research Libraries News 36:299–301 [Oct. 1975]).

FORMULA A—

The formula for calculating the number of relevant print volumes (or microform volume-equivalents) to which the library should provide prompt access is as follows (to be calculated cumulatively):

1. Basic Collection . . . . 85,000 vols.
2. Allowance per FTE Faculty Member . . . . . . 100 vols.
3. Allowance per FTE Student . . . . 15 vols.
4. Allowance per Undergraduate Major or Minor Field* . . . . . 350 vols.
5. Allowance per Masters Field, When No Higher Degree is Offered in the Field* . . . . 6,000 vols.
6. Allowance per Masters Field, When a Higher Degree is Offered in the Field* . . . . 3,000 vols.
7. Allowance per 6th-year Specialist Degree Field* . . . . . 6,000 vols.
8. Allowance per Doctoral Field* . . . . 25,000 vols.

A "volume" is defined as a physical unit of any printed, typewritten, handwritten, mimeographed, or processed work contained in one binding or portfolio, hardbound or paperbound, which has been cataloged, classified, and/or otherwise prepared for use. For purposes of this calculation microform holdings should be included by converting them to volume-equivalents. The number of volume-equivalents held in microform should be determined either by actual count or by an averaging formula which considers each reel of microform as one, and five pieces of any other microformat as one volume-equivalent.

Libraries which can provide promptly 100 percent as many volumes or volume-equivalents as are called for in this formula shall, in the matter of quantity, be graded A. From 80-99 percent shall be graded B; from 65-79 percent shall be graded C; and from 50-64 percent shall be graded D.

* See Appendix I, "List of Fields."

FORMULA B—

The number of librarians required by the college shall be computed as follows (to be calculated cumulatively):

For each 500, or fraction thereof, FTE students up to 10,000 . . . . . 1 librarian
For each 1,000 or fraction thereof, FTE students above 10,000 . . . . 1 librarian
For each 100,000 volumes, or fraction thereof, in the collection . . . . 1 librarian
For each 5,000 volumes, or fraction thereof, added per year . . . . . 1 librarian

Libraries which provide 100 percent of these formula requirements can, when they are supported by sufficient other staff members, consider themselves at the A level in terms of staff size; those that provide 75–99 percent of these requirements may rate themselves as B; those with 55–74 percent of requirements qualify for a C; and those with 40–54 percent of requirements warrant a D.

FORMULA C—

The size of the college library building shall be calculated on the basis of a formula which takes into consideration the size of the student body, requisite administrative space, and the number of physical volumes held in the collections. In the absence of consensus among librarians and other educators as to the range of non-book services which it is appropriate for libraries to offer, no generally applicable formulas have been developed for calculating space for them. Thus, space required for a college library's non-book services and materials must be added to the following calculations:

a. *Space for readers.* The seating requirement for the library of a college wherein less than fifty percent of the FTE enrollment resides on campus shall be one for each five FTE students; the seating requirement for the typical residential college library shall be one for each four FTE students; and the seating requirements for the library in the strong, liberal arts, honors-oriented college shall be one for each three FTE students. In any case, each library seat shall be assumed to require twenty-five square feet of floor space.

b. *Space for books.* Space required for books depends in part upon the overall size of the book collection, and is calculated cumulatively as follows:

	Square Feet/Volume
For the first 150,000 volumes	0.10
For the next 150,000 volumes	0.09
For the next 300,000 volumes	0.08
For holdings above 600,000 volumes	0.07

c. *Space for administration.* Space required for such library administrative activities as acquisition, cataloging, staff offices, catalogs, and files shall be one-fourth of the sum of the spaces needed for readers and books as calculated under (a) and (b) above.

This tripartite formula indicates the net assignable area necessary for all library services except for non-book services. (For definition of "net assignable area" see "The Measurement and Comparison of Physical Facilities for Libraries," produced by ALA's Library Administration Division. See Appendix II.) Libraries which provide 100 percent as much net assignable area as is called for by the formula shall qualify for an A rating as regards quantity; 75–99 percent shall warrant a B; 60–74 percent shall be due a C; and 50–59 percent shall warrant a D.

Editor's Note: ACRL Members may order single copies of the Evaluative Checklist by sending a self-addressed label and $.30 in postage to the ACRL office. Nonmembers should include $1 with their order.

College & Research Libraries news

No. 11, December 1972

ACRL News Issue (B) of College & Research Libraries, Vol. 33, No. 7

GUIDELINES FOR TWO-YEAR COLLEGE LEARNING RESOURCES PROGRAMS

Approved by the ACRL Board of Directors on June 29, 1972. These guidelines supersede and replace the final draft of the "AAJC-ACRL Guidelines for Two-Year College Library Learning Resource Centers" (CRL News, v.32, no.5, October 1971, p.265-278) and the "Standards for Junior College Libraries" (CRL, v.21, no.3, May 1960, p.200-206).

American Library Association
(Association of College and
Research Libraries)
American Association of Community and
Junior Colleges
Association for Educational Communications
and Technology

Two-Year College. Any institution of higher education which offers less than a baccalaureate degree and which requires its students either to be high school graduates or beyond high school age. Comprehensive community colleges, public and private junior colleges, and technical institutes are included.

Learning Resources. Includes library, audiovisual and telecommunications and encompasses instructional development functions and instructional system components. (See Glossary for expanded definitions.)

Introduction. Two-year colleges constitute one of the most dynamic sectors in American higher education. The increasing number of students and the growing number of new junior and community college institutions reflect a ground-swell of concern toward extension of universal higher education. A statement describing adequate learning resources and services has been difficult to formulate for such institutions because of factors such as the widely diversified purposes and sizes of the institutions —private and public, the high proportion of commuting students, the comprehensiveness of the curricula, the willingness of administrators and faculty to experiment unhampered by tradition, and the heterogeneity of background among those enrolled. Although the diversity among the institutional patterns makes the establishment of generally applicable guidelines difficult, all two-year institutions need qualitative recommendations based on professional expertise and successful practices in leading institutions which can be used for self-evaluation and projective planning.

The evolution of libraries away from their traditional function as repositories of books has been parallel to the evolution of audiovisual centers away from their traditional function as agencies for showing films. There has been a confluence of accelerated development in both areas which is inextricably interwoven in the technological revolution in education. Contemporary Learning Resources Programs in two-year colleges are supportive of institution-wide efforts. Such programs should provide innovative leadership coupled with a multiplicity of varied resources which are managed by qualified staff who serve to facilitate the attainment of institutional objectives. Paramount to the success of such programs is the involvement of Learning Resources staff with teaching, administrative, and other staff members in the design, implementation, and evaluation of instructional and educational systems of the institution.

These guidelines are diagnostic and descriptive in nature. They have been prepared to give direction to two-year colleges desiring to develop comprehensive Learning Resources Programs. This document is designed to provide criteria for information, self-study, and planning, not to establish minimal (or accreditation) standards. Application of the criteria should be governed by the purposes and objectives of each college. Since they represent recommended practices, any variant procedures should be supported by cogent reasons directly related to institutional objectives.

Nothing in these guidelines should be construed as an effort to superimpose an administrative or organizational structure upon an institution. There is no expectation that every institution should be forced into the same mold. The guidelines are more concerned with functions related to the instructional program rather than with specific organizational patterns. Although it is expected that these functions will be grouped into administrative (or supervisory) units within the Learning Resources Program, the nature of grouping and the resulting number of units must be determined by the unique requirements, resources, facilities, and staff of the college. The degree of autonomy granted each unit will also vary considerably. In some institutions, perhaps because of size, the units may be fairly task specific, with supervisory (rather than administrative) heads, and with little budgetary autonomy. Examples of such units include: an audio-tutorial laboratory; a bibliographic control center; media production; technical processes; etc. In other institutions, each unit may subsume a number of related activities, or carry out direct instructional assignments of a broad scope, and have an administrative head and a high degree of budgetary autonomy. Examples of such units include: an audiovisual center; a computing center; a library; a telecommunications center; etc. In all institutions, however, the units report to a chief administrator at the level of dean or vice-president, responsible for overall coordination of the Learning Resources Program. The extent of his ¹irect supervision of the units will be determined by the nature of the units and the degree of autonomy granted them.

Many aspects of traditional library and audiovisual services in the two-year college and the integration of these services have not been studied adequately for long-range projection of needs. Until such studies have been made these guidelines may serve as the foundations for research and for experimentation in organization, structure, and services.

The changing and expanding role of two-year colleges in America today may well result in institutions quite different from those in operation at the present time. These guidelines, therefore, may require significant upward revision when such institutions reach a new stage in their development. At that point, they may well need greater resources and greatly extended services. All concerned should be alert to this coming challenge.

THE ROLE OF THE LEARNING RESOURCES PROGRAM

Many diverse elements contribute to the quality of instruction as it contributes to the development of two-year college students. No one of these is dominant or isolated from the others. Faculty, students, finances, teaching methods, facilities, resources, and educational philosophy all play significant roles in the educational environment of the institution.

Education is more than exposure through lectures and rote learning to the knowledge, ideas, and values current in society. Education is a process for communicating means for resolving the range of problems continuously encountered by man in living and in pursuing an occupation. The student must be able to explore fields of knowledge which will enhance his potential and be relevant to him. The means of exploration include active participation in the classroom and the laboratory, self-directed study, and the use of individualized instructional resources. Trained professional assistance is necessary in the design of instructional systems which contribute to the enrichment of the learning environment as well as to the support of students and faculty. The design of the instructional system, utilizing a configuration of resources, is a joint responsibility of administration, teaching faculty, and the Learning Resources staff.

The student's success in achieving instructional objectives is heavily dependent on access to materials. Both student and faculty member function at their best when Learning Resources Programs are adequately conceived, staffed, and financed. More than almost any other element in the institution, Learning Resources Programs express the educational philosophy of the institution they serve.

Because of its direct relationship to the institutional and instructional objectives, the Learning Resources Program has a fourfold role: (1) to provide leadership and assistance in the development of instructional systems which employ effective and efficient means of accomplishing those objectives; (2) to provide an organized and readily accessible collection of materials and supportive equipment needed to meet institutional, instructional, and individual needs of students and faculty; (3) to provide a staff qualified, concerned, and involved in serving the needs of students, faculty, and community; (4) to encourage innovation, learning, and community service by providing facilities and resources which will make them possible.

GLOSSARY

The terms listed below are used throughout these guidelines as defined.

Two-year college. Any institution of higher education which offers less than a baccalaureate degree and which requires its students either to be high school graduates or beyond high school age. Included under this term are the following types of both public and private institutions: (1) institutions offering courses similar to the liberal arts curricula in the first two years of a senior college or university; (2) institutions which provide for the first two-year programs as branches or extension centers of senior colleges and universities, in anticipation of transfer to the parent institution or some other college at the junior year; (3) institutions for post-high-school-aged students whose concern is primarily vocational or technical and which are administered as specialized institutions of higher education; (4) comprehensive institutions offering both liberal arts and occupational programs of post-high-school level. Comprehensive community colleges, public and private junior colleges, and technical institutes are included.

Learning Resources Program. An administrative configuration within the institution responsible for the supervision and management of Learning Resources Units, regardless of the location of these components within the various physical environments of the institution.

Learning Resources Unit. A subordinate agency within the Learning Resources Program sufficiently large to acquire organizational identification as distinct from individual assignment and with an administrative or supervisory head, and which may have its own facilities, staff, and budget. How many of these units would make up the Learning Resources Program, and the functions assigned to each, will vary from institution to institution.

Instructional development functions. The solution of instructional problems through the design and application of instructional system components.

Instructional system components. All of the resources which can be designed, utilized, and combined in a systematic manner with the intent of achieving learning. These components include: men, machines, facilities, ideas, materials, procedures, and management.

Instructional product design. The process of creating and/or identifying the most effective materials to meet the specific objectives of the learning experience as defined by instructional development.

Production. The design and preparation of materials for institutional and instructional use. Production activities may include graphics, photography, cinematography, audio and video recording, and preparation of printed materials.

Staff. The personnel who perform Learning Resources Program functions. These persons have a variety of abilities and a range of educational backgrounds. They include professional and supportive staff.

Professional staff. Personnel who carry on responsibilities requiring professional training at the graduate level and experience appropriate to the assigned responsibilities.

Supportive staff. Personnel who assist professional staff members in duties requiring specific skills and special abilities. They make it possible for the professional staff to concentrate their time on professional services and activities. Their training may range from four-year degrees and two-year degrees to a one-year certificate, or extensive training and experience in a given area or skill.

System(s) approach. The application of instructional system components.

Materials. Divided into three categories: written, recorded, and other materials (see below).

Written materials. All literary, dramatic, and musical materials or works, and all other materials or works, published or unpublished, copyrighted or copyrightable at any time under the Federal Copyright Act as now existing or hereafter amended or supplemented in whatever format.

Recorded materials. All sound, visual, audiovisual, films or tapes, videotapes, kinescopes or other recordings or transcriptions, published or unpublished, copyrighted or copyrightable at any time under the Federal Copyright Act as now existing or hereafter amended or supplemented.

Other material. All types of pictures, photographs, maps, charts, globes, models, kits, art objects, realia, dioramas, and displays.

I. OBJECTIVES AND PURPOSES

A. *The college makes provision for a Learning Resources Program.*

The kinds of educational programs offered at nearly every two-year college require that adequate provisions be made for a Learning Resources Program, which should be an integral part of each institution. Learning Resources Programs should efficiently meet the needs of the students and faculty and be organized and managed for users. The effect of combining all learning resources programs under one administrative office provides for the maximum flexibility, optimum use of personnel, material, equipment, facilities, and systems to permit increased opportunities for the materials best suited for the user's needs.

B. *Learning Resources Programs have a statement of defined purpose and objectives.*

The need for clear definition of the role and purposes of the college and its various programs is highly desirable. Since Learning Resources Programs are a vital part, the objectives within the college they serve need to be defined and disseminated in an appropriate college publication. Within this framework, the following overall purposes of the Learning Resources Program are delineated:

1. *Learning Resources Programs exist to facilitate and improve learning.*

The emphasis is upon the improvement of the individual student, with a wide choice of materials to facilitate his learning. Such emphasis requires a staff committed to effective management of instructional development functions and effective utilization of instructional system components.

2. *Learning Resources Programs, like the instructional staff, are an integral part of instruction.*

Students who discover by themselves, or who are encouraged by the staff or faculty to seek out, the materials appropriate to their curriculum sequence of courses should be provided options to regular classroom instruction to achieve credit for a particular course. *Such alternatives should be developed and made available to the students.* The staff provides information on new materials, acquires them, or produces them, working cooperatively with the faculty on instructional development.

3. *Learning Resources Programs provide a variety of services as an integral part of the instructional process.*

a. Instructional development functions, which include task analysis, instructional design, evaluation, and related research.

b. Acquisition of learning materials, including cataloging and other related services.

c. Production

d. User services which include reference, bibliographic circulation (print and nonprint material), transmission or dissemination, and assistance to both faculty and students with the use of Learning Resources.

e. Other services, such as the computer operation, bookstore, campus duplicating or printing service, the learning or developmental lab, various auto-tutorial carrels or labs, telecommunications, or other information networks might be included within the functions and purposes of the college's overall organization and objectives.

4. *Learning Resources Programs cooperate in the development of area, regional, and state networks, consortia or systems.*

Every two-year college, whether privately or publicly supported, has a responsibility to help meet the resource material need of the larger community in which it resides. Attention is placed on ways in which each college can serve that community; in turn, the community serves as a reservoir of material and human resources which can be used by the college.

If the internal needs of the college and its students and staff are met, then coordination of its resources and services with those of other institutions to meet wider needs is mandatory. Reciprocal participation in consortia with other institutions for the development of exchanges, networks, or systems provides the colleges with materials and services that otherwise could not practically be provided.

II. Organization and Administration

A. *The responsibilities and functions of Learning Resources Programs within the institutional structure and the status of the chief administrator and heads of Learning Resources Units are clearly defined.*

The effectiveness of services provided depends on the understanding by faculty, college administrators, students, and Learning Resources staff of their responsibilities and functions as they relate to the institution. A written statement, endorsed by the institution's trustees or other policy-setting group, should be readily available.

To function adequately, the chief administrator of a Learning Resources Program (whose title may vary in different institutions) reports to the administrative officer of the college responsible for the instructional program and has the same administrative rank and status as others with similar institution-wide responsibilities. These responsibilities are delineated as part of a written statement so that he has adequate authority to manage the internal operations and to provide the services needed.

B. *The relationship of a Learning Resources Program to the total academic program necessitates involvement of the professional staff in all areas and levels of academic planning.*

Provision of learning materials is central to the academic program. As a result, the professional staff has interests which are broad and go beyond the scope of its day-to-day operations. The professional staff members are involved in all areas and levels of academic planning. The chief administrator and heads of Learning Resources Units work closely with other chief administrators of the college, and all professional staff members participate in faculty affairs to the same extent as other faculty.

The professional staff members are involved in major college committees. As far as possible, the professional staff members ought to function as liaison participants in staff meetings of the various departments.

C. *Advisory committees composed of faculty and students are essential for the evaluation and extension of services.*

As a rule, there should be a faculty advisory committee appointed by the appropriate administrative officer of the college, elected by the faculty, or selected by the procedure generally followed in the formation of a faculty committee. It should include representatives of the various academic divisions of the college and consist of both senior and junior members of the faculty, chosen carefully for their demonstrated interest beyond their own departmental concerns. The committee functions in an advisory capacity and acts as a connecting link between the faculty as a whole and the Learning Resources Program. It should not concern itself with details of administration.

A student advisory committee (or a joint advisory committee with the faculty) serves as a liaison between the student body and the Learning Resources Program. The committee should work closely with the chief administrator, an ex-officio member; he may use it as a sounding board for new ideas in developing a more effective program of services.

D. *The chief administrator is responsible for the administration of the Learning Resources Program, which is carried out by means of established lines of authority, definition of responsibilities, and channels of communication through heads of Learning Resources Units as defined in writing.*

E. *Internal administration of a Learning Resources Program is based on staff participation in policy, procedural, and personnel decisions.*

The internal organization is appropriate to the institution, and within this framework is based upon a considerable amount of self-determination, guided by the need for meeting common goals. Regular staff meetings and clearly devised lines of authority and responsibility are necessary. All staff members share in the process by which policies and procedures are developed; all staff members have access to heads of Learning Resources Units and the chief administrator.

Each professional and supportive staff member knows which activities are his responsibility and to whom he is accountable. Each Learning Resources Unit requires a staff manual which provides policy and procedural statements, duty assignments and other organizational matters, and items of general information.

F. *Budget planning and implementation of a Learning Resources Program is the responsibility of the chief administrator.* (See Section III.)

G. *The accumulation of pertinent statistics and maintenance of adequate records is a management responsibility.*

Adequate records are needed for internal analysis and management planning and to provide data for annual and special reports needed by the college, accrediting associations, and government agencies. Effective planning can be made only on the basis of available information. Statistics providing a clear and undistorted picture of activities, acquisitions of materials and equipment, utilization of materials, equipment and personnel, and annual expenditures are essential for federal, state, and college use. These statistics and records are collected in terms of the definitions and methods of reporting set forth in federal and professional publications. Appropriate data must also be collected and analyzed with regard to the instructional programs and the effectiveness of Learning Resources on these programs. Data of this type serve as the basis for important instructional decisions affecting the institution, faculty, students, and Learning Resources Program.

H. *Adequate management includes the preparation and dissemination of information to administration, faculty, and students concerning activities, services, and materials.*

The close interrelationship which exists with instructional departments on the campus demands that information about the Learning Resources Program be readily available. An annual report and other planned informational reports are essential for this purpose. Among other possible publications are bibliographies, acquisitions bulletins, current awareness lists, handbooks for faculty and students, releases to student and community publications through regular college channels, campus broadcasts, and utilization of other communications services which will reach students and faculty.

I. *Responsibilities for all learning resources and services should be assigned to a central administrative unit.*

Centralized administration is desirable in order to provide coordination of resources and services, to develop system approaches to needs, and to effectively utilize staff. Materials, on the other hand, should be located in the areas where learning takes place. Inventory control of all materials and equipment should be the responsibility of the Learning Resources Program and its units. All such collections of materials should be considered the resources of the entire college and not limited in utilization to separate departments.

J. *Multicampus districts take advantage of the opportunity for close cooperation, exchange of resources, and shared technical processes while providing full resources and services for every campus.*

Each campus in a multicampus, two-year college district has its instructional and individual needs met on its campus. Learning Resources needed by off-campus programs are supplied by the campus sponsoring the program. There is no need, however, for duplication of routine technical processes and production facilities where these can be centralized more economically. Organizational structure within the district should facilitate cooperation and exchange of resources.

III. BUDGET

A. *Learning Resources Program budget is a function of program planning. It is designed to implement the realization of institutional and instructional program objectives.*

It is the responsibility of the chief administrator to see that each unit of a Learning Resources Program receives due attention in the budget and that the allocation of funds is based on sound principles of management.

B. *Budget planning for the Learning Resources Program reflects the campus-wide instructional material needs, is initiated by the administrative head, and is changed in consultation with him.*

Adequate budget, essential to provide good services, is based upon needs of the curriculum and functions of the Learning Resources Program. Through his own consultations with the heads of Learning Resources Units, the administrative head acquires the information needed to prepare the budget, with ample time to present and explain the budget request to the college administration as part of the budget process. Whenever consideration is given to adjustments or reallocation of funds or applications for grants, consultation is also indicated.

C. *Separate categories are maintained in the budget for salaries, student wages, purchase and rental of all types of materials and equipment, production of instructional materials, supplies and contractual services (including data processing services), repairs, replacement and new equipment, travel of staff to professional meetings, and other related items.*

For management purposes, costs relating to the various types of materials and services are separately identifiable. Where specialized facilities are a part of the Learning Resources Program, it is desirable that cost for these be identifiable as well.

D. *Financial records are maintained by, or are accessible to, the Learning Resources Units.*

Costs analyses and financial planning are dependent upon the adequacy of records, with sufficient additional information to enable comprehensive planning and effective utilization of all funds available. These records are not necessarily the same records as are needed in the business office.

E. *All expenditures, other than payroll, are initiated in the Learning Resources Units with payment made only on invoices verified for payment by the staff.*

Purchases are initiated by the staff through preparation of purchase order or requisition. Institutional business operations require approval of all invoices by the operating departments.

F. *To the legal extent possible and within the policies of the Board of Trustees, purchases of materials are exempted from restrictive annual bidding.*

Materials often are unique items obtainable from a single source. Equivalent prices and speedier service often can be obtained by direct access to the publisher or manufacturer rather than through a single vendor. Satisfactory service requires prompt delivery so that the needs which determined their acquisition might be met; a larger discount might justifiably be rejected if it entails a delay in filling the order. Satisfactory service rendered by a vendor in the past may more than outweigh the confusion and interruption of service inherent in frequent changes of vendors through annual bidding requirements for learning materials.

G. *Purchase of materials is based on curricular requirements and other factors, and thus made throughout the year rather than annually or semiannually.*

Expenditures are based on need, availability, and practical considerations such as processing time, rather than through fixed sequences which inhibit the functions of the unit.

H. *Learning Resources Program equipment is purchased through a systems approach.*

Learning Resources equipment may serve two purposes: (1) instructional supportive systems, and (2) instructional developmental systems. The purchase of any Learning Resources Program equipment, like all functions of the Learning Resources Program, should be carried out through a systems approach based on well-defined institutional and instructional objectives.

I. *Selection of Learning Resources Program equipment to be purchased for implementation of instruction is based on valid criteria.*

Performance quality, effective design, ease of operation, cost, portability, cost of maintenance and repair, and available service are among the criteria which should be applied to equipment selection.

Most important, however, is how the item or items will fit into planning for maintenance and improvement of curriculum programming as set forth in continuous instructional design plans. Responsibility for evaluating, selecting and recommending purchase of equipment is that of the Learning Resources staff.

J. *Cooperative purchasing of materials and equipment should be effected where possible.*

In an effort to secure the best materials and equipment at the lowest cost, cooperative purchasing should be developed with other area institutions.

IV. INSTRUCTIONAL SYSTEM COMPONENTS

A. Staff

1. *The chief administrator of the Learning Resources Program is selected on the basis of acquired competencies which relate to the purposes of the program, educational achievement, administrative ability, community and scholarly interests, professional activities, and service orientation.*

He has a management responsibility and is concerned and involved in the entire educational program of the institution as well as with the operation of the Learning Resources Program. He is professionally knowledgeable about all types of materials and services and is capable of management of instructional development functions. Because the ultimate success of a Learning Resources Program is to a large extent dependent upon the ability of the administrative head to perform his multiple duties effectively, the recruitment and selection of the administrative head is of paramount importance.

2. *The administrative (or supervisory) heads of the separate Learning Resources Units are selected on the basis of their expertise in and knowledge of the function and role of the particular Learning Resources Unit which they will manage and to which they will give leadership.*

3. *A well-qualified, experienced staff is available in sufficient numbers and areas of specialization to carry out adequately the purposes and objectives of the Learning Resources Program.*

Depending upon the size and programs of the institution, the hours operated, the physical facilities, and the scope and nature of the services performed, the number and specializations of professional and supportive staff will vary from one institution to another.

4. *All personnel are considered for employment on the recommendation of the administrative head and, upon employment, are responsible to him through the appropriate administrative structure for the performance of assigned duties.*

The effectiveness of a Learning Resources Program is determined by the performance of the staff. It is essential, therefore, that all personnel—professional or supportive—be recommended for employment to the chief administrator on the advice of the Learning Resources Unit head who will be involved in the supervision of the new staff member.

5. *Professional staff members should have degrees and/or experience appropriate to the position requirements.*

Professional training is appropriate to assignment in the Learning Resources Program. Additional graduate study or experience in a subject field should be recognized for all personnel as appropriate to such assignments.

Professional staff members are assigned duties. They are accountable for the operational effectiveness of the Learning Resources Program as designated by the chief administrator and heads of units. They may be supervisors as well as professional consultants to the faculty and advisors to students.

6. *Every professional staff member has faculty status, faculty benefits, and obligations.*

Professional staff benefits include such prerogatives as tenure rights, sick leave benefits, sabbatical leaves, vacation benefits, retirement and annuity benefits, provisions for professional development, and compensation at the same level which is in effect for teaching faculty or for those at comparable levels of administration. When Learning Resources personnel work on a regular twelve-month schedule, salary adjustments will be necessary to compensate for additional service days. Where academic ranks are recognized, such are assigned to the professional staff based on the same criteria as for other faculty, and are independent of internal assignments within the Learning Resources Program.

There is the obligation of faculty status to meet all faculty and professional requirements, advanced study, research, promotion, committee assignments, membership in professional organizations, sponsorships, publication in learned journals, etc., which the institution expects of faculty members.

7. *Professional development is the responsibility of both the institution and the professional staff member.*

Personal membership and participation in professional activities is expected of all staff members. Further graduate study should be encouraged and rewarded. The institution is expected to encourage and support professional development by providing among other benefits: consultants for staff development sessions; travel funds for regular attendance of some staff members and occasional attendance for every staff member at appropriate state or national meetings, workshops and seminars; and special arrangements for those staff members who serve as officers or committee members or participate on a state or national program.

8. *Teaching assignments by Learning Resources staff members are considered dual appointments in calculating staff work loads.*

When members of Learning Resources staff are assigned regular teaching responsibilities in training technicians or other classroom assignments, the hours scheduled in the Learning Resources Program are reduced by an equivalent time to allow preparation and classroom contact hours.

9. *Supportive staff members are responsible for assisting the professional staff in providing effective services.*

Responsibility for each level of supportive staff will be determined by the needs of the institution and the appropriate administrative structure. The number and kind of supportive staff needed will be determined by the size of the college and the services provided. The educational background and experience of such supportive staff should be appropriate to the tasks assigned.

The supportive staff may be supervisors as well as technical assistants or aides. In many instances, graduates of four-year degree programs and two-year technical programs will meet the training required; in other cases, one-year programs may be sufficient; or skills may have been learned through extensive work experience in a related position.

10. *Student assistants are employed to supplement the work of the supportive staff.*

Student assistants do not, however, replace provision of adequate full-time staff, nor can their work be matched on an hour-to-hour basis with that of regular full-time employment.

They are important because of the variety of tasks they can perform effectively. They encourage other students to use the facilities and services, and they serve as significant means of recruitment for supportive and professional positions.

B. *Facilities*

1. *Planning of new or expanded facilities is accomplished with the participation and concurrence of the chief administrator in all details and with wide involvement of users and staff.*

The chief administrator and his staff work with the architect and the administration in every decision and have prime responsibility in the functional planning of the facility. Employment of a knowledgeable media specialist or library building consultant results in a more functional and useful building operation and should be given serious consideration. In the case of specialized facilities, special technical consultants may be required. As a result of poor design, functions of many buildings fail because those persons who will be working in or using the building have not been involved in planning. Staff, faculty, student representatives, and others who will utilize the facilities should be consulted.

2. *In the design of classrooms and other college facilities where Learning Resources are to be used, Learning Resources specialists should be consulted.*

The effective use of an instructional system is dependent upon the availability of a suitable environment for the use of specified Learning Resources. Frequently, architects and other college staff are not aware of all of the technical requirements of such an environment.

3. *The physical facilities devoted to Learning Resources and Learning Resources Units are planned to provide appropriate space to meet institutional and instructional objectives and should be sufficient to accommodate the present operation as well as reflect long-range planning to provide for anticipated expansion, educational and technological change.*

The location and extent of space provided for development, acquisition, design, production, and use of learning resources is the responsibility of the chief administrator of Learning Resources, and should be designed to implement explicit, well-articulated program specifications developed by the Learning Resources and instructional staff of the college. Such a program should include flexible provisions for long-range development and phasing. The alteration, expansion, or consolidation of facilities also should be guided by carefully delineated program objectives which are known and understood by Learning Resources personnel, the instructional and administrative staff of the college, and the Board of Trustees. Factors to be considered when developing facilities requirements from the program specifications include projections of the student enrollment, the extent of community services, growth in the varieties of service, growth of materials collections, staff needs, and the impact of curricular development and technological advances.

4. *Facilities of Learning Resources Units should be located conveniently for use by both students and instructional staff.*

Learning Resources services for administration, acquisition, and cataloging should be centralized for more efficient operation. Planning should provide for convenient locations of facilities for storing and using equipment and materials close to the learning spaces or central to student traffic flow in which they are to be used. Where existing facilities will not permit this arrangement, an effort should be made to reduce confusion and frustration by making clear to the user the specific function of each facility.

The number of users varies in all units from peak periods when crowded conditions make service difficult to times when few students are present. Physical arrangements should make continued service with minimal staff possible during quiet times and at the same time provide for augmented service at other periods.

5. *Internal arrangement of service and work areas is planned with consideration as to flexibility, relationship between areas, and function, with particular attention to staff needs.*

Flexibility is essential to meet advances in technology and changes in instructional requirements. Areas within the Learning Resources Unit are grouped to aid the user and to permit the staff to perform duties effectively. Services provided are dependent upon staff, whose efficiency is in turn dependent upon adequate office, workroom, and storage space. The production facility should provide for consultation and demonstration space. It should be equipped to permit the demonstrating and previewing of all components of an instructional system. A staff conference room, apart from the administrative head's office, is desirable in all but the smallest institutions.

6. *The physical facilities provide a wide variety of learning and study situations.*

Students require various types of facilities for learning and study. Some require programmed learning equipment; others learn best by use of isolated individual study areas. In some circumstances they need to study together as a group or relax in comfortable lounge chairs. Proper arrangement and sufficient space for utilization of instructional equipment and materials should be provided for individualized instruction, browsing, and media production.

7. *The physical facilities are attractive, comfortable, and designed to encourage use by students.*

Attractive and well-planned areas encourage student utilization. Air-conditioning and comfortable heating, proper lighting, acoustical treatment, regular custodial care, prompt maintenance of equipment, and regular and systematic repair of damages are necessary. Attention to the needs of the physically handicapped should be met in regard to restrooms, external and internal traffic flow, and doors.

8. *Space requirements, physical arrangements, and construction provide for full utilization of specialized equipment.*

Specialized facilities are necessary for certain types of equipment. For example, data processing services, listening and viewing equipment, media production, and use of other types of electronic equipment require special consideration in terms of electrical connections, cables, conduits, lights, fire protection, security, and other factors which affect service.

C. *Instructional Equipment*

1. *Necessary instructional equipment is available at the proper time and place to meet institutional and instructional objectives.*

Centralized control of inventory and distribution of all equipment is needed. A thorough and continual evaluation is desirable to insure that enough of the appropriate equipment is available.

2. *Classroom and Learning Resources Program use of equipment is managed in the most effective manner to minimize operational mishaps and insure effective utilization.*

Assistance from Learning Resources staff is available as a regular service when needed and for the maintenance of equipment. Except for more complex equipment, the instructor and student should be responsible for the operation of the equipment.

3. *Learning Resources and instructional equipment are selected and purchased on the basis of specific criteria.* (See Section III.)

D. *Materials*

1. *Materials are selected, acquired, designed, or produced on the basis of institutional and instructional objectives, developed by the faculty, students, and administration in cooperation with Learning Resources.*

A written statement regarding acquisition and production of learning materials has such an important and pervasive effect upon the instructional program and the services of the Learning Resources Program that all segments of the academic community should be involved in its development. The statement should be readily available in an official publication.

Learning Resources Programs provide materials presenting all sides of controversial issues. The position of the American Library Association, and comparable associations, on the subject of censorship is firmly adhered to.

2. *Materials may be acquired and made available from a variety of sources.*

In an effort to meet the needs of the instructional process and cultural enrichment, it will be necessary to acquire materials through:

a. purchase of commercially available materials;

b. lease or rental of materials where purchase is neither possible or practical in terms of cost, utilization, or type;

c. loan through free loan agencies;

d. acquisition of materials as gifts;

e. design and production of materials not readily available.

3. *Materials must be accessible to authorized individuals.*

Although there is no uniformly accepted system to make all resources available, the materials must be properly organized and the necessary staff, facilities, and hardware provided. Highly sophisticated systems for computer, video, and audio access for retrieving, manipulating, and displaying information might be necessary.

4. *Final management decision as to the order in which materials are to be purchased or produced is the responsibility of the chief administrator or his delegated subordinate.*

Within the established framework of the written statement on acquisition and production, and the budgetary restraints, the final management decision and priority judgment must be the responsibility of the chief administrator and his duly designated subordinates.

5. *Representative works of high caliber which might arouse intellectual curiosity, counteract parochialism, help to develop critical thinking and cultural appreciation, or stimulate use of the resources for continuing education and personal development are included in the collection even though they do not presently meet direct curricular needs.*

One function of higher education is to develop adult citizens intellectually capable of taking their places in a changing society. Provision of materials beyond curricular needs is essential for this goal.

6. *Materials reflect ages, cultural backgrounds, intellectual levels, developmental needs, and vocational goals represented in the student body.*

Two-year college students represent all strata of community and national life. To meet their needs, the collection must contain materials of all kinds and at all levels. Those students who require basic remedial materials, those who seek vocational and technical training or retraining, those who seek an understanding of their culture, and those who are utilizing their retirement years for personal stimulation should each find the materials which can serve their interests and solve their problems. Special care is taken to include representative materials related to the needs of cultural or racial minorities as well as materials reflecting divergent social, religious, or political viewpoints.

7. *A board policy is developed concerning gifts to a Learning Resources Program.*

Generally, gifts are accepted only when they add strength to the collection and impose no significant limitations on housing, handling, or disposition of duplicate, damaged, or undesirable items. It is recognized that gifts frequently require more time to screen, organize, catalog, and process than new materials. Stor-age space and staff time requirements must be considered in accepting gift materials. In acknowledgment of gifts, attention should be called to government recognition of such contributions for tax purposes, as well as to the impropriety of any appraisal by the recipient of a donation.

8. *In local reproduction of materials for instructional use, care is taken to comply with copyright regulations.*

Laws restrict the copying of many items without permission. Procedures and guidelines must be established regarding reproduction of copyrighted materials and made easily accessible.

9. *The reference collection includes a wide selection of significant subject and general bibliographies, authoritative lists, periodical indexes, and standard reference works in all fields of knowledge.*

Every two-year college requires extensive bibliographical materials for use in locating and verifying items for purchase, rental, or borrowing, for providing for subject needs of users, and for evaluating the collection.

10. *Newspapers with various geographical, political, and social points of view on national and state issues are represented in the collection.*

Newspapers should reflect community, national, and worldwide points of view. Back files of several newspapers are retained in print or microform.

11. *Government documents are required as significant sources of information.*

Some two-year colleges which are document depositories receive government publications as a matter of course. All Learning Resources Programs should acquire regularly such publications.

12. *Files of pamphlets and other ephemeral materials are maintained.*

An effective and up-to-date pamphlet file is a strong resource in any college. Included are vocational and ephemeral materials developed through systematic acquisition of new materials, including subscriptions to pamphlet services and requests for free materials. References in the catalog to subjects contained in pamphlet files are desirable in providing the fullest access to the materials. Periodic weeding of the collection is essential.

Manufacturers' and publishers' catalogs and brochures which describe new materials and equipment are needed to supplement published lists and to provide up-to-date information.

13. *A collection of recorded and other materials should be available for individual use as well as for meeting instructional needs.*

14. *The conservation of materials, as well as the elimination of those which are obso-*

lete, should be developed as part of on-going procedures.

The materials in the collection should be examined regularly to eliminate obsolete items, unnecessary duplicates, and worn-out materials. Prompt attention must be given to damaged materials so that repairs and replacement (including rebinding of printed materials or replacement of portions of projected or recorded materials) are handled systematically, along with prompt action to replace important items, including those discovered to be missing.

15. *The Learning Resources Unit functions as an archive for historical information and documents concerning the college itself.*

An effort should be made to locate, organize, and house institutional archives to the extent defined by the administration.

V. SERVICES

A. *Users of Learning Resources have the right to expect:*

1. That facilities, materials, and services are available to meet demonstrated instructional needs for their use;
2. That an atmosphere be provided which allows sensitive and responsive attention to their requirements;
3. That professional staff be readily available for interpretation of materials and services and for consultation on instructional development;
4. That physical facilities be maintained to make use comfortable and orderly;
5. That requests for scheduling, circulation, distribution, and utilization of materials and related equipment be handled expeditiously;
6. That acquisition, production, and organization of materials meet their instructional and personal needs.

VI. INTERAGENCY COOPERATIVE ACTIVITIES

A. *Cooperative arrangements for sharing of resources are developed with other institutions and agencies in the community, region, state, and nation.*

To provide the best possible service to the students and faculty in the two-year college, close relationships with other local institutions and agencies and with institutions of higher education in the area are essential. Through consortia, media cooperatives, and loan arrangements, institutions can share resources. The college may need to make arrangements so that its students may use the area facilities and resources. When an undue burden is placed on a neighboring institution, financial subsidy may be appropriate.

B. *The institution is willing to consider participation in cooperative projects, such as shared cataloging, computer use, and other services which may be mutually beneficial to all participants.*

By cooperative planning much expense and wasteful duplication can be avoided in the community and region. Learning Resources personnel and institutional administrators need to be alert to cooperative activities of all kinds and to be willing to explore the possibilities of participation for their own institution.

C. *Responsibility for the collection and preservation of community history and for the accumulation of other local and statistical data is shared with other institutions and is coordinated with them.*

(Copies of this article are available from ACRL.) ■■

Statement on
Quantitative Standards for
Two-Year Learning Resources Programs

FOREWORD

The following statement on quantitative standards for two-year college learning resources programs has been prepared by the Ad Hoc Subcommittee to Develop Quantitative Standards for the "Guidelines for Two-Year College Learning Resources Programs." A draft of the statement appeared in the March 1979 issue of *College & Research Libraries News*.

In June 1979 the Ad Hoc Subcommittee revised this draft. At the ALA Annual Meeting in June 1979, the ACRL Board voted to ratify the revised statement. "Statement on Quantitative Standards for Two-Year Learning Resources Programs" is hereby published in its final form for the information of ACRL members.

INTRODUCTION

When the "Guidelines for Two-Year College Learning Resources Programs"* was completed in 1972, it was planned that a supplementary statement of quantitative standards should be developed. This document is the intended supplement, designed to meet the recurring requests for suggested quantitative figures for help in planning and evaluating programs. No absolutes are presented here; too many variables must be considered for this to be possible. In addition, although extensive use has been made of existing statistics when these were appropriate,† no conclusive research provides quantitative measurements of some factors. In such cases the professional judgment and extensive experience of the members of the committee have been the basis for the recommendations.

---

*American Association of Community and Junior Colleges—Association for Educational Communications and Technology—American Library Association, "Guidelines for Two-Year College Learning Resources Programs," *Audiovisual Instruction*, XVIII, p.50–61 (Jan. 1973); *College & Research Libraries News*, XXXIII, p.305–15 (Dec. 1972).

†For example, extensive computer analysis was made of the 1975 HEGIS statistics, which had the only comprehensive coverage of audiovisual holdings. These statistics were analyzed by FTE, by types of materials, and by other factors. The quartiles developed have been used extensively by the committee. Stanley V. Smith, *Library Statistics of Colleges and Universities: Fall 1975 Institutional Data* (U.S. Dept. of Health, Education and Welfare, National Center for Education Statistics, 1977).

Adherence to every single element in the Learning Resources Program (as defined in the "Guidelines") is not considered essential in this document. For example, collection size is viewed as relating not to book holdings alone or to audiovisual holdings alone but rather to total bibliographical unit equivalents (as defined in section on collections).

The significant variable accepted for most elements is enrollment expressed as full-time equivalent (FTE) students. The tables reflect from under 1,000 FTE to the largest enrollments for a single Learning Resources Program. Should the total enrollment be more than twice the FTE, collection, staff, and space requirements will exceed the quantities in the tables. Levels of attainment of Learning Resources Programs will vary. Two levels are addressed in this document in each enrollment bracket: "minimal" (indicated in the tables by *M*) and "good" (indicated by *G*). A program consistently below the *M* level for its size is probably not able to provide services needed. A program consistently above the upper, or *G* level, will usually be found to have the capability of providing outstanding services.

It cannot be expected that these quantitative standards will remain constant. To reflect changes in two-year colleges, results of additional research, new technological and professional developments, experience in the use of this statement, and changes in the economic and educational conditions in the nation, it is recommended that a review committee be appointed three years from the date of initial adoption and at three-year intervals thereafter.

STAFF

Staff components are defined in the "Guidelines." The positions in table 1, which include the director, are full-time equivalents for staff working thirty-five to forty hours a week for twelve months a year, including vacations and holidays, in a Learning Resources Unit in which most processing occurs on campus. Staff in a central unit, such as a processing center for a multicampus district, should be in proportion to the services rendered each campus.

Staffing of branches, extension centers, commercial level production facilities, computer operations, printing services, extensive learning or developmental laboratories, bookstore operations, or on-the-air broadcasting are not included in the table. Most institutions will need to modify the

TABLE 1
STAFF

Full-Time Equivalent Enrollment	Level	Professional	Support
Under 1,000	M	2	4
	G	4	6
1,000–3,000	M	2.5	5
	G	4	10
3,000–5,000	M	3.5	9
	G	6	18
5,000–7,000	M	6	15
	G	8	24
Additional for each 1,000 FTE over 7,000	M	.5	1
	G	1	3

staffing pattern to include such factors as longer or shorter workweeks and annual contracts.

BUDGET

Budget formulas in a true sense are not possible in two-year colleges because of wide variances in practice from institution to institution. For example, film rentals may be charged to departmental budgets, and staff fringe benefits may or may not be included in the budget for Learning Resources Programs. In addition to these, various other services, such as learning or developmental laboratories, which are definitely part of such programs, will not always be so charged in the institutional budgets.

The formulas are further complicated where there are centralized services, satellite operations, and continuing education responsibilities, so that an absolute formula is not possible without examining all elements of staff, materials, services, and the delineations listed in IIIC of the "Guidelines" at each campus.

Experience indicates, however, that a fully developed Learning Resources Program will usually require from 7 to 12 percent of the educational and general budget of the institution, whether these are separately identified as learning resources or diffused in a multiple number of accounts.

COLLECTION SIZE

Size of the collection available on any two-year college campus is best expressed as "bibliographical unit equivalents." Where a multicampus district maintains some materials centrally, these holdings should be distributed for statistical purposes proportional to use by the various campuses.

Bibliographical unit equivalents (BUE) consist of written, recorded, or other materials. Each item in the following three groups is one BUE.

Written Materials
1. One cataloged bound volume.
2. One periodical volume.

3. One cataloged document.
4. One reel of microfilm.
5. One cataloged microfiche.
6. Five uncataloged microfiche.
7. Five microcards.
8. One cataloged musical work.
9. One periodical currently received.

Recorded Materials
10. One videocassette or videotape reel.
11. One reel of 16mm motion picture film.
12. One cataloged 8mm loop film.
13. One cataloged 35mm slide program.
14. One cataloged set of transparencies.
15. One cataloged slide set or filmstrip.
16. Fifty cataloged 2 x 2 slides, not in sets.
17. One cataloged sound recording (disc, reel, or cassette).
18. Five films rented or borrowed during an academic year.

Other Materials
19. One cataloged map, chart, art print, or photograph.
20. One cataloged kit.
21. One cataloged item of realia, model, or art object.
22. Any other comparable cataloged item(s).

Table 2 shows the total number of BUEs used to measure the collection. Normally, written materials should constitute at least 70 percent of the BUEs. All other proportions of the totals may be adapted to the Learning Resources Program of the institution. Flexibility in determining the informational needs of the program then makes it possible to choose to purchase either a book or an audiovisual item, a periodical subscription, or any other materials. No two-year college should be without some BUEs in each of the five categories used in table 2. Technical institutes with extremely specialized programs may reduce the total BUE requirements as much as 40 percent.

ANNUAL ACCESSIONS

If the materials are to meet the instructional needs of the institution served, continued acquisitions accompanied by continued weeding are needed even where holdings exceed recommendations. New materials are needed for presentation of new information and new interpretations or the collection becomes dated and decreases in educational value. New courses added to the curriculum and new instructional programs require new materials to meet classroom and individual needs of students. As enrollment increases there is need for more duplication and for broader approaches to topics already represented in the collection.

Five percent of the collection size should be the minimum annual acquisition for each Learning Resources Program. This percentage does not include replacements of lost or stolen items or materials to support new courses or curricula, which should be additional.

TABLE 2
COLLECTION SIZE

FTE Enrollment	Level	Written Materials Periodical Subscriptions	Other Written Materials	Recorded Materials Motion Pictures & Videotapes	Other Recorded Materials	Other Materials	BUE Collection Size Totals
Under 1,000	M	200	20,000	15	350	50	20,615
	G	300	30,000	125	1,350	350	32,125
1,000– 3,000	M	300	30,000	125	1,350	350	32,125
	G	500	50,000	350	3,200	1,200	55,250
3,000– 5,000	M	500	50,000	350	3,200	1,200	55,250
	G	700	70,000	700	5,350	2,350	79,100
5,000– 7,000	M	700	70,000	700	5,350	2,350	79,100
	G	800	85,000	1,250	8,500	4,500	100,100
Additional each 1,000 FTE over 7,000	M	5	6,000	13	10	5	6,133
	G	30	12,000	150	405	305	12,890

TABLE 3
SPACE REQUIREMENTS

Full-Time Equivalent Enrollment	Print Materials and Services Minimum	Maximum	Audiovisual Materials and Services Minimum	Maximum	Related Instructional Services	Total Assignable Square Feet
1,667	7,500	9,250	5,000	6,750	750	15,000
2,500	9,503	13,055	5,000	8,552	950	19,005
5,000	15,495	21,693	7,748	13,946	1,550	30,990
8,333	23,000	32,200	11,500	20,700	2,300	46,000
10,834	28,503	39,904	14,251	25,652	2,850	57,005
14,167	35,488	49,683	17,744	31,939	3,549	70,975
16,667	40,650	56,910	20,325	36,585	4,065	81,000

SPACE REQUIREMENTS

Space standards for two-year colleges have already been developed by the Learning Resources Associaton of California Community Colleges and should be utilized for permanent facilities to be in use for ten or more years. Their *Facilities Guidelines,*‡ if adjusted to FTE by use of the formula provided, will serve as a satisfactory standard.

Table 3 has been adapted from the *Facilities Guidelines* using absolute FTE to allow easy comparison when that publicaton is not available. The premises upon which the original was based deserve more attention than is possible in these standards.

To be added to the total square feet in table 3 is any additional space needed for related instructional services for individualized instruction, such as learning laboratories, study skills center, language laboratories, etc. Also to be added are internal offices, office service areas (file rooms,

‡Learning Resources Association of the California Community Colleges, *Facilities Guidelines for Learning Resources Centers: Print, Non-print, Related Instructional Services* (P.O. Box 246, Suisun City, CA 94585, 1978), $25.

vaults, duplicating rooms, internal corridors, office supply rooms, etc.), office-related conference rooms and conference room services (kitchenettes, sound equipment storage, etc.), internal classrooms and laboratories, and nonassignable space (janitor's closets, stairways, public corridors, elevators, toilets, and building utility and operational facilities).

EQUIPMENT FOR DISTRIBUTION

There is need for sufficient equipment for distribution to classrooms beyond equipment necessary for individual utilization of audiovisuals in the learning centers. Recommendations are limited to major types of equipment. Opaque projectors should be available even in minimal programs; quantity will depend upon utilization. Overhead projectors should be available in all classrooms. Recommendations in table 4 are for classroom equipment distribution only and assume a replacement schedule not longer than five years.

Quantitative formulas for some equipment are inherent in use. In a laboratory situation, type and quantity of equipment will depend upon what the course or program is. Permanent sound and projection equipment will be installed in large lecture halls. All classrooms will have per-

TABLE 4
EQUIPMENT FOR DISTRIBUTION

Uses per Year	16mm Projector	Super 8mm Projector	Video-cassette Player	Slide Projector	Audio-casette Player	Record Player
1–100	2–9	2–9	2–9	2–24	2–49	2–9
101–1,000	10–24	10–24	10–24	25–49	50–99	10–24
1,001–3,000	25–44	15–19	25–32	50–64	100–174	25–35
3,001–5,000	45–49	20–24	33–49	65–99	175–249	36–49
5,000+	50+	25+	50+	100+	250+	50+

manently installed projection screens and room-darkening drapes or shades and will have connections and outlets for closed-circuit television where it exists

In determining the number of pieces of equipment, a reasonable distribution of demand is assumed, i.e., that all use will not be concentrated on a peak period of either the days or the academic year. Random access or broadcast delivery systems will also affect the needs for equipment.

PRODUCTION

All Learning Resources Programs should provide some production capability according to the needs and requirements of the curricula, the availability of commercial materials, and the capability of the delivery system. Production, except where part of an instructional program or meeting a specific institutional need, is not an end in itself. Neither is it related to institutional size.

Basic production capability for all campuses consists of minimal equipment items for:

Still photography (1 35mm camera and arrangements for developing film elsewhere).

Ability to make and duplicate sound recordings.

Sign production.

Graphics layout and lettering.

Laminating and dry-mounting.

Ability to make overhead transparencies.

Simple illustrations.

Videoplaying and duplication.

One camera videotaping and videodubbing.

Intermediate production capability consists of all elements above and in addition equipment items for:

Photographic black-and-white printing and processing.

Ability to edit sound recordings.

Two-camera video production.

Advanced production when justified consists of all above and in addition equipment items for:

Simple studio videoproduction in color.

Simple studio for sound recording and editing.

Optional production (justifiable only when needed for programs for cooperative distribution or highly sophisticated institutional needs) in addition consists of:

Color television directing, production, and editing.

16mm motion picture directing, production, and editing.

Color photographic developing and processing.

Guidelines for Library Services to Extension/Noncampus Students: Draft of Proposed Revisions

FOREWORD

The following draft of proposed revised *Guidelines for Library Services to Extension/Noncampus Students* has been prepared under the auspices of the ACRL Standards and Accreditation Committee. The decision to revise the existing guidelines was based on a nationwide survey of randomly selected academic libraries. The findings of the survey were further supported by individual comments made during the ACRL/COPA Accreditation Institute held in June 1980 in New York City. The thinking among some of those queried was that more explicit guidelines were needed.

If guidelines are to be revised, then should they be general or specific? Qualitative or quantitative? Should an evaluative checklist be included in a set of evaluative guidelines? The responses to these issues were studied and analyzed. There seemed to be a slight preference for general as opposed to specific guidelines, against quantitative guidelines, and for an evaluative checklist. When the same responses were grouped into four geographic regions, only one region preferred general guidelines (Northeast) while preferences of the other three (South, Midwest, West) were split between general and specific guidelines; a similar pattern was observed on the question of quantitative guidelines. Two regions favored an evaluative checklist (South and Midwest), one region was evenly split (West) and one was opposed (Northeast).

On the basis of these responses the proposed revised *Guidelines for Library Services to Extension/Noncampus Students* has been prepared. Following the proposed guidelines is *An Evaluative Checklist for Reviewing Library Services to Extension/Noncampus Students*. To facilitate the ACRL membership review of the document, the proposed guidelines and the accompanying checklist are published here.

A special hearing to review this document is planned for the January 1981 ALA Midwinter Meeting in Washington, D.C. Persons wishing to react to this document are encouraged to send their comments before the end of November to: George V. Hodowanec, William Allen White Memorial Library, Emporia State University, Emporia, KS 66801. Individual comments will be incorporated into a revised draft that will be available before the January 1981 hearing.

Membership of the Standards and Accreditation Committee at the time this project was first discussed included Marjorie C. Dennin, director of Learning Resources, Annandale Campus, Northern Virginia Community College; James T. Dodson (chair), director, University of Texas at Dallas Library; Jane G. Flener, associate director, University of Michigan Libraries; Peter C. Haskell, director, Franklin and Marshall College Library; George V. Hodowanec, director of the library, Emporia State University; Jay K. Lucker, director of libraries, Massachusetts Institute of Technology; Elizabeth M. Salzer, librarian, J. Henry Meyer Memorial Library of Stanford University Libraries; and Barbara J. Williams, director, South Carolina State College Library. Since June of 1980, the following membership changes have occurred: Patricia A. Sacks, director of libraries, Muhlenberg and Cedar Crest colleges, replaced James T. Dodson as chair of the committee and Irene B. Hoadley, director of libraries, Texas A&M University, replaced Jane Flener.

The growing importance of off-campus programs offered by colleges and universities is quite evident by the rapid expansion within the last fifteen years of part-time degree programs. By and large library services to extension/noncampus students have not kept pace with this rapid growth, and as a result, are inadequate in many respects. Because of the dynamic and innovative nature of library services to extension/noncampus students, it is imperative that the ACRL membership review and comment on these proposed revised guidelines.—*George V. Hodowanec.*

Draft of Proposed Revisions

What follows is a set of proposed revised guidelines for library services to noncampus/extension students based on the original guidelines published in 1967. As the guidelines have been revised, so have the assumptions upon which they are based.

Assumptions

1. As with campus courses, library services are an integral part of the quality of credit noncampus/extension or night courses offered by an academic institution.
2. If a university or college assumes a responsibility for the provision of library services for its

campus courses, it should also assume the responsibility for providing adequate library support for its noncampus/extension courses. This provision may be achieved through a variety of ways, but the ultimate responsibility rests with the institution.
3. The level of support for noncampus/extension courses, including printed materials as well as nonprint or audiovisual materials, should mirror the level of support for campus courses at both the graduate and undergraduate levels. The following types of noncampus courses necessitate library support as determined by instructors of noncampus/extension courses and library extension personnel:
   a. Credit courses: require the active support of library resources as an extension of the classroom.
   b. Independent study: this type of course often involves the active pursuit of a variety of library resources by a student and thus the full range of library services is necessary.
   c. Courses offered through electronic media: since in many cases the student in this type of course has limited personal access to the instructor, library services often must take up the slack. In many cases, students requiring materials for such courses must obtain them from libraries.
   d. Noncredit courses: this type of noncampus course has the broadest span of subjects and therefore library needs are difficult to assess. Since the course is not for credit, often the need for print materials is not as intense. However, library resources should be available and at times such resources may be essential to the course.

Definitions

It is necessary to the clarity of the proposed revised guidelines that one term be defined.

Noncampus/extension course: This term applies to any course offered by a college or university which does not utilize normal campus classrooms and facilities during normal campus class times. The term covers courses which meet as a class off the main campus, courses which may meet on campus but not during times when normal campus activities are in operation, and courses offered through electronic media or correspondence.

In reference to library services, a noncampus course is any course which does not have access to full library services on equal par with regular campus courses.

The term, with these connotations, is used as follows:

noncampus/extension courses
noncampus/extension/library services, resources, facilities
noncampus/extension student

In order to insure the provision of adequate

library services, resources, and facilities for the noncampus/extension student, what follows serves as guidelines for the institution's responsibility of providing library support for its noncampus/extension course offerings.

GUIDELINES

1. Finances

Noncampus/extension library services cannot be assured unless adequate financing is provided, therefore:

a. Library services for noncampus/extension purposes should be financed on a regular basis.

b. Funds should be budgeted specifically for the purpose of providing library resources to noncampus/extension students.

c. The amount spent for noncampus/extension students should be comparable to the per student expenditures for campus students and/or proportional to the level and complexity of campus programs.

2. Personnel

The task of providing library resources, services, and facilities for noncampus/extension courses must be assumed by competent library personnel, therefore:

a. Library personnel should be given the specific responsibility for identifying information needs and making appropriate arrangements for delivery of materials and services to noncampus courses.

b. Staffing requirements for off campus programs depend upon the nature and level of the courses offered. They should be comparable to the staffing requirements identified in the *Standards for College Libraries* (Formula B).

c. It is the task of library personnel in charge of noncampus/extension needs to consider, in consultation with necessary faculty and library staff, the library needs for any existing or proposed noncampus/extension course and then determine how these needs can be provided for. If, in the opinion of the librarian and the instructor, adequate library resources cannot be made available, the course should not be approved.

3. Facilities

One of the following arrangements should be met in an effort to satisfy the need for library facilities to noncampus/extension students:

a. Establishment of a branch library should be considered if a large number of classes are offered in an off campus area.

b. Contract with local public libraries or any other library in the area to provide facilities to noncampus/extension students.

c. Arrangement with the instructor of the noncampus/extension class to transport resources needed by students from the main campus to the class location.

d. Provision of a cooperative branch library service among area academic libraries. If service does not exist but is feasible, plans should be made to formulate such.

4. Resources

The provision of library resources is a crucial aspect to any noncampus/extension course, therefore:

a. The noncampus/extension library service coordinator will make sure that all the resources needed by students in preparing for a noncampus/extension course are made available either through cooperative arrangement with other libraries or systematic collection development.

b. Depending on the nature and level of off campus programs, the rate of collection development for noncampus/extension programs, whether in terms of dollars or resources, should be comparable to the main campus.

5. Services

The following library services should be provided to noncampus/extension students:

a. Access to library resources and assistance in library use should be available to noncampus/extension students as is normally available to campus students.

b. Noncampus/extension students should have the opportunity to take library orientation tours at the library which will extend library services to them during the course of the semester.

c. Noncampus/extension students should have access to periodicals, reserve collections, and any other collections normally available to campus students.

d. Access to online literature search service should be available to noncampus/extension students as is normally available to campus students.

EVALUATIVE CHECKLIST FOR REVIEWING LIBRARY SERVICES TO NONCAMPUS/EXTENSION STUDENTS: DRAFT

The following evaluative checklist for library noncampus/extension services is not intended to provide a precise and totally objective picture of a library's ability to meet the needs of its noncampus/extension students. However, if thoughtfully completed, it will suggest strengths and weaknesses in a library's program for noncampus/extension services. The checklist is broken down into five major components of noncampus/extension services: budget, staff, facilities, resources, and services. While an evaluator should realize that such a breakdown is not all-inclusive, it does incorporate many of the elements of a successful library noncampus/extension program.

In format and structure this checklist was guided by, and is indebted to, "An Evaluative

Checklist for Reviewing a College Library Program" developed by ACRL.

DIRECTIONS FOR USE

A set of guidelines for each component is offered before the checklist. Based on these guidelines, a continuum of four statements concerning parts of that component follows. These statements represent the checklist. The evaluator should determine which of the four statements best describes the library.

To the left of each statement are three numbers, ranging from 1 to 12. If the statement chosen accurately describes the library, circle the middle number (2, 5, 8, or 11). If the evaluator feels the conditions of the library are below those described by the statement, circle the higher numbers (3, 6, 9, or 12). If the conditions at the library are above those of the statement, circle one of the lower numbers (1, 4, 7, or 10). Circle *only one* of the numbers in the 1 to 12 grouping.

Component 1: Budget for Noncampus/Extension Services

1. Library services for noncampus/extension purposes would be financed on a regular basis.
   1.1 Funds should be budgeted specifically for the purpose of providing library resources to noncampus/extension students.
2. The amount spent for noncampus/extension students should be comparable to the per student expenditures for campus students and/or proportional to the level and complexity of campus programs.

A. Budget Allocation

1 2 3   Funds specifically for noncampus/extension student library services are regularly allocated as part of the annual library budget.

4 5 6   Noncampus/extension student services are not specifically allocated funds, but some expenditures are made regularly for this purpose.

7 8 9   Funds are used for noncampus/extension students services only occasionally.

10 11 12   No funds are provided for noncampus/extension student library services.

B. Budget Amounts

1 2 3   The amount spent for noncampus/extension services is comparable to the per student expenditures for campus students.

4 5 6   The amount spent for noncampus/extension services approaches but seldom equals the amount spent per student for campus students.

7 8 9   The amount spent for noncampus/

extension services is well below the amount spent per student for campus students.

10 11 12   No amount is spent for library noncampus/extension students.

Component 2: Staff for Noncampus/Extension Services

1. Library personnel should be given the specific responsibility for identifying information needs and making appropriate arrangements for delivery of materials and services to noncampus/extension courses.
2. Staffing requirements for off campus programs depend upon the nature and level of the courses offered. They should be comparable to the staffing requirements identified in the *Standards for College Libraries* (Formula B).
3. It is the task of library personnel in charge of noncampus/extension needs to consider, in consultation with necessary faculty and library staff, the library needs for any existing or proposed noncampus/extension course and then determine how these needs can be provided for. If, in the opinion of the libraries and the instructor, adequate library resources cannot be made available, that course should not be approved.

A. Responsibility for Noncampus/Extension Services

1 2 3   Library personnel are given the specific responsibility for providing library services to noncampus/extension courses.

4 5 6   Library needs for noncampus/extension courses are handled regularly by what library personnel is available.

7 8 9   Library needs for noncampus/extension courses are only occasionally handled by what library personnel is available.

10 11 12   No library personnel have the responsibility for handling library needs of noncampus/extension students or courses.

B. Support Staff for Noncampus/Extension Services

1 2 3   Support staff for noncampus/extension library needs is provided in accordance with the staffing requirements of the *Standards for College Libraries* (Formula B).

4 5 6   Support staff is provided to assist in noncampus/extension library needs, but not always in accordance with staffing requirements.

7 8 9   Occasionally support staff is provided but seldom in accordance with staffing requirements.

10 11 12   No support staff is provided to assist in noncampus/extension library needs, contrary to staffing requirements.

C. Staff Duties for Noncampus/Extension Services

1 2 3   Library personnel in charge of noncampus/extension library needs regularly consult with faculty and library staff and assess each proposed noncampus/extension course.

4 5 6   Library personnel frequently assess the needs for noncampus/extension courses.

7 8 9   Library personnel assess the needs of noncampus/extension courses only in particular cases or upon request by a student, faculty member, etc.

10 11 12   No assessment of noncampus/extension library needs is made by library personnel.

Component 3: Facilities for Noncampus/Extension Services

1. One of the following arrangements should be met in an effort to satisfy the need for library facilities to noncampus/extension students:

   1.1 The establishment of a branch library in the area where most noncampus/extension courses are offered so that noncampus/extension students may have access to the facility.

   1.2 A contract with local public libraries or any other library in the area to provide facilities to noncampus/extension students.

   1.3 An arrangement with the instructor of the noncampus/extension class to transport resources needed by students from the main campus to the class location.

   1.4 The provision of a cooperative branch library service among area academic libraries. If no service exists but is feasible, plans should be made to formulate such.

A. The Provision of Facilities for Noncampus/Extension Students

1 2 3   Library facilities for noncampus/extension courses and students are consistently and adequately provided. These facilities are sufficient to accommodate necessary resources.

4 5 6   Library facilities are usually provided for noncampus/extension courses and students.

7 8 9   Library facilities are seldom provided for noncampus/extension courses and students.

10 11 12   Library facilities are never provided or are provided only by impetus of the instructor of a noncampus/extension course.

Component 4: Resources for Noncampus/Extension Services

1. The noncampus/extension library service coordinator will make sure that all the resources needed by students in preparing for a noncampus/extension course are made available either through cooperative arrangement with other libraries or systematic collection development.

2. Depending on the nature and level of off campus programs, the rate of collection development for noncampus/extension programs, whether in terms of dollars or resources, should be comparable to the main campus.

A. Provision of Resources

1 2 3   All necessary resources for noncampus/extension courses are regularly provided by the library service coordinator through some sort of arrangement.

4 5 6   An effect is usually made to provide necessary resources for noncampus/extension courses, and most courses are regularly provided for.

7 8 9   Resources are seldom provided for noncampus/extension courses and often those resources which are provided are insufficient.

10 11 12   No effort is made to make resources available for noncampus/extension courses.

B. Rate of Collection Development

1 2 3   The library has an active collection development program for noncampus/extension courses and that development is comparable to the collection development efforts on the main campus.

4 5 6   The library has collection development for noncampus/extension courses, but the rate of collection development is not comparable to that at the main campus.

7 8 9   Collection development for noncampus/extension courses occurs incidentally. Little effort is made to expand that collection.

10 11 12   No collection development is provided for noncampus/extension courses.

Component 5: Noncampus/Extension Library Services

1. Access to library resources and assistance in library use should be available to noncampus/

extension students as is normally available to campus students.

2. Noncampus/extension students should have the opportunity to take library orientation tours at the library which will extend library services to them during the course of the semester.

3. Noncampus/extension students should have access to periodicals, reserve collections, and any other collections normally available to campus students.

    3.1 Access to online literature search services should be available to noncampus/extension students as is normally available to campus students.

A. *Availability of Services*

1 2 3 Access to library resources and assistance in library use is available to noncampus/extension students on a comparable basis to what is provided the campus students.

4 5 6 Efforts are made to provide noncampus/extension students with library resources and assistance in library use approaching a comparable basis to what is provided the campus students.

7 8 9 Occasionally efforts are made to provide noncampus/extension students with library resources and assistance in library use, but as a whole services are not on a comparable basis to what is provided the campus students.

10 11 12 Few or no library services are available to noncampus/extension students.

B. *Library Orientation*

1 2 3 Arrangements have been made which insure that noncampus/extension students have the opportunity to take library orientation tours at the library which extends library services to them during the semester.

4 5 6 Noncampus/extension students are not assured library orientation tours, but such tours generally are provided.

7 8 9 Library orientation tours are available to noncampus/extension students only upon request and not necessarily at the library which extends services to them during the semester.

10 11 12 Noncampus/extension students have no opportunity to take library orientation tours at the library which extends library services to them, either because no arrangements have been made for such tours or no library has been provided.

C. *Access to Periodicals, Collections, Search Services*

1 2 3 Noncampus/extension students have access to all materials available to campus students and online literature search services are provided as is normally available to campus students.

4 5 6 Noncampus/extension students have some access to library materials but library privileges comparable to campus students are not provided. Limited access to online services are also provided compared to those provided to campus students.

7 8 9 Noncampus/extension students have only limited library privileges, which may or may not include online search services.

10 11 12 Noncampus/extension students have no access to library materials and no access to online literature search services.

PROFILE OF NONCAMPUS LIBRARY SERVICES

The following chart is provided to tabulate and summarize the judgment recorded on the evaluative checklist. To develop a profile, transfer the marks from each item of the checklist to this sheet. Connect the marked circles by straight lines. Then turn the sheet to a horizontal position to observe the resulting graph. The result should indicate those components of noncampus library services in which the library is either strong or weak and in need of improvement. ■■

		Strong											Weak
Budget	Component 1												
	Item A	1	2	3	4	5	6	7	8	9	10	11	12
	Item B	1	2	3	4	5	6	7	8	9	10	11	12
Staff	Component 2												
	Item A	1	2	3	4	5	6	7	8	9	10	11	12
	Item B	1	2	3	4	5	6	7	8	9	10	11	12
	Item C	1	2	3	4	5	6	7	8	9	10	11	12
Facilities	Component 3												
	Item A	1	2	3	4	5	6	7	8	9	10	11	12
Resources	Component 4												
	Item A	1	2	3	4	5	6	7	8	9	10	11	12
	Item B	1	2	3	4	5	6	7	8	9	10	11	12
Services	Component 5												
	Item A	1	2	3	4	5	6	7	8	9	10	11	12
	Item B	1	2	3	4	5	6	7	8	9	10	11	12
	Item C	1	2	3	4	5	6	7	8	9	10	11	12

Registrants

Sidney August
Director, Division of Educational
    Resources
Community College of Philadelphia
34 South 11th Street
Philadelphia, PA 19107

George Bailey
2129 Villa Maria Road
Claremont, CA 91711

Ruth E. Bauner
1207 B. West Freeman
Carbondale, IL 62901

James F. Bemis
Executive Director, Northwest
    Association of Schools and Colleges
Commission on Colleges
3700-B University Way, N.E.
Seattle, WA 98105

Henry Birnbaum
University Librarian
Pace University
New York, NY 10038

Marjorie Dennin
Director, Learning Resources Center
Northern Virginia Community College
8333 Little River Turnpike
Annandale, VA 22203

James T. Dodson
Director of Libraries
University of Texas at Dallas, Box 643
Richardson, TX 75080

George L. Gardiner
Director, Kresge Library
Oakland University
Rochester, MI 48063

Dr. Nicholas E. Gaymon
Director of Libraries
Florida A&M University
Tallahassee, FL 32307

Johnnie Givens
Metrics Research Corporation
180 Allen Rd., Suite 200 South
Atlanta, GA 30328

Peter C. Haskell
Director of the Library
Franklin and Marshall College
Lancaster, PA 17604

George V. Hodowanec
Director, William Allen White Library
Emporia State University
Emporia, KS 66801

Philip Johnson
Graduate Dean
Oakland University
Rochester, MI 48063

Arthur E. Jones
Librarian
Drew University
Madison, NJ 07940

James V. Jones
Director, University Libraries
Case Western Reserve University
11161 East Boulevard
Cleveland, OH 44106

Millicent Kalaf
Staff Associate, New England
    Association of Schools and Colleges,
    Inc.
131 Middlesex Turnpike
Burlington, MA 01803

Dr. Francis J. Kerins
President, Carroll College
Helena, MT 59601

Robert Kirkwood
Executive Director, Commission on
  Higher Education
Middle State Association of Colleges
  and Schools
3624 Market Street
Philadelphia, PA 19104

Toni Kuzma
Director of Learning Resources
Somerset County College
P.O. Box 3300
Somerville, NJ 08876

Ronald Leach
Charles V. Park Library
Central Michigan University
Mount Pleasant, MI 48859

Jay Lucker
Director, Massachusetts Institute of
  Technology Libraries
Room 14S-216
Cambridge, MA 02139

Dr. James R. Macklin
Librarian, Macon Junior College
Macon, GA 31206

Thurston E. Manning
Director, Commission on Institutions of
  Higher Education
North Central Association of Colleges
  and Schools
1221 University Avenue
Boulder, CO 80302

Roland Moody
Dean of Libraries and Learning
  Resources
Northeastern University
Boston, MA 02115

Phoebe Oplinger
Director, Central Piedmont Community
  College Library
1201 Elizabeth Ave., P.O. Box 4009
Charlotte, NC 28204

Warren S. Owens
Dean of Instructional Services
University of Idaho
Moscow, ID 83843

Charles F. Perkins
Director of Library and Learning
  Resources
Massachusetts Bay Community College
50 Oakland Street
Wellesley, MA 02181

Jay Poole
Editor, *Choice*
100 Riverview Center
Middletown, CT 06457

Dr. James T. Rogers
President, Brenau College
Gainesville, GA 30501

Patricia Sacks
Director of Libraries
Muhlenberg and Cedar Crest Colleges
Allentown, PA 18104

Elizabeth M. Salzer
Head Librarian, J. Henry Meyer
  Memorial Library
Stanford University
Stanford, CA 94305

Jasper Schad
Director, Library/Media Resources
  Center
Box 68, Wichita State University
Wichita, KS 67208

Dr. Barbara Scott
Librarian, Birmingham-Southern
  College
Birmingham, AL 35204

Brooke E. Sheldon
School of Library Science
Texas Woman's University
Denton, TX 76204

Dr. Jessie C. Smith
University Librarian
Fisk University
Nashville, TN 37203

Carla Stoffle
Assistant Chancellor for Educational
    Services
University of Wisconsin-Parkside
Kenosha, WI 53141

Gordon W. Sweet
Executive Director, Commission of
    Colleges
Southern Association of Colleges and
    Schools
795 Peachtree Street, N.E.
Atlanta, GA 30308

Richard Talbot
40 High Point Drive
Amherst, MA 01002

Johanna E. Talman
Library Director
California Institute of Technology
Pasadena, CA 91109

Dr. Patricia A. Thrash
Associate Director, North Central
    Association, Commission on
    Institutions of Higher Education
820 Davis Street
Evanston, IL 60201

Dr. Kenneth Tidwell
Associate Executive Director
Commission on Occupational Education
    Institutions, Southern Association of
    Colleges and Schools
795 Peachtree Street, N.E.
Atlanta, GA 30308

Julie Carroll Virgo
Executive Director, Association of
    College and Research Libraries
50 E. Huron Street
Chicago, IL 60611

Dr. Harold Wade
Southern Association of Colleges and
    Schools
795 Peachtree Street, N.E.
Atlanta, GA 30308

J. O. Wallace
Director of Learning Resources
San Antonio College Library
1001 Howard Street
San Antonio, TX 78284

David C. Weber
Director of Libraries
Stanford University
Stanford, CA 94305

Duane Webster
Association of Research Libraries
1527 New Hampshire Avenue N.W.
Washington, DC 20036

Kenneth E. Young
President, The Council on Post-
    secondary Accreditation
One Dupont Circle, Suite 760
Washington, DC 20036

Selected Annotated Bibliography
Ree DeDonato

The following bibliography is the result of an online search run in several data bases: ERIC, LISA (Library and Information Science Abstracts), SOCIAL SCISEARCH (Social Science Citation Index), and COMPREHENSIVE DISSERTATION INDEX. A ten year period beginning 1970 was searched.

MacVean, Donald S. *An NCATE Evaluation of a University Library: A Case History.* 1979. (ERIC Document ED 171240)
This report documents the procedures and problems encountered during the evaluation of Western Illinois University's library by the National Council for Accreditation of Teacher Education (NCATE) and proposes recommendations for future evaluations of university libraries. Basic problems with the NCATE evaluation involved: (1) an unqualified library evaluator; (2) the absence of a library specialist on the visiting team and the failure of the provost and dean of education to check on visiting team qualifications; (3) providing detail about the library in the institutional report, which resulted in misinterpretation by the evaluator, and (4) the lack of library evaluation due to vague standards and unqualified evaluators. It is recommended that visiting team members should be more conscientiously selected from rosters of nominees provided by NCATE's constituent and associate organizations, and that NCATE should arrange with one of the library associations to nominate persons qualified to evaluate college and university libraries. In particular, NCATE should revise its standards on libraries so that they are more specific and meaningful.

Totten, Herman L. *Identification of Library Elements in Statements of Accrediting Standards: A Review of the Literature.* Working Paper, ACRL Ad Hoc Committee to Revise the 1959 *Standards for College Libraries.* 1974. (ERIC Document ED 121350)
A review of the literature on college library standards was conducted in order to tabulate the elements found in the latest statements of accrediting agencies and library organizations. First, the published standards and guidelines of library associations and accrediting agencies were considered individually. A chart was devised for tabulating these sixteen publications against twenty elements possible for inclusion in standards. Information from two studies of accrediting agencies was also examined and tabulated in a similar way. These studies considered requirements for libraries made by twenty-one accrediting organizations in such areas as law, business, health, etc. The elements most often checked on both charts were resources, staff, finances, services, facilities, and administration.

Webb, Mary Alice. *A Study of the Perceptions of the Presidents, Academic Deans and Learning Resources Administrators in the Public Community Colleges in Florida Regarding the 1972 Library Standards, 'Guidelines for Two-Year College Learning Resources Programs:* Ph.D. Dissertation, The Florida State University, 1980. (*Dissertation Abstracts* Order No. 8016305)

Ree DeDonato is reference librarian at Northwestern University.

The purpose of this study was to examine and compare the perceptions of presidents, academic deans, and learning resources administrators in the public community colleges in Florida to determine to what extent similarities and significant differences exist regarding the 1972 *Guidelines for Two-Year College Learning Resources Programs*. A three-part survey questionnaire was sent by direct mail to the three groups of Florida community college administrators. The first part of the questionnaire solicited personal and institutional information. The second part, the focal part of the survey, gathered perceptions of the administrators regarding statements from *Guidelines* relative to learning resources areas: objectives and purposes, organization and administration, budget, staff, facilities and instructional equipment, and materials. Part III surveyed opinions regarding the need for quantitative standards to implement the qualitative *Guidelines*. Space was also provided for comments. A Likert-like scale of five numbered places allowed the respondent to assign a degree of importance to statements from *Guidelines*. Information was supplied by check marks in other parts of the questionnaire. All responses to the questionnaire were tabulated in numbers and percentages of the population reporting. These figures were placed in tables. Results of the survey of perceptions revealed many similarities in the perceptions of Florida community college presidents, academic deans, and learning resources administrators. However, perceptions varied within the individual groups as well as among the three groups; perceptions varied frequently from the lowest to the highest level on the scale. Responses from presidents tended to be less scattered on the scale than those from academic deans or learning resources administrators. Results showed some differences in perceptions of the academic deans vis-à-vis presidents and learning resources administrators regarding several sensitive statements in *Guidelines*. The most significant variances in perceptions concerned the rank and status of the chief learning resources administrator, the staff, instruction, and the budget. Out of the total of seventy-seven administrators, 62 percent believed that quantitative standards were necessary to implement the qualitative *Guidelines*. Learning resources administrators recognized greater need for the quantitative standards than did either academic deans or presidents. Academic deans saw the least need. The majority of the administrators in favor of the quantitative standards believed that the standards should be based on a formula which could be applied to colleges of varying sizes. However, in spite of the agreement that there was a need for quantitative standards, questions were raised about applying the standards.

Yates, Dudley V. *An Analysis of the Bases Used by Library Evaluators in the Accrediting Process of the Southern Association of Colleges and Schools*. Ph.D. dissertation, The Florida State University, 1973. (ERIC Document ED 140800)

Seventy-seven of the ninety library evaluators of the Southern Association of Colleges and Schools (SACS) responded to a 1973 questionnaire to determine (1) if evaluative criteria used are based with an authority other than SACS; and (2) if certain methods, procedures, and techniques employed by evaluators could be used to construct an ideal evaluator profile. Evaluators considered themselves competent and self-sufficient to evaluate libraries without strict adherence to SAC's standard. They expressed a need, however, for guidance from SACS through quantitative guidelines, checklists, and questionnaires, and have developed their own. A profile was constructed based on procedures used by evaluators.

The study concluded that minimal guidance is given to evaluators, and that there is minimal communication between SACS and evaluators. The study recommended that SACS should: (1) produce and distribute publications to evaluators identifying differences between suggestions and recommendations; (2) give first-time evaluators copies of good past reports; (3) assign library evaluators to libraries and not other institutional aspects; and (4) make the library standard modern and flexible, containing normative data and quantitative guidelines. Further research on evaluator competency and other libraries and accrediting associations was recommended. Cover letter, questionnaire, and bibliography are appended.

Yates, Dudley V. *The Impact of Regional Accrediting Agencies Upon Libraries in Postsecondary Education.* 1976. (ERIC Document ED 135337)

In this age of accountability, accreditation commissions face criticism from higher education professions and the public. Although agencies have committed their energies to protect the general public from inferior educational institutions, they appear to be insensitive to the effects of changes in education. There is a need to rank schools of higher education, and, since institutional programs are reflected by the support of their academic libraries, the lack of uniformity in library evaluation theory and practice is a critical problem. Accrediting agencies must define acceptable levels of library services and resources to become more accountable to the public. Selected results of a survey of Southeastern Library Association members on library evaluation are mentioned.

Additional References

Carpenter, Ray L. "College Libraries: A Comparative Analysis in Terms of the ACRL Standards." *College & Research Libraries,* 42 (January 1981), pp. 7-18.

A quantitative analysis of the 1977 HEGIS data bearing on college libraries in terms of the ACRL *Standards for College Libraries* (1975) concludes that most of the libraries do not meet *Standards'* criteria for collection size and development, staff, and budget. Variable in *Standards* not included in the HEGIS data are not analyzed.

Hardesty, Larry and Bentley, Stella, "The Use and Effectiveness of the 1975 *Standards for College Libraries*." Manuscript. 25 p. 1981.

A Survey was made to determine if the 1975 *Standards for College Libraries* are used and whether they are considered to be effective. The results show that they are used, that there is a great deal of interest in having standards, and that most college library directors feel that the 1975 *Standards* are in general very useful. Specific recommendations for change and for better implementation of *Standards* are made.

Leach, Ronald George, *Identification and Modification of Criteria and Procedures for Evaluating College and University Libraries by North Central Association Accreditation Teams.* Ph.D. dissertation, Michigan State University, 1980.

The purpose of this study was to assess North Central evaluators' opinions about evaluating libraries during the accreditation process, to review existing literature in search of library evaluative criteria, and to propose new guidelines for evaluating libraries as part of the accrediting process. The investigation looked at the following two questions:

1) Lacking library specialists on visitation teams or guidelines to assist nonspecialists, how do evaluators assess the effectiveness of the library program in relation to the mission of the institution?
2) What criteria would be useful to assist evaluators in making an informed judgment about the overall effectiveness of the library program?

A proposed set of guidelines is suggested.

Travis, Jo Ann, *Library Standards for Proprietary Junior Colleges of Business.* Masters Paper, University of North Carolina at Chapel Hill, 1978.

DO NOT RETURN IN JIFFY BAG